The teaching of modern languages in the primary school

It has been argued for some time that to improve language learning in Britain we need to start earlier, as many other European countries do. Up to now only Scotland has really begun to implement primary foreign languages on a national scale, but there is a growing groundswell of opinion in support of its development throughout the UK.

This book is addressed to policy-makers and teachers who are considering the possibility of getting involved in the teaching of MFL in the primary school. It will help them to decide whether they are ready to embark on such a move; it will draw them into a discussion about the issues they will need to consider and it will provide substantial practical guidelines to support the development of classroom practice.

Patricia Driscoll is a languages teacher and has conducted research on modern foreign languages in the primary school for her doctorate at Canterbury Christ Church University College and **David Frost** is a researcher and lecturer in the field of school improvement at the University of Cambridge School of Education.

First published 1999
by Routledge
2 Park Square, Milton Park, Abingdon, Oxon, OX14 4RN

Simultaneously published in the USA and Canada
by Routledge
270 Madison Ave, New York NY 10016

Transferred to Digital Printing 2006

Typeset in Garamond by Routledge

British Library Cataloguing in Publication Data
A catalogue record for this book is available from the British
Library

Library of Congress Cataloguing in Publication Data
The teaching of modern foreign languages in the primary school/
edited by Patricia Driscoll and David Frost.
Includes bibliographical references.
1. Languages, Modern–Study and teaching (Elementary)–Great
Britain. I. Driscoll, Patricia II. Frost, David
LB1580.G7T43 1999   98-41841
372.65'044–dc21   CIP

ISBN 0–415–18382–0 (hbk)
ISBN 0–415–18383–9 (pbk)

Publisher's Note
The publisher has gone to great lengths to ensure the quality of
this reprint but points out that some imperfections in the
original may be apparent

For Patrick and Olivia

Contents

12 Developing primary MFL: a teacher-led, community-focused
    approach   181
    DAVID FROST

13 A research agenda for modern languages in the primary
    school   197
    RICHARD JOHNSTONE

Illustrations

Figures

Tables

Contributors

Michael Byram is Professor of Education at Durham University. He has been involved in teaching foreign languages in Britain and in other countries for more than 20 years. He is interested in the relationship of language learning and cultural learning in foreign language courses and has published several books on the subject including *Teaching and Learning: Language and Culture* (1994, Clevedon: Multilingual Matters) and *Teaching and Assessing Inter-cultural Communicative Competence* (1997, Clevedon: Multilingual Matters). He is currently editing the *Encyclopaedia of Language Teaching and Learning*.

Peter Doyé is Professor of English at the School of Education, Technische Universität Braunschweig, Germany. In the 1970s he conducted an extensive research project on Primary English in German schools. He is author of a number of books and articles on various aspects of foreign language education and co-editor of the *Zeitschrift für Fremdsprachenforschung*.

Patricia Driscoll has been engaged in research in the primary MFL field in connection with her PhD at Canterbury Christ Church University College since 1995. She has taught modern foreign languages in secondary schools and also taught English as a foreign language across the full age range. For a number of years she worked in industry both in Britain and abroad. She is currently engaged in collaboration with other researchers across Europe under the auspices of the European Commission Training and Mobility of Researchers Programme.

Michael Evans is a member of the University of Cambridge School of Education where he teaches the Modern Languages pathway on the PGCE. He has written about French and Spanish literature and the methodology of literature in the target language. He has recently completed research on pupils' attitudes towards Europe and the influence of school on the development of European identity and citizenship. He has also studied the effect of the use of Information and Communication Technology (ICT) on foreign language teaching and learning, and has been directing the university's participation in a LINGUA-funded collaborative project entitled 'The Use of Multimedia for Foreign Language Learning at Primary and Lower Secondary School Levels'.

David Frost is currently a member of the school improvement team at the University of Cambridge School of Education. He has published mainly in the field of teacher development and school improvement although he has also written about careers education and guidance and pastoral care. His most recent book is entitled *Reflective Action Planning: A Guide to Teacher-led School Improvement* (1997, London: David Fulton Publishers). The book arises from the CANTARNET teachers' school improvement network he established in Kent.

Alison Hurrell is a lecturer in Modern Languages at the Northern College of Education, Aberdeen where she works with both BEd Primary and PGCE Secondary students. Prior to that she taught in secondary schools for over twenty years. Between 1989–92 she played a leading role in the Scottish National Pilot for Modern Languages in the Primary School as the Field Development Officer and has since worked as co-author of the National In-Service Training Programme for primary teachers in French. She has co-authored secondary course books and a Reading Scheme for early years learners of French.

Richard Johnstone is a Professor of Education and Head of the Department of Education at the University of Stirling. He is also Director of the Scottish Centre for Information on Language Teaching and Research (CILT). He has directed many research projects for SOEID on the teaching and learning of foreign or second languages, and has written several books on the subject. His most recent work has included responsibility for the evaluation of national pilot projects in modern languages in Scottish primary schools.

Lesley Low is a Research Fellow in the Institute of Education at the University of Stirling. She was the principal researcher on the evaluation of the national pilot projects for foreign languages in the primary school in Scotland. She is currently collaborating with colleagues in other European countries to identify effective ways of supporting initiatives in early foreign language learning. She has published widely in the field.

John Muir is an Adviser in Primary Education and Coordinator of the MLPS programme for the Highland Council in Scotland. He is the author of a number of books including the *Classroom Clangers* series of humorous anecdotes from parents, pupils and teachers. He has been a contributory author to several primary schemes, for example, Longmans *Science Connections*. He writes regularly for educational journals, including the *Times Educational Supplement Scotland*.

Shelagh Rixon is a lecturer in the Centre for English Language Teacher Education at the University of Warwick, where she has special responsibility for postgraduate courses for primary school level English as a Foreign Language teacher. She has worked on primary language projects for the British Council and has published training and teaching text books including *Tip Top* (1989, Basingstoke: Macmillan), *How to Use Games in Language Teaching* (1981, Basingstoke: Macmillan) and a number of articles in the field of language teaching at primary school level.

Glynis Rumley is a member of the Kent local authority advisory team. Having taught in secondary schools she has been the Project Officer for the Primary Modern Languages Project for some years and has led training sessions for teachers throughout Kent and elsewhere. She is co-author of the *Pilote* materials.

Peter Satchwell has worked as a head of languages in a comprehensive school, as languages adviser for Surrey LEA, and more recently as a University PGCE tutor. For the past fifteen years he has been keenly interested in the introduction of language teaching into primary schools and has provided in-service training sessions in various parts of the country. He chairs the national Primary Languages Network based at CILT and is the co-author (1995) of *Young Pathfinder 1: Catching them Young* (1995, London: CILT). He has written extensively on primary MFL.

Keith Sharpe is a Professor of Education and Head of Department of Education at the University of Liverpool. He taught in primary schools for many years and until recently was Director of Primary Education at Canterbury Christ Church University College. He played a leading role in the development of a modern foreign languages programme for Kent primary schools and has published a number of articles on the subject of primary MFL. His recent research is a comparative study of British and French primary schools.

Abbreviations

ALL	Association of Language Learning
BCLE	Bureau de coopération linguistique et éducative
CBEVE	Central Bureau for Educational Exchanges and Visits (see Appendix I)
CILT	Centre for Information on Language Teaching and Research
CPD	Continuing Professional Development
DES	Department for Education and Science (now DfEE)
DfE	Department for Education
DfEE	Department for Education and Employment
EC	European Commission
EFL	English as a Foreign Language
ELI	European Language Institute
EYL	EFL for young children
FL	Foreign Language
GCSE	General Certificate of Secondary Education
GPS	General professional studies
HEI	Higher education institute
HMI	Her Majesty's Inspectorate
ICT	Information and Communication Technology
INSET	In-service training
IQEA	Improving the Quality of Education for All
ITT	Initial Teacher Training
IUFM	Instituts Universitaires de Formation des Maîtres
KS1	Key Stage 1
KS2	Key Stage 2
KS3	Key Stage 3
KS4	Key Stage 4
L1	The first language
L2	The second language
LEA	Local Education Authority
MFL	Modern foreign languages
MLPS	Modern languages in the primary school

NC	National Curriculum
NCITT	National Curriculum for Initial Teacher Training
NFER	National Foundation for Educational Research
NPQH	National Professional Qualification for Headship
NQT	Newly Qualified Teacher
PG	postgraduate
PGCE	Postgraduate Certificate in Education
QCA	Qualifications and Curriculum Authority
QTS	Qualified Teacher Status
SA1	subject application 1
SALT	Scottish Association of Language Teachers
SAT	Standardised Assessment Tasks
SCAA	Schools Curriculum and Assessment Authority
SCILT	Scottish Centre for Information on Language Teaching and Research
SK1	subject knowledge 1
SK2	subject knowledge 2
SOED	Scottish Office Education Department (until 1995)
SOEID	Scottish Office Education and Industry Department
TPR	total physical response
TTA	Teacher Training Agency
TVEI	Technical and Vocational Educational Initiative
UG	undergraduate

Introduction

Philosophers of education have struggled over the years to establish the idea of a curriculum based on rational principles; a curriculum untainted by the meddling of social engineers and populist politicians. Nevertheless, it may be inevitable that the curriculum will reflect to some extent the social, economic and political climate of the time. An earlier proposal to extend the teaching of modern foreign languages (MFL) to all British primary schools was officially rejected 25 years ago because no substantial gain in later attainment at the secondary school could be demonstrated; the government lost its nerve and primary modern foreign languages was not extended. Perhaps the time was simply not right but now, in the closing months of the twentieth century, we believe that it is appropriate to review that decision and take a fresh look at the possibility of teaching modern foreign languages to primary-aged children.

The decision following the Burstall Report (1974) was a considerable disappointment because there had been such a high level of enthusiasm and interest in the pilot scheme, 'French From Eight (1963–1974)'. Despite this, the time was less than propitious in a number of ways. This was the era in which there was a collision between the optimistic expansionism and creativity of the post-war curriculum movement and the harsh reality of the economic recession and the stirrings of the educational accountability debate. There was another clash evident at that time; on the one hand, there was the child-centred ideology expressed in the Plowden Report (DES, 1967) influencing the *debate* about, if not the actual practice of primary pedagogy and on the other hand, the strongly behaviourist methodology which dominated modern foreign languages teaching at that time. Until the widespread introduction of comprehensive schools, MFL was considered an elitist subject, taught only in selective grammar schools, so the proposal to introduce it into the primary schools in the early 1960s was quite radical; it offered the possibility of extending languages teaching to all children, a move which would have presented a considerable challenge since there was no experience of teaching the subject within mixed ability classes.

But times have changed. As we approach the millennium, the Labour government elected in 1997 is firmly pro-European and there is a far higher degree of pan-European economic and cultural co-operation than in the early 1970s. The learning of modern foreign languages plays a central role in these developments not simply because of its practical application within the economic sphere but also because of its obvious links to the development of a conception of citizenship which extends beyond national boundaries.

Learning a language is a valuable and worthwhile enterprise at any age because it provides the possibility of practical communication; it is also a source of valuable intellectual stimulation and enjoyment; it cultivates broader perspectives and insights into other cultures and enables people to gain insights into their own culture and language through contrast. But an early start to foreign language learning has particular advantages which are discussed in a number of chapters in this book. Learning a language is a long process and so we need to make sure that young people have the maximum opportunity for language learning whilst still at school and before the demands of their adult working lives are upon them.

The publication of this book coincides with the conducting of a national inquiry into the UK's capability in languages. The inquiry, funded by the Nuffield Foundation will ask questions not only about our current capability, but also about the policies and strategies needed to enable Britain to 'fulfil its economic, strategic, social and cultural responsibilities and aims and aspirations of its citizens' (Nuffield, 1998). The establishment of this inquiry is perhaps just one of a number of significant indications of a society engaged in reviewing its cultural resources egged on by a new government committed to the idea of Britain taking its rightful place at the European table.

It is a shared belief on the part of all contributors to this book that any review of our languages capability must surely conclude that the official neglect of modern foreign languages in the primary school is completely unacceptable. Doubtless there will be those who will argue that the learning of foreign languages is unnecessary given that English is used for business transactions and electronic communications almost everywhere in the world. Indeed, the terms of reference for the Nuffield inquiry invites such an argument by listing as one of its initial questions: 'What kind of foreign language capability is appropriate for a country whose first language is a major world language?' But, such arguments would be based on an extremely narrow view of the nature of language learning and its role in the broader social and cultural education of our young people. In Chapter 9 Michael Byram and Peter Doyé discuss in some detail the question of the teaching of cultural awareness and the way it is inextricably linked to language learning.

It is anachronistic that Britain is without a policy for the development of modern foreign languages at the primary stage particularly now that 'literacy' has recently been declared a national educational priority. There are some fairly obvious implications of this for language awareness; arguably one of the most effective ways of understanding the structure of a language is to compare it with the structure of another language.

The decisive action to extend MFL to all primary schools in Scotland has shown us a viable alternative to the secondary school model within the British context. In the Scottish scheme there is no fixed syllabus and the foreign language is linked to other curriculum areas so that there is no need to find a substantial amount of extra curriculum time. Scottish children are discovering at an earlier age that languages are accessible to them and so we can be confident that Scottish children at least are growing up with a greater sense of European community and their place in it. This is not to suggest, however, that the Scottish development is without its difficulties, as is discussed by Lesley Low in Chapter 3 of this volume, or that the model could be successfully implemented without modification in the rest of the UK.

In the last decade a large number of primary head teachers in the rest of Britain have taken the initiative on an *ad hoc* basis and have introduced MFL; this has led to a rich diversity of practice of course and there are successful programmes of one sort or another running in primary schools the length and breadth of Britain. This diversity and ways of understanding it are explored in some depth by Patricia Driscoll in the first two chapters. In particular, these papers help us to look at the role of teacher expertise in relation to primary MLF. The diversity of practices and views about policy and practice is reflected in the variation in terminology employed by the contributors to this book. The editors are using the term 'primary MFL' as does Keith Sharpe in Chapter 11 but those who have been involved in the Scottish development will tend to use the term MLPS (Modern Languages in the Primary School). These minor differences can be irritating to readers new to the subject matter but it is hoped that this book will play a significant part in the development of the debate about the importance of language learning for primary schoolchildren and will contribute to the emergence of a greater degree of consensus in this field.

The book does not begin with or include papers which put forward arguments for the inclusion of primary MFL in the National Curriculum although readers new to the subject will gain some insight from Chapter 1; rather, it is assumed that the arguments for primary MFL are unassailable and the value of such programmes is obvious. The book is addressed to policy-makers, teachers and other interested parties who are considering the possibility of getting involved in the teaching of modern foreign languages in the primary school. It is hoped that the book will help them to decide whether they are ready to embark on such a move; it will draw them into a discussion about the issues they will need to consider and it will provide substantial practical guidelines to support the development of classroom practice. Obviously, a book such as this cannot solve the problem of 'curriculum overload' but it is already clear since the Secretary of State announced the slimming down of the primary curriculum in January 1998, that schools are taking the opportunity to 'offer tasters in other subjects, including modern languages if they wish' (DfEE 1998). So we hope that this book is arriving at a time when it begins to be possible for LEAs and clusters of schools to take the initiative in this area.

Part I, 'Policy and Rationale', offers an overview of the debate and a substantial analysis of the nature of teacher expertise related to pedagogical practice. This discussion addresses fundamental issues such as: what should be the main aims and purposes of a modern languages programme in the primary school?; who is to teach primary MFL and what kind of expertise will they need?; where can it be located within the primary curriculum and at what age can children begin to learn MFL? Lesley Low offers a helpful exploration of a wide range of policy issues related to these questions in Chapter 3.

Part II, 'Classroom Issues', the longest section, contains a number of chapters which offer practical guidance: Alison Hurrell's chapter draws on her experience as a development officer and trainer with the Scottish pilot scheme to provide an excellent and eminently practical exploration of teaching and learning the four skills in modern languages. The question of the use of the target language as the medium of instruction is dealt with by Peter Satchwell, chairman of the Primary Languages Network at CILT (Centre for Information and Research in Language Teaching). From his perspective as an LEA advisor taking a leading role in the Scottish Modern Languages in the Primary School initiative, John Muir is able to report on detailed strategies for embedding modern languages teaching in the primary curriculum. Similarly, Glynis Rumley, who has been a major force for change in Kent, provides detailed guidance on ways to integrate modern languages teaching into the primary classroom through strategies which are primarily designed to develop positive attitudes to language learning. Shelagh Rixon reports on her comprehensive survey of resources and materials both for language and cultural learning in the classroom and for the purposes of teacher development. The question of 'intercultural competence' is addressed in the chapter by Michael Byram and Peter Doyé which is in itself a manifestation of the desire of many of us to forge strong cultural and academic links across national boundaries. The chapter is a rigorous examination of the question of what counts as the teaching of cultural awareness and what is required for successful learning in this area. Michael Evans' account of an evaluation of European partnership projects fostered under the Comenius umbrella provides us with a clear view of the relationship between language learning and the development of a European consciousness and identity.

Part III, 'Future Development', deals with research and development themes. Keith Sharpe's chapter assumes the possibility of a national strategy to teach MFL in primary schools and examines the implications for initial teacher education. He provides a helpful analysis of the training needs of the various categories of people who might apply for training places were they to be allocated to the training institutions. David Frost's chapter, by contrast, assumes the continued absence of such a national strategy and argues instead for a community-based curriculum development strategy which would empower primary teachers and local communities to take primary MFL forward in ways which match their local circumstances.

In the concluding chapter Dick Johnstone helps us to gain access to recent international research in the field of primary MFL teaching which, because it is published in a number of languages and places across Europe, is normally beyond our reach. Johnstone sets out an agenda for research across Europe as a whole which reminds us of the need to avoid a limited, purely Anglo-centric view of the issues and to enter into the discourse as Europeans.

References

Burstall, C., Jamieson, M., Cohen, S. and Hargreaves, M. (1974) *Primary French in the Balance*, Slough: NFER.

DfEE (1998) *Blunkett Strengthens Curriculum Focus on the Basics*, press release: 006/98 – 13 January 1998.

Department of Education and Science (1967) *Children and Their Primary Schools*, (The Plowden Report), London: HMSO.

Nuffield Languages Inquiry (1998) *Where Are We Going With Languages?* www.nuffield.org

I

Policy and rationale

Modern foreign languages in the primary school

A fresh start

Patricia Driscoll

The creation of the single European market and currency, the relaxing of trade restrictions, and closer political and industrial links have highlighted the value of cross-cultural communication, a fundamental part of which is learning languages. Languages enable us to access the potentially greater prospects arising from the growing mutual interconnection and interdependence of communities around the world. The recent resurgence of interest in primary modern foreign languages (MFL) in almost every country in Western Europe reflects a growing realisation that pupils need to be equipped with the competences, attitudes and skills to cope successfully with the social and economic changes which are transforming life in Europe. Primary MFL is not only an investment for the future but it also reflects our values as European citizens and our conception of what it means to be educated.

In England, Wales and Northern Ireland there is a wide range of MFL provision in primary schools in at least 40 LEAs (CILT 1995) and, following a successful pilot phase, Scotland has embarked on an extension programme to introduce MFL to all primary schools. The development of primary MFL is complex, involving differing views of both its aims and purposes and its approaches to instruction. There are strong indications of official support and interest from a number of national bodies (DES, 1990; Dearing, 1993; SCAA, 1997; DfEE, 1998) but as yet no funding has been made available nor any national guidelines laid down. So, at a time of unprecedented national control and externally determined standards for pupils' achievement in all other curriculum subjects, individual schools, groups of schools and in some cases whole LEAs are experimenting with curriculum designs and pioneering a variety of new approaches to teaching foreign languages in the primary school.

The aim of this chapter is to sketch in the nature of this diversity and to explore the parameters of the field of primary MFL. The chapter is divided into three sections: the first section examines some of the key issues in the debate about the inclusion of modern foreign languages in the primary curriculum; the second discusses the diversity in primary MFL programmes in terms of their aims and approaches to instruction; the final section examines a framework for distinguishing between different types of provision and explores the implications for planning.

Key issues in the debate about the inclusion of MFL in the primary curriculum

The recent development of commitment to the European ideal is reflected by the fact that parents increasingly expect primary schools to include a foreign language into the existing curriculum (CILT, 1995). In recent years parental power has been strengthened in two major ways: first, a greater number of parents are required to be included on schools' governing bodies, so the 'voice' of the community is highlighted more than ever before in many aspects of schools' strategic planning and, second, parents are now able to exert influence on the curriculum by opting for schools of their choice. As a consequence, headteachers may be encouraged to include MFL to 'add value' to their schools. Where schools are not meeting the needs of parents or where the provision is perceived as inadequate, parents who can afford to pay are turning towards commercial 'clubs', which offer MFL tuition privately to small groups of young children.

Part of the drive to include MFL into the primary school is likely to stem, on the one hand, from a common-sense belief that 'practice makes perfect' and, on the other hand, from a conviction that 'young is best' in terms of foreign language acquisition. The assumption in the first case is that, by extending MFL downwards into the primary school, more time can be spent practising and learning the language and more language content can be included. In the second case it is assumed that young children possess natural attributes which allow them to acquire languages more efficiently than older learners. Singleton (1989) suggests that this conviction is part of our 'folk wisdom', based perhaps on the obvious speed with which young children master their first language and, the way they appear, when they emigrate, to acquire a better pronunciation and more 'native' grammatical usage and word choice in another language in comparison with the older members of their families.

The age factor

However, as yet there is little conclusive research evidence to support the proposition that there exists an overall critical age for foreign language learning except in naturalistic conditions (Lapkin *et al.*, 1991). But, the debate is ongoing. Older learners appear to out-perform younger learners in the rate of language acquisition because they have a better grasp of grammatical patterns which transfer from their mother tongue to the foreign language (Ausubel 1964; Hawkins 1987; Collier 1989); they have had more practice in sustaining conversations (Scarcella and Higa 1981); they are more efficient at acquiring facts and concepts (Asher and Price, 1967; Oller and Nagato, 1974; Burstall *et al.*, 1974; Snow and Hofnagel-Hohle, 1978); they have developed a greater cognitive maturity and have better general learning strategies and skills (Collier, 1989; Johnstone, 1994).

There is, however, strong empirical evidence to support younger pupils' superiority in oral and aural performance irrespective of formal or informal settings (Singleton, 1989; Hawkins, 1987). Young learners appear to possess a superior 'sound' system which enables them to imitate sounds more accurately and increasing age shows a decline in the quality of native-like pronunciation (Tahta *et al.*, 1981; Vilke, 1988). A further advantage for young learners is their natural tendency to respond enthusiastically to new challenges in contrast with the self-consciousness that afflicts adolescents when performing in a foreign language. Young people are also more receptive in terms of attitude formation and the development of their identity and self-concept. Burstall, C., *et al.* (1974) noted that one of the results of an early start was that primary beginners demonstrated more positive attitudes to speaking French than secondary beginners. The evaluation of the Scottish pilot project (Low *et al.*, 1993, 1995) found that the pupils who had been taught in the primary school showed particular ability in listening and speaking, although reading and writing were also introduced successfully.

The time factor

The amount of time spent actively learning a foreign language is considered to be a significant factor in achieving high levels of proficiency (Vilke, 1988; Radnai, 1996), or even, the most important predictor of success (Carroll, 1975). Although a number of other factors such as the aptitude and attitude of the learner and the effectiveness of the teaching have a powerful impact on pupils' achievement, Vilke (1988) estimated that over 1000 hours of contact time are needed for learners to achieve proficiency in a foreign language. In English secondary schools the amount of time provided for modern languages is set at less than half that amount so, even though learning years may not hold equal weight, additional hours can be provided by extending MFL downwards into the primary school. The primary provision can promote specific competences which are developed at a more sophisticated level in the secondary school as well as offer a rich holistic learning experience which is different in nature from the secondary provision.

The question of objectives

So far there has been a tendency to evaluate the early teaching of modern languages purely in terms of linguistic objectives and the building of foundations for improved language acquisition later in schooling rather than the broader educational value of foreign language learning at such a formative time of schooling. The quest for hard evidence is driven to some extent by a desire to justify the cost of MFL in the primary school by pointing to possible obtainable goals at some point in the future. The interest in linguistic gain may also be influenced by the preoccupation of many of the leading professionals in the primary MFL field, who are predominantly language specialists rather than primary specialists and who may have made a considerable investment both personally and professionally in the pursuit of linguistic excellence.

At the heart of learning is the development of language competence, but it is vital at this stage of learning that foreign language provision makes a valuable contribution to the primary child's overall personal development, cultivates their communication skills and their understanding of the world. Vivet (1995) stresses the importance of considering the young pupil's needs rather than seeing primary MFL programmes as a preparation for the future.

> Foreign languages can introduce children to a world of sounds, positive sensations, new discoveries and stimulating acquisitions which go far beyond the narrow boundaries of a monolingual and monocultural education. Considerable benefit is drawn from such experience long before children become adults.
>
> (Vivet, 1995: 6)

One of the difficulties for the teacher in the early years of language learning is that the full benefits of knowing a language are only experienced once the learner has sufficient knowledge of the language to be able to use it for their own purpose (Vivet, 1995; Tost Planet, 1997). The teacher needs to find ways to stimulate the pupil's desire to acquire a limited knowledge and engage in relatively unsophisticated conceptual learning tasks and activities particularly in comparison with their other work at the upper level of Key Stage 2. Learning a language is a long haul, and motivation is a key factor in the process: if pupils are not motivated they cannot learn. The primary curriculum provides a wealth of opportunities for the foreign language to be exploited within other primary topics and the memorisation of stock phrases can be connected to the pupils' experience through story telling, songs and play activities which help to generate an enjoyable motivating environment for foreign language learning.

Stepping outside the security of the mother tongue can be difficult for some learners in the initial stages and pupils can develop confidence in the family atmosphere and caring culture of the primary school with fellow class mates they know well and with whom they have learnt all manner of basic skills over the years (Sharpe, 1991). This point is illustrated by the comments of a secondary teacher in a research interview.

Before they did primary French the children would arrive at the school and I would say nearly every year we had a child who became a school refuser because they were timid and they didn't like speaking...in all subjects, but the reason that would be given was that French was the thing that they were terrified of, having to come in and speak in class. I haven't had that at all from anybody since the primary French came in, and I think the reason is that they have got over that in a nice cosy atmosphere in their primary school with all their mates, with a teacher they know. I mean if they're coming here they don't know us – they don't know the other children and they always think everybody is better than them. They always think everybody's laughing at them and I think that the primary French has cut that out and they can come in and they are a lot more confident.

We have learnt a substantial amount about the early teaching of modern languages from studies around the world, but, without reference to the culture and context in which pupils learn, it is a little like studying fish without reference to the water. The two major research projects in Britain in the last 30 years (Burstall *et al.*, 1974 and Low *et al.*, 1995), were both designed to examine the efficacy and benefits of particular initiatives. The reports have given us considerable insight into the possibilities and dilemmas of teaching MFL to primary-aged pupils in Britain, but there is a need for more research. In British schools at present there is a wealth of diversity from which we can gather information on how teachers and schools are achieving the 'best fit' between teaching foreign languages and other primary subjects, and how primary teachers who are experts in oracy and literacy matters are extending their expertise to incorporate MFL.

Curriculum diversity in primary MFL programmes

There is no standard formula for the organisation and presentation of foreign languages in primary schools; provision varies not only from one LEA to another but between schools within a locality. The two most significant factors which frame the diversity and determine the nature of other characteristics within any programme are the teaching aims and the approaches to instruction although the competence of the teacher is also a significant factor as will be discussed in greater detail in Chapter 2.

Teaching aims

When the National Curriculum was first devised for the secondary school, it was decided to design the assessment targets with a ten-level attainment scale in keeping with all other subjects that start at the age of 5 rather than at the age of 11. With a clear understanding that at some future stage MFL would start earlier, at which point, levels one to three could be achieved in the primary school (DES, 1990). The implications of this are that the aims of MFL in secondary schools would be adopted for the younger learners and that the primary provision would be seen simply as the beginning of the language learning process as a whole. The educational purposes proposed by the Modern Foreign Languages Working Party (DES, 1990) are very broad and consist of both language and cultural components; they also stress the need to cultivate positive attitudes and general language learning skills in pupils.

The language component of MFL teaching

In terms of language development, the educational goals of modern languages teaching are:

• to develop language effectively and appropriately;
• to develop insights into the structure and awareness of the nature of language;
• to develop a sound base of skills, language and attitudes for further study.

(DES, 1990: 3)

In secondary schools, developing language competence tends to take the foreground and is prioritised to some extent because of the central role it plays in the external public examinations. In primary schools, the aim of language competence may be more low key and the broader aims of language awareness, developing language learning skills and the cultivation of positive attitudes towards language learning may take the foreground. So we could say that there is a continuum defined by the levels of intensity and complexity of the linguistic content; at one end of the continuum are Language Acquisition programmes which aim to develop a measure of language proficiency in pupils; at the other end, there are Sensitisation programmes which promote a broader 'base line' competence in language learning skills and a more elementary competence in a foreign language. The distinction between Sensitisation and Language Acquisition programmes (*sensibilisation* and *apprentissage*) derives from the French debate about the aims of primary MFL. Sensitisation programmes are often referred to as Language Awareness programmes, but I have made the distinction here because Language Awareness programmes need not incorporate any *actual* foreign language learning.

Language awareness is an essential and intrinsic part of all foreign-language learning. It both provides an 'education of the ear' (Hawkins, 1987) and offers 'a forum where language diversity can be discussed' (Hawkins, 1984: 4) so pupils develop insights into the roots and origins of words. Pupils' understanding of the structure and concept of language is also strengthened which promotes overall basic literacy (Johnstone, 1994).

Both Sensitisation programmes and Language Acquisition programmes are an initiation into learning a foreign language. They encourage pupils to take an active role in using 'bits' of language creatively. In the first instance a stock of 'formulaic' phrases are practised, and over time, pupils develop the skills and confidence to manipulate the language for their own purpose. The defining line between Language Acquisition programmes and Sensitisation programmes is rather vague in practice as their aims are not mutually exclusive; it is more a matter of emphasis. The broader educative value of Sensitisation programmes are also powerful elements of Language Acquisition programmes and Sensitisation programmes do not preclude the possibility of pupils developing language competence; it is merely that it is not developed to the same degree.

Sensitisation programmes

There are a number of programmes in the country which aim to develop a basic competence and confident 'handling' of simple phrases and vocabulary in one or more 'foreign' language. Sensitisation models suggest an experience which is essentially primary, emphasising as it does the value of developing the present skills and interests of pupils. The language content is more than incidental but continuity of learning and future attainment is not stressed. Sensitisation programmes may also include a strong element of language awareness which links the foreign language to mother tongue learning, although this is not always the case.

Language Acquisition programmes

Language Acquisition models emphasise performance, with strong structuring and progression of the learning. Tost Planet (1997), in his discussion of some of the fundamental issues raised by a range of experts in this field brought together under the aegis of the Council of Europe, expressed the argument that the aim of sensitisation in relation to foreign languages and cultures is an insufficient aim for primary schools and that 'real' foreign language learning should be the aim although the approach should not be modelled upon teaching in secondary school.

However, such a Europe-wide perspective tends to underplay the particular cultural and linguistic contexts of individual countries. Other European countries operate with English as a global language with all that implies about exposure through popular culture, computer technology and commerce, and many communities across Europe are exposed to a neighbouring language which may have a high profile in the home environment. Whereas in Britain, if children do not encounter other European languages and cultures in school, they are unlikely to be exposed to them at all as part of their daily lives, apart from in Wales and Scotland where Welsh and Gaelic are spoken by some and are used in radio and television broadcasts. Sensitisation programmes may therefore be more valuable in the British context because they help to ameliorate the limitations of the mono-cultural and mono-lingual environment within which many people live.

Communicative competence

In recent years the communicative competence approach, which stresses the importance of pupil interaction and involvement, has dominated language teaching. The central goal of communicative competence is to enable learners to communicate effectively and appropriately in the foreign language and, although accuracy and the grammatical structure are important, priority is given to the essential meaning.

Communicative competence is difficult to define. It is not structured around a single approach with prescribed teaching methods (Richards and Rogers, 1986), nevertheless, a framework of the major components for the purposes of teaching has been outlined in a number of models (Canale, 1983; Van Ek, 1986). These models identify a range of components which underpin communication such as the social code and socially acceptable norms of conversational exchanges, so that the learner can internalise the grammatical structure, pronunciation and vocabulary within a cultural context of 'native-likeness'.

The cultural component of MFL teaching

Teaching aims also vary in terms of the cultural component. The report from the Working Party which formed the framework for the National Curriculum (DES, 1990) was very explicit that cultural awareness should be given systematic attention in MFL teaching. Language is a primary element of culture and, without reference to the native culture, foreign language learning might well be reduced to lists of vocabulary, phrases and rules. MFL, more than any other part of the curriculum, can help develop pupils' understanding and appreciation of other cultures and ways of life, as well as help develop a critical perceptive of their own cultural 'norms'. Morgan (1995) points out that the overall goal of cultural awareness is the understanding of the target culture.

> We need to be given detailed information about the target country... and the ways of life...If we see acquisition of information and understanding of the underlying values as the first two steps of understanding foreign culture, we then also need to recognise that a detailed understanding of our own culture is necessary. This process can add a further

two stages to the development of cultural learning: a comparison of one's own culture and that of the target country and finally a standing outside those cultures to recognise the relativity of each.

(Morgan, 1995: 10)

Cultural understanding is a long-term goal and primary schools can begin the process by developing pupils' curiosity about other countries and laying the foundations for empathy towards the people. Primary schools which provide some form of MFL are more likely to make links with schools abroad; to invite native speakers into the classrooms and offer pupils the opportunities for exchanges and visits to countries in mainland Europe, all of which can boost language learning and provide useful and relevant cultural exposure for pupils. Contact with the 'native' people and country is noted as an important aspect of integrative motivation; if pupils start to develop a genuine empathy towards the country and the people it is likely that they will develop more positive attitudes towards learning the language (Gardner and Lambert, 1972; Schumann, 1978; Mitchell et al., 1992). Hawkins (1996) suggests that the capacity for empathy declines with the onset of adolescence; if this is the case, then it makes sense to capitalise on younger learners' openness to the unfamiliar and acceptance of differences in others.

The majority of pupils do not see themselves as products of their own cultural environment (Valdes, 1986) and the development of their awareness of the differences and commonalties between cultures and customs helps pupils to recognise the importance of culture on people's lives. The process of comparing cultures side by side gives pupils the freedom to make informed and educated choices and the opportunity to reflect on their own lives and values in a more detailed way. Without such insights into cultural variations, an individual is more likely slavishly to embrace the systems and perceptions of those around him which has implications for the growth of prejudices in some quarters.

Approaches to instruction

MFL programmes in primary schools vary not only in terms of their teaching aims but also in terms of the approach to instruction. Rixon (1992) noted that the main contrast in approaches to instruction in primary MFL can be drawn between programmes which adopt an overt teaching approach and those which favour a holistic one. In the overt teaching approach the foreign language is timetabled as an additional subject in the curriculum and the language itself is the central focus of the lesson. The language content is organised in topic areas and usually taught systematically; the topics may be quite separate as they would be in the secondary school or they might be drawn from and influenced by other subjects in the curriculum.

Depending on the level of competence of the teacher, the foreign language can be used spontaneously as a means of communication: for organising the learning activities and interacting with the pupils on a variety of levels within the timetabled slot.

The holistic approach integrates the MFL in a variety of ways into the existing primary curriculum (Sharpe, 1992; Johnstone, 1994). There is a great oral tradition in the primary school which makes it an ideal context in which to incorporate modern language teaching (Hawkins, 1987; Sharpe, 1992). If the classroom teacher is responsible for the provision, there are a vast number of opportunities for the foreign language to be integrated spontaneously into the daily activities and embedded within the teaching of other subjects, so pupils learn to appreciate that a foreign language can be used for genuine communication and as a 'real' and normal part of life (Sharpe, 1991). The teacher can also consolidate the learning of the foreign language whenever opportunities arise throughout the school day. Below there are three examples of ways in which languages teaching can be integrated into the curriculum by the classroom teacher.

First, the teacher can conduct classroom business in the target language. There are only a limited number of ways to call a register or say goodbye to children at the end of the day irrespective of which language is used, so this initial step of integrating MFL requires simple routinised phrases and a very basic vocabulary and knowledge of linguistic functions. Second, the target language can be used for general classroom interaction: organising, praising and encouraging children in their work and general 'chatting'. This type of integration ranges from limited and isolated phrases, learnt by heart, such as *écoutez* or *très bien*, to an extensive and spontaneous use of the target language throughout the day. In Chapter 4 Hurrell gives an excellent example of this type of integration where the specialist teacher, speaking in a foreign language, tends to a pupil's hurt knee. Finally, activities conducted in the foreign language can be interwoven into the core curriculum. At the most modest level the target language can be used to reinforce a task already 'covered', for example, reciting times tables, (see Chapter 7). In Chapter 6, Muir describes in excellent detail a more intense form of integration where a foreign language is embedded and interwoven into other subject areas of the curriculum. The immersion approach is at the strong end of this type of integration where the target language is used as a medium to teach another subject, which is rare in British state schools. The range and amount of foreign language learning integrated into the daily life of the classroom particularly in the two latter examples depend to a degree on the competence and confidence of the teacher more than any other factor, which has implications for training and resources.

The majority of holistic models include a stand-alone component to introduce, practise, and reinforce the language systems and vocabulary and as preparation for activities which take place throughout the day. They are nevertheless economic in terms of curriculum time because the foreign language is exploited predominantly for the purposes of communication throughout the day. As pupils become accustomed to being addressed in a foreign language and confident of their 'role', these activities take little more time than if they were conducted in English.

Distinguishing between different types of provision

Building on Johnstone's typology, Figure 1.1 consists of two continua: one axis is concerned with the intensity and extent of the language content and the other is concerned with the level of overt teaching and the extent to which the programme is integrated into the curriculum (Johnstone, 1994). Discussions about these various approaches tend to assume a clear choice of model, but it has to be recognised that whatever model might have been chosen, there will tend to be a shift in the specification of provision due to the realities and vicissitudes of the local context. There may be changes, for example, in the allocation of curriculum time or the linguistic expertise and position of the teacher, to the extent that the provision could be identified as a quite different type. A programme might be designed to incorporate a relatively high level of language content using high frequency of integration, but if the classroom teacher lacks the proficiency and another member of staff 'drops in' to the classroom for the purposes of teaching the foreign language, high levels of integration would be difficult to sustain. Equally, if a fluent semi-specialist teacher leaves the school and an enthusiastic novice takes on the responsibility, then high levels of language content cannot be guaranteed. Conversely, a classroom teacher who lacks confidence can be 'kitted out' with a self-contained programme of materials and provided with support to enable him or her to teach for up to 30 minutes a week. If that teacher is replaced by one who is more fluent, then the language content may well be doubled.

It is important to note that, even where there is an LEA-led programme in which schools have agreed to follow the same basic programme, there is still likely to be a shift at the individual school level depending on the time allocation, the confidence and competence of the teacher and the attitude of the head teacher and other colleagues.

Implications for planning

Given the evident diversity of practice, those approaching primary MFL for the first time might be tempted to make their choice of approach on the basis of wishful thinking but success lies in a realistic assessment of prevailing conditions and the actual context. Inevitably there will be a creative tension between what is considered ideal in terms of the age of the pupils and the beliefs about foundations for future learning, and the actuality, in terms of

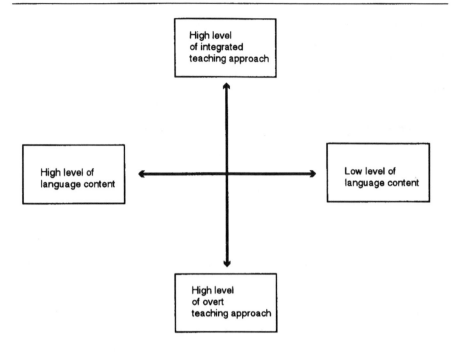

Figure 1.1 A framework for viewing provision

the availability of curriculum time, the level of available teacher expertise and the capacity for the provision of appropriate training. Table 1.1 contrasts some of the differences between approaches which can be grouped under the headings of 'Language Acquisition' and 'Sensitisation' models.

Language Acquisition models require more curriculum time than Sensitisation models to enable pupils to benefit from the linguistic instruction and to master the complex language structures. The teacher exerts explicit control over the knowledge and promotes specialised and specific communicative skills whereas in Sensitisation programmes the teacher facilitates a limited use of a foreign language and highlights motivational and attitudinal aspects of learning. Language Acquisition programmes are more likely to introduce four skills, which affects the time factor; Radnai (1996) noted that reading and writing activities require more teaching and learning time than oral skills, so lessons need to be longer. If the foreign language is integrated into the curriculum, pupils benefit in particular from the frequent oral practice and interaction as well as from a teaching slot once or twice a week.

Language Acquisition programmes tend to start in the upper stages of Key Stage 2 once pupils have mastered basic literacy skills in English. If high levels of foreign language input are provided in Key Stage 1 and continued throughout primary schooling, the demand on the teacher's

Table 1.1 The planning implications of different models

Aim	Language acquisition model	Sensitisation model
Curriculum outline	Intense subject content. More likely to incorporate 4 skills. Highlights specialised knowledge and skills. Need for long term planning	Limited subject content. More likely to incorporate 2 skills. Highlights motivational and attitudinal aspects of learning Less long term planning needed
Teacher's subject knowledge	More demanding on teacher's linguistic knowledge and skills.	Less demanding – a teacher requires purposeful knowledge of the content and limited 'conversational' command of classroom language.
Curriculum time (length and frequency)	Requires between 4%–8% (1–2 hours per week)	Requires between 2%–4% (up to an hour a week).
Age	Usually in the upper stages of junior school – progression is an important factor	Can start at any age, even the early years – with songs, rhymes and some classroom commands.
Choice of language	Usually one language (because demanding on curriculum time)	Can offer a flavour of more than one language
Evaluation and assessment	Emphasis on performance and product. Monitoring and assessment important tools – use of explicit measurable objectives.	Emphasis on enjoyment and willingness to 'have a go'. Difficult to determine external procedures.
Progression and continuity to secondary school	Progression and continuity key features. Influences the learning programme in secondary school and has implications for the transfer of information and liaison with the secondary school.	Intrinsically a primary experience, a foundation in learning how to learn a language. Progression to secondary school less of a key factor for success.

subject knowledge at the upper stages of Key Stage 2 is considerable and the impact on the secondary syllabus and external examination criteria dramatic. Sensitisation programmes can start at any age even in pre-school and a variety of languages can be encountered. Children can 'progress' from Sensitisation models and begin a more intense programme in the upper stages of Key Stage 2 which they then continue through to the secondary school.

Language Acquisition programmes tend to offer pupils the opportunity to study only one language as there simply isn't the curriculum time available for pupils to study two languages at this level of intensity. It is important in Language Acquisition programmes that the secondary schools take account of pupils' foreign language knowledge and skill and that pupils continue studying the same language so their progress is assured. In recent years there has been a massive language diversification programme in secondary schools so, if Language Acquisition programmes are adopted at the primary stage, there needs to be even greater collaboration between the secondary school and its feeder primaries in order to be clear about which language is to be learnt.

In comparison, Sensitisation programmes are less prescriptive; they usually require much less curriculum time so primary teachers have the freedom to offer taster courses in two or even three languages. This extends the pool of possible linguistic expertise available in the primary school and also means that progression and continuity are not such key issues. Whilst teachers may have realistic expectations of the outcomes of Sensitisation programmes, parents and pupils may expect substantial levels of proficiency from the weekly half an hour and be disappointed if the language cannot be continued in the secondary school. Children may have developed a considerable interest in a particular language and be highly motivated; they may perceive their level of proficiency to be higher than it really is and may therefore resist or even resent starting a different language in the secondary school. Consequently, parents and pupils need to be informed about the aim of any provision and why schools are choosing one language over another.

It is important to find appropriate methods of monitoring pupils' progress. Sensitisation programmes emphasise the present accomplishment of pupils, their achievement tends not to be measured against linguistic objectives, but progression and continuity of learning particularly throughout the primary school are crucial if skills are to be developed and motivation sustained. Progression and continuity of language competence are at the core of Language Acquisition programmes and pupils who study a language for a number of years are expected to make a marked improvement in terms of fluency, accuracy and the complexity of language content. This is an important feature in the primary stage but also at the point when pupils transfer to the secondary school.

For continuity to be successful there needs to be effective communication between primary and secondary teachers and a flow of information so that pupils' knowledge and skills can be built upon and a mutual understanding of diverse teaching and learning objectives can be developed. With the level of diversity that exists in primary MFL provision, it is difficult to imagine how effective continuity can best be achieved, but there are a number of key issues which need to be considered.

First, there needs to be adequate planning and sequencing to address each of the four skills to ensure an incremental growth of grammatical control and fluency as well as the expansion of vocabulary. Second, there needs to be joint planning of topics so that pupils can progress from one topic to another. Third, materials and resources need to be presented in sequence to avoid repetition. Finally, colleagues in both the primary and secondary schools may need to examine the teaching styles that pupils experience in each context, to see what can be done to ensure that the transition does not entail a discontinuity of learning.

Conclusion

There is no doubt in my mind that teaching modern languages to primary schoolchildren is a worthwhile enterprise, in particular because of the advantages that children of this age have in terms of their oral and aural ability but also, in a more general sense, we can see massive advantages in engaging young children in what Hawkins (1987) calls 'the apprenticeship of language learning' which entails the development of global perspectives and positive attitudes both to language learning and to other cultures. The emphasis on oral/aural development and attitude formation should not eclipse the role of reading and writing: we are only just beginning to embrace the new technology which enables children to communicate with their counterparts all over the world through e-mail and to access information through the world wide web. These skills rest on the ability to read and write in other languages. In addition, by providing MFL exposure in the primary school pupils have more time to practise and reinforce a variety of linguistic skills.

I have argued in this chapter that whatever the merits of various theoretical positions, the design of the primary MFL provision has above all to be responsive to the actual local context and to take account of the level and nature of the available expertise. This is not to deny that there may well be an ideal scenario in terms of the age of the child, the allocation of time and the expertise of the teacher but if we are to succeed in giving primary children the benefits of MFL, we have to be realistic and accept that practice has to be shaped by actual circumstances. We also need to be realistic in our expectations of what can be achieved in the primary school, exaggerated claims of possible achievement may have a de-motivating effect for pupils, parents and policy-makers alike. Learning anything in the primary classroom takes a long time even when the subject content is reinforced and supported in the home environment.

For many, programmes which are at the language acquisition end of the continuum may constitute the ideal because of their emphasis on performance and the fact that they can give children a head start in one language. For others, programmes which lie at the sensitisation end of the continuum are ideal because they develop the child's understanding about language learning and prioritise positive attitudes and confidence in using small amounts of language. This type of provision also has the advantage of practical viability in circumstances where resources are scarce; it at least provides the possibility of getting started at a time when primary schools are struggling to cope with so many other initiatives.

We must accept of course that the implementation of primary MFL will not be free of difficulty; coherence in curriculum design and in practice within schools and across clusters of schools may be difficult to attain in the initial stages. There will be difficulties, for example, arising from transition and the choice of the languages to be taught and small primary schools will have a difficult task to achieve progression for children in classes containing more than one age range. Johnstone (1994) reminds us that it took The Netherlands 20 years to work through these sorts of problems before primary MFL was finally established as part of the compulsory curriculum. So, it seems clear to me that we cannot afford to wait for the arguments to be resolved and for consensus about the ideal design to emerge.

In the final analysis, it is a matter of values. It is no longer tenable for policy-makers to ignore the anomalous situation where at the official level we declare that we are European while on the ground parents and teachers are having to take action to respond to these cultural and political developments as best they can without the support of national resources. I would argue that, as Europeans, primary schoolchildren are entitled to language learning and we can no longer avoid the need to take concerted action at the national level to support this initiative.

References

Asher, J. and Price, B. (1967) 'The Learning Strategy of the Total Physical Response: Some Age Differences', *Child Development*, 38.

Ausubel, D. (1964) 'Adult Versus Children in Second Language Learning: Psychological Considerations', *Modern Language Journal*, 48.

Burstall, C. (1970) *French in the Primary School: Attitudes and Achievement*, Slough: NFER.

Burstall, C., Jamieson, M., Cohen, S. and Hargreaves, M. (1974) *Primary French in the Balance*, Windsor: NFER.

Byram, M., Escarte-Sarries, V. and Taylor, S. (1991) *Cultural Studies and Language Learning: A Research Report*, Clevedon: Multilingual Matters.

Canale, M. (1983) 'From Communicative Competence to Language Pedagogy', in J.C. Richards and R. Schmidt (eds) *Language and Communication*, London: Longman.

Carroll, J. B. (1975) *The Teaching of French as a Foreign Language in Eight Countries*, New York: Wiley and Son.

CILT (1995) *Modern Languages in Primary Schools: CILT Report 1995*, London: CILT.

Collier, V. P. (1989) 'How Long? A Synthesis of Research on Academic Achievement in a Second Language', *TESOL Quarterly*, 23/3 509–31.

Dearing, R. (1993) *The National Curriculum and its Assessment*, London: SCAA.

DES (1990) *Modern Foreign Languages for Ages 11 to 16: Proposals of the Secretary of State for Education and Science and the Secretary of State for Wales*, London: HMSO.

DfEE (1998) *Blunkett Strengthens Curriculum Focus on the Basics*, Press Release 006/98, London: DfEE.

Edelenbos, P. and Johnstone, R. (eds) (1996) *Researching Languages at Primary School: Some European Perspectives*, London: CILT.

Gardner, D. B. and Lambert W. E. (1972) *Attitudes and Motivation in Second Language Learning*, Massachusetts: Rowley.

Hawkins, E. (1984) *Awareness of Language: An Introduction*, Cambridge: Cambridge University Press.

——(1987) *Modern Languages in the Curriculum*, Cambridge: Cambridge University Press.

——(1996) 'Languages Teaching in Perspective', in E. Hawkins (ed.) *30 Years of Language Teaching*, London: CILT.

Johnstone, R. (1994) *Teaching Modern Languages at Primary School*, Edinburgh: SCRE.

Lapkin, S., Hart, D. and Swain, M. (1991) 'Early and Middle French Immersion Programs: French Language Outcomes', *Canadian Modern Language Review*, 48, 1.

Low, L., Brown, S., Johnstone, R. and Pirrie, A., (1995) *Foreign Languages in Primary Schools: Evaluation of the Scottish Pilot Projects 1993–1995 Final Report*, Stirling: CILT.

Low, L., Duffield, J., Brown, S. and Johnstone, R. (1993) *Evaluating Foreign Languages in Primary Schools*, Stirling: Scottish CILT.

Mitchell, R., Martin, C. and Grenfell, M. (1992) *Evaluation of the Basingstoke Primary Schools Language Awareness Project: 1990/1991 Final Report, Occasional Paper No 7*, Southampton: Centre for Language in Education.

Morgan, C. (1995) 'Cultural Awareness and the National Curriculum', *Language Learning Journal*, 12, September.

Oller, J. and Nagato, N. (1974) 'The Long Term of FLES: An Experiment', *Modern Language Journal*, 5.

Radnai, Z. (1996) 'English in Primary Schools in Hungary', in P. Edelenbos and R. Johnstone (eds) *Researching Languages at Primary School: Some European Perspectives*, London: CILT.

Richards, J. C. and Rogers, T. S. (1986) *Approaches and Methods in Language Teaching*, Cambridge: Cambridge University Press.

Rixon, S. (1992) 'English and other languages for younger children: practice and theory in a rapidly changing world', *Language Teaching*, 25, 2.

SCAA (Schools Curriculum and Assessment Authority) (1997) *Modern Foreign Languages in the Primary Curriculum*, London: SCAA.

Scarcella, R., and Higa, C. (1981) 'Input, negotiation, and age difference in second language acquisition', *Language Learning*, 32, 2.

Schumann, J. (1978) 'The Acculturation Model for Second Language Acquisition', in R. Gingras (ed.) *Second Language Acquisition and Foreign Language Teaching*, Arlington: Center for Applied Linguistics.

Sharpe, K. (1991) 'Primary French: More Phoenix than Dodo Now', *Education 3–13*, March.

——(1992) 'Communication, Culture, Context, Confidence: The Four "Cs" in Primary Modern Language Teaching', *ALL Language Learning Journal*, 6.

Singleton, D. (1989) *Language Acquisition and the Age Factor,* Clevedon: Multilingual Matters Ltd.

Snow, C. and Hofnagel-Hohle, M. (1978) 'The Critical Period for Language Acquisition: Evidence from Second Language Learning', *Child Development,* 49.

Tahta, S., Wood, M. and Loewenthal, K. (1981) 'Foreign Accents: Factors Relating to Transfer of Accent from the First Language to a Second Language', *Language and Speech,* 24, 3, pp. 265–72.

Tost Planet, M. A. (1997) 'Objectives and Contents', in P. Doyé and A. Hurrell (eds) *Foreign Language Learning in Primary Schools,* Strasbourg: Council of Europe.

Valdes, J. M. (1986) 'Language, Thought and Culture', in J.M. Valdes (ed.) *Culture Bound: Bridging the Cultural Gap in Language Teaching,* Cambridge: Cambridge University Press.

van Ek, J. (1986) *Objectives for Foreign Language Learning,* Vol. I: *Scope,* Strasbourg: Council of Europe.

Vilke, M. (1988) 'Some Psychological Aspects of Early Second-language Acquisition', *Journal of Multilingual and Multicultural Development,* 9, 1 and 2.

Vivet, A. (1995) 'Sens et rôle des langues dans le développement des enfants', in Council of Europe, *Report on Workshop 17,* Strasbourg: Council of Europe.

2

Teacher expertise in the primary modern foreign languages classroom

Patricia Driscoll

Modern foreign languages (MFL) is the only National Curriculum subject excluded from the primary school. Pupils learn all other curriculum subjects from the age of 5 but modern languages provision is delayed until the age of 11. One of the main reasons for this is the formally accepted view that there are insufficient teachers with appropriate expertise to teach it (Dearing, 1993). As the Modern Languages Working Party pointed out in 1990, 'Full-scale teaching of foreign languages in primary schools...is not at present possible, not because children at this age cannot successfully learn a language but because very few teachers in primary schools are equipped to teach it' (DES, 1990: 5).

This perceived deficiency in primary teachers' knowledge and skill presupposes criteria for good practice, which in the absence of national guidelines, tend to be based on the experience of teaching MFL in the secondary sector. Whilst the educational goals of MFL at the secondary level may equally apply to primary pupils (Doyé and Hurrell, 1997), the differences both in the organisation of primary schools (Sharpe, 1991) and the age-range of the pupils, present us with a challenge to formulate a new approach to learning. The teaching of MFL in secondary schools is strongly influenced by external criteria such as the GCSE (General Certificate of Secondary Education) examinations, but, rather than mimic this practice, primary schools need to develop one which is conducive to the particular nature of the primary context.

In this chapter I examine how experienced teachers approach the process of teaching MFL in primary schools, in order to generate fresh understanding about the range and scope of the professional expertise needed to teach the subject successfully throughout the primary sector. I draw upon data gathered in an ethnographic study which featured two contrasting approaches to teaching French in the primary school in two separate local education authority (LEA) areas. In one LEA, specialist peripatetic teachers teach French within a timetabled slot; in the other, the teacher is a generalist who incorporates MFL into the traditional primary curriculum. My initial exploration in a number of schools enabled me to develop two models of primary MFL, and although each teacher had idiosyncratic characteristics and worked autonomously within their classrooms, there were distinct patterns of practice which distinguished the teaching in the two LEA areas.

The main sources of data are field notes from participant observation in the classroom, and both taped interviews and informal conversations with teachers, pupils, head teachers and local authority officers. I also collected considerable data on pupil learning outcomes, but for the purpose of this chapter I shall focus particularly on the impact of teachers' knowledge and expertise on the teaching processes.

Since the advent of the National Curriculum, the importance of primary teachers' knowledge has been at the forefront of the educational debate, in particular the relationship between the depth of teachers' subject knowledge and the quality of the teaching process. Research such as Shulman's in the USA (Shulman, 1986, 1987) has been influential and leading British educational figures (particularly Alexander *et al.*, 1992) have produced work which has supported a marked shift towards greater subject specialisation. The recent development of interest in primary MFL has to be seen in the context of this discourse.

One important factor which distinguishes the specialist from the generalist teacher is that the former has gained considerable proficiency and competence in the target language, through higher academic study which usually includes residential experience in the country where the language is spoken. They have usually been trained using the communicative competence approach, the central goal of which is to enable learners to communicate effectively using the language for real purposes. The teacher needs to select the most appropriate methods in order to provide opportunities for pupils to internalise a mass of language and to develop confidence in responding suitably to unpredictable situations using the language they know. The National Curriculum for secondary pupils has emphasised the maximum use of the target language, and communication in the target language is viewed not only as the major learning outcome but also as a means of achieving this outcome (Brumfitt, 1995). Although there are benefits to be gained by extensive use of the target language, it is not a prerequisite of the communicative competence approach.

In addition to cultivating language competence, part of the teacher's task is to provide opportunities for cultural development and to broaden pupils' understanding of their own culture as well as that of others. This has important implications for the teacher's own cultural knowledge and awareness; the teacher needs to be able to access relevant cultural information and step outside of their own culture in order to obtain a fresh perspective. Doyé (1995) argues that for teachers to facilitate intercultural learning in their pupils they themselves need to be international and intercultural learners so they can see cultural variables side by side (see also Byram and Doyé in this volume).

In the main, British people are not exposed to the language and culture of other European countries in the way that other Europeans are exposed to the Anglo-American language and culture through the media, and so on. The specialist teachers in the study tended to visit France more regularly than the generalist teachers who had difficulty in finding opportunities to remedy the gaps in their cultural and linguistic knowledge.

The primary generalist teachers may not have extensive specific subject knowledge but they do have a different kind of professional knowledge to bring to the task. Sharpe argues that primary teachers already possess effective pedagogic strategies to teach MFL and a reflective awareness of what constitutes good practice; furthermore, he points out that primary schools are much better placed to teach a programme of communicative competence as the foreign language can be used for real purposes of communication in the pupils' daily lives (Sharpe, 1991, 1992). Primary school teachers require a substantial breadth of subject knowledge particularly to teach at the upper stages of Key Stage 2 and considerable expertise to organise and transform the knowledge of different subjects, so that pupils across a wide ability range understand what is being taught, find meaning in the experience and are stimulated to learn.

The purposes of learning a foreign language according to the Modern Foreign Languages Working Party's report (DES, 1990) are wide-ranging and consist of a number of dimensions, amongst which are: the development of an awareness into the nature of language; the ability to communicate in the foreign language; insights into the 'foreign' culture and civilisation, insights into the pupils' own culture, and positive attitudes towards foreign language learning and the speakers of foreign languages.

The implications of this for teaching are very complex and require different types of knowledge and a range of processes and strategies to ensure that the various elements of MFL are incorporated into the learning experience. The teachers in the study combined and prioritised these dimensions in a variety of ways; these choices were based on practical considerations such as the physical and time restrictions of the classroom environment or the limitations of their expertise and curriculum resources and were informed by their beliefs about the nature of the subject. This chapter examines some of the main differences between the teaching process of the specialist and generalist teacher and considers the choices that were made. It is presented in three main sections. In the first section, I briefly describe the structure and organisation of the two programmes featured in the study. In the second section, I examine the management of the teaching and learning activities and, in the final section I examine the management of the social relationships which influences the conditions for learning.

The structure and organisation of the programmes

The specialist teachers were frequently 'on the move' and taught a number of classes in up to four schools a day, teaching similar if not the same content in each lesson. As such, they were 'outside' of the decision-making process within the school and often French was 'bracketed' in planning meetings. The teachers were directly employed by the LEA's Adviser for MFL and were assigned to particular schools. The generalist teachers spent most of the day with the class, taught a wide range of subjects and were responsible for the co-ordination of up to three curriculum areas including French.

There was a great variation in the amount of time allocated to teaching MFL in each LEA. The programmes taught by the specialists were allocated up to 120 minutes a week depending on the size of the school, and the programmes taught by the generalist teachers were allocated approximately 25 minutes per week, although French was also used for classroom commands throughout the day.

There was a greater scope in terms of the vocabulary and the complexity of grammar and function in the programme taught by the specialist and the pupils were introduced to the four linguistic skills; speaking, listening, reading and writing. In comparison, the programme taught by the generalist focused mainly on the two skills of listening and speaking.

The generalist teachers were allocated a teaching pack which consisted of a video to help present the language and cultural information and teaching notes which set out a number of teaching activities. The teaching aids for the specialists were flash cards and an audio cassette for listening comprehension. Pupils were provided with printed 'cartoon-style' booklets for their written work.

The management of the teaching and learning

The linguistic proficiency of the teacher had a powerful impact on the way the teaching was managed. The specialist teachers used the target language continuously throughout the lesson as a medium of communication, even when the learner replied in English. By contrast, the generalist teachers lacked the relaxed facility for using the target language in a natural way; their usage appeared rather formulaic and artificial, more like reciting lines from a play in the early stages of rehearsal. This difference in expertise was most apparent in the way the teacher used ordinary classroom language, for example when organising classroom routines, or when greeting the class rather than when teaching the content part of the lesson itself.

Classroom language is very complex and requires the teacher to respond to the unpredictable nature of classroom life without the support of teaching aids or materials. Macaro (1997) points out that the complexity of classroom language can be seen in the large number of verbs which are required to organise and manage the learning in comparison with the number of verbs used in teaching the actual content. In my own study, a generalist teacher, who frequently visited France said during an interview:

> I did 'A' Level French, I mean hundreds of years ago, but I think you retain enough to know the vocabulary and to be able to pronounce the words. My problem is the verbs, you know, if I'm wanting to do a sentence like today um...; As tu mangé...? you see I had to sort out what ending it had and, you know, I can sort of visualise the accent but I can't get the verbs... so I am a little bit hesitant about doing too many sentences in case I give them wrong information.

In relation to the management of the subject content aspect of the lessons, the difference in the teachers' personal linguistic skills was not so apparent as they were more intent on encouraging as much pupil participation as possible and the specialist used chunks of language that were more 'pitched' at the pupils' level of knowledge and competence. During the timetabled slot the generalist teachers were supported by the resources, so if difficulties arose they could check their 'facts' with the teachers' notes and their pronunciation with the video. The generalist teachers were encouraged to integrate the foreign language into the whole curriculum during the training programme, but without resources specifically designed to exploit topics in other subject areas, the teacher's linguistic competence allowed them to do no more than use a limited number of French phrases. The generalist teachers expressed a growing confidence in their knowledge base, accuracy and pronunciation with every passing year of 'doing' the project and some reported on being 'word perfect'. But this competence was limited to the confines of the programme and routine phrases.

Classroom language and activities

The specialist teachers used the target language as a medium to express wishes, organise tasks, to praise, ask and answer questions and to chat about incidentals of the day. As they greeted the class at the beginning of the lesson they tended to talk in an elaborate way about what had happened on the way to the school, or a forthcoming event. This heralded their arrival, and established French as a means of communication. During this phase the teachers frequently spoke 'out loud' to themselves, sometimes in a rather exaggerated way, 'Oh là là... où est mon stylo?, ahh...le voilà. So the pupils were surrounded by 'Frenchness'.

The generalist teacher had the opportunity to use French throughout the day for general classroom language and activities. There were, however, two major difficulties, the first related to the purpose of the communication and the second related to the complex role of the classroom teacher. On the one hand, if the teacher asked a pupil a genuine question opposed to a drill-and-practice question e.g. 'Where have you been?', she required a clear and comprehensible answer, so French was rarely used. On the other hand, during a busy morning of counting swimming money, sorting out costumes for the school assembly, and collecting in signed consent forms for the school trip the teacher had difficulty in speaking in French easily and confidently whilst concentrating on so many other tasks. The relatively simple 'routinised' class-room commands such as *levez-vous* and *posez tes crayons* were frequently used, as were purposeful routine activities which required small amounts of the target language, such as taking the register. The extract below is a typical example of how the generalist teachers took the register at least once a week:

T: Bonjour, tout le monde.
T: Brrr, il fait froid n'est pas?
T: Please put your projects on the table and then get ready for your groups. (*the children were divided into ability groups for the core subjects and moved classes*)
T: En français s.v.p. (*calling out the names*)
T: Mary?
P: Oui Madame.
T: Helen?
P: Elle est absente.
T: Qu'est-ce qu'elle a?
Ps: Elle est malade.
T: Peter? (*no answer*)
P: Il est malade.
T: Peut-être il est absent, peut-être qu'il est en retard. (*register called for the whole class*)
T: Bon, alors qu'est-ce qu'on va manger aujourd'hui?
T: Patrick?
P: Je vais manger un sandwich à l'école.
T: Daniel?
P: Je vais manger le déjeuner à l'école, *etc.*
T: Get all your things ready for the maths swap...

Taking the register is part of the pupil's daily life and although both the teacher and the pupil reverted to English when they needed to speak outside the routinised pattern of the register, the children learnt how to communicate confidently for a real purpose. Classroom activities such as these conducted in French took roughly the same amount of time as that in English and were therefore an economic way of incorporating French into the curriculum. The generalist teachers also integrated short idealised French 'conversations' usually in question form at odd times of the day, such as:

T: Quel temps fait-il aujourd'hui? (*pupils put up their hands, the teacher chose a pupil to respond*)
P: Il fait chaud aujourd'hui.
T: Bien (*several pupils were asked and a variety of phrases about the weather offered as an alternative to the first*)
T: OK, it's almost time for assembly,...oh yes, I've had a complaint about the way some of you stack the lunch boxes after lunch... please be more careful, you're letting the class down...

These snippets of language were more in the mode of the 'drill and practice method' and could not be described as genuine exchanges of information. Pupils needed to suspend their belief that the teacher (who was very busy) was really interested in talking to them about the weather, their co-operation in 'playing the game' was required together with considerable concentration in recalling the phrases they were learning.

The classroom language (date, register, greetings, weather, etc.) appeared to be 'taught' to the pupils mainly at the beginning of the year and practised throughout the year in comparison with the content language of the lesson where the structures and vocabulary were sequenced usually at the pace of the course book or video. Chanting French words was a strategy frequently used by the teacher during the day to signal to children that order needed to be restored. The children, for example, would count upwards in twos or threes as they were clearing up after a 'messy' art activity or wet play.

Lesson content

The linguistic content in both the specialist and generalist programmes was structured into topic areas and the teachers introduced each topic more or less as it appeared in the published material. The underlying structure of the specialists' lessons consisted of three basic phases: the *introductory phase* orientated pupils to the content of the lesson and usually included a revision of previous work; the *activity phase* focused specifically on practising the phrases, vocabulary or function and the *consolidation phase* enabled pupils to reinforce or demonstrate what they had learnt. The latter was usually in written form and was used for monitoring and assessment.

The generalist lessons also consisted of phases but they were much more fluid; frequently the activity and consolidation phases were combined and the assessment was less visible and interwoven into the process of the lesson. There was a tendency towards whole class teaching at the beginning of each phase. The generalist teachers tended to incorporate more group work in games whereas the specialist teachers promoted more individual work, particularly at the 'consolidation phase' of the lesson when pupils worked in their work books.

Below, I have set out some of the differences in character of each model using extracts from the field notes.

The specialist's lessons

The specialist teacher tended to follow the lesson plan more consistently and games were usually included at the end of the lesson after the 'workload' had been completed, if there was any time left or as a reward.

In the *introductory phase* of the lesson the specialist teacher sketched out the general plan of the lesson, asked about homework, and prepared the pupils for the new material and any activities. One of the specialist teachers usually structured the revision of previous work around a question and answer session where pupils asked each other questions in turn around the class. The teacher listened carefully to the pupils and helped them extend the length of their utterances or 'scaffolded' their understanding with clues in the form of mime, facial expressions or gestures, for example:

P: Tu préfères vert eerrer rouge? (*teacher stopped the questioning by writing on the board*) Tu préfères…ou …
T: (*the teacher stressed the sound*) ou.
P: Tu préfères le vert ou le rouge? (*pupils stressed the sound*)
P: Je préfère le rouge.
T: Montre-moi quelque chose de rouge. (*the pupil picked up a red pencil*)
T: Vas-y. (*gesturing for another pupil to ask a question*)
P: Tu préfères un lapin ou un cheval?
P: Je préfère un lapin.
T: Pour manger?
P: (*pupil looked confused*)
T: Pour manger? (*rubbing her tummy*) Yum yum.
T: Ou comme un animal à la maison?
P: Un animal à la maison.
P: Tu aimes la maison?
P: Oui.
T: Pourquoi?
P: err Elle est grand.
T: Grande, bien (*teacher corrected the pronunciation, quietly*)

In the *activity phase* the teacher used a variety of activities to extend and reinforce the linguistic tasks: paired dialogues, 'un sondage' and listening comprehension were frequent features. The specialist lessons were speckled with incidental references to how a French person might express themselves, or with cultural nuances which gave a taste of the unique and essential character of France. Although some of the cultural references were stereotypical in nature, such as 'French people eat horse meat', the teachers also referred to personal anecdotes about French life drawn from their own experiences which reflected their enthusiasm and commitment to France. The cultural references occurred spontaneously throughout the lessons, and covered facts about France and stories about French culture which were frequently used to 'cement' or revise a teaching point, as this extract from the data illustrates for instance:

(The pupils were learning about shopping, and they had had difficulty in remembering 'charcuterie'.)

T: Où est ce-qu'on achète le jambon? (*teacher appoints the pupil*)
P: Char um (*pupils attempts the word, several pupils were asked without the correct response*)
T: Charcuterie.

The teacher spoke for some time about the 'age-old' prevalence of the charcuterie in French towns, and about the French custom of 'take away' prepared food and cooked meats, linking with the notion of the delicatessen in the UK and how the American name had been imported rather than the French name. She finally showed the pupils the meaning of the word. She wrote on the board: Chair = Flesh Cuit = Cooked.

T: The cooked flesh shop.

The children laughed and remembered the word and its meaning in subsequent lessons.

The *consolidation phase* usually involved a writing or copy-writing exercise; the pupils worked on their own while the teacher walked around the class, marking books, helping with spelling or misunderstandings. During this phase the teachers spoke to individual pupils about their work and often spent time revising or reinforcing grammatical points. The range of pupils' understanding of key concepts was made more visible during this phase and teachers frequently gave impromptu teaching sessions 'inspired' by the desire to correct an error or a misunderstanding made apparent by the written word. In interviews the specialist teachers spoke of the importance of laying a good linguistic foundation for the pupils, and their aims in correcting mistakes stemmed from a concern about pupils 'getting into bad habits' which may cause grammatical confusion or incorrect usage later in learning.

The generalist's lessons

In comparison, the lessons were relatively informal with a much slower pace, mediated by the pupils' understanding. The activities and tasks were explained in English, with specific dialogues, games, or songs conducted in the target language. In comparison to the specialist teachers, the generalist teachers rarely changed the tone or pitch of their voices, nor did they use mime or facial expressions as teaching aids. The level of questioning was noticeably less demanding on the pupil and the teachers rarely prompted the children to extend their dialogues or 'answers' with further information or longer utterances. The cultural dimension in the generalist lessons was not extensive and usually limited to stimulation by the video which accompanied the course. The teachers reported that although the video featured incidents about French culture, there was little easily accessible cultural information. The teachers spoke frequently about the need for *all* the pupils to feel confident with a few phrases, and the importance of pupils' enjoyment and comprehension in using relatively small amounts of French in as many different activities as possible. Consequently the children were frequently out of their seats engaged in some form of 'doing'. One of the teachers often spoke of the light relief of French after 'a morning of preparing for the SAT tests or hours of "secondary" geography'.

During the *introductory phase*, previously learnt subject matter was revised, usually in the form of question and answer with the teacher at the front of the class addressing individual pupils in turn rather than pupils addressing each other. The following transcription depicts a typical start to the lessons:

T: Let's do some French.
T: Comment t'appelles-tu?
P: Je m'appelle Jodi.
T: John, if you please....(*pupil chewing his pen*)
T: Quel âge as-tu, John?
P: J'ai dix ans.
T: Bien.
T: Comment s'appelle-t-il?
P: Jamie.
T: Où habites-tu?, etc.

The interaction in the lesson was not dominated by the teacher's use of the foreign language and the dialogue was shared almost equally between the teacher and the pupil. Some of the teachers used the video to deliver the language content, the children were required to repeat the phrases spoken by the voices on the video; the teacher often translated phrases into English rather than requiring the pupils to scan for gist. The video depicted a number of cultural differences which the teacher pointed out as they occurred, for example, the French children shaking hands. Other teachers used the video intermittently to revise what had been learnt, and introduced new vocabulary by drawing on the board.

In the *activity phase* the teacher would sometimes use the hall for the follow up activity, as this extract from the field notes show:

All the children got into equal-sized groups and 'the runner' was nominated, the group were given an equal number of picture cards depicting animals. The teacher called out 'un phasme', the group selected the stick insect card from the cards they had in their hands, the runner 'snatched' the card and ran to the teacher. The first runner to reach the teacher won a point for the group. (Lots of excitement and cries of 'that's not un phasme it's a souris'.)

In the summer, the larger spaces such as the playground or school fields would be used by the class to practise items of vocabulary or structures. These outdoor activities appeared to enhance the fun and enthusiasm for the lessons (which the teachers reported was already very high) because the pupils could make more noise, laugh and generally enter into the competitive spirit which appeared to 'sweep along' even the most timid of pupils. For example,

> A number game – played in the playground, with the hoops used for PE. The teacher wrote numbers between 70 and 79 within hoops in the playground, the teacher shouted 'soixante douze', all the children ran from one hoop to another trying to find the number. Once the number was found they all tried to stand within the hoop.

This was particularly effective for those pupils who had difficulty with numbers as they could follow the 'stronger pupils' for a while who knew their numbers and yet still feel part of the activity. At other times the pupils stayed in the classroom, but there would often be some form of activity linked to the learning. The lessons were full of movement with the emphasis on games, but a closer inspection revealed that all the pupils were involved with the tasks and the children listened very carefully and tried hard to participate.

Planning, progression and differentiation

The teachers all had to make decisions about how best to manage the content, organise the activities, motivate the pupils, meet their needs and give them feedback all within a limited time which required considerable planning. All the teachers in the study had taught French for a number of years and there was little evidence of pre-planning in relation to reviewing the 'subject matter' in either the course or video texts which was an indication of their considerable confidence in the content of the syllabus and resources. Both the generalist and specialist teachers geared the planning of lessons around an activity or a sequence of activities in a single lesson and the overall framework of the term's work was determined by the topics as they appeared in the published course. The specialist teachers tended to plan for quieter, more controlled language activities such as paired role play and they took care not to leave the classroom untidy. As one specialist teacher said during an interview,

T: They get all 'up in the air' if we do too many games and songs, and then I have to hand them back to Peggy (*the classroom teacher*) and they're not ready to carry on with their other work.

In contrast, the generalist teachers did not have to worry about such difficulties because they had ongoing responsibility for the class and were not under pressure to prepare the class to be 'handed back' to another teacher at the end of the lesson. The generalist teachers frequently planned the lesson in connection with a 'doing' activity that used paints and scissors as the following quote indicates:

T: I'm going to try and finish pets off for now so we can concentrate on 'Noël'. We've got cards to do, (*in French*), and I want to try a mobile with French weather scenes (labelled in French – as a gift to take home).

The study revealed some interesting differences in the management of cross-phase liaison in relation to MFL. Every term the specialist teachers, from the feeder primary schools, met together with the secondary school MFL teacher responsible for 'cross-phase' liaison to discuss pupils' achievements, future plans and any concerns. The teachers aimed for a parity of language experience across the cluster group of primary schools, to maximise the progression of pupils' learning. The teachers spoke with a common purpose about the teaching methods and techniques and shared a strong sense of responsibility to pupils' achievements of linguistic proficiency. The approach to systematic planning and evaluation in terms of pupils' performance and production of what had been learnt, lent itself to a greater transfer of information regarding pupils' progress. The specialist teachers tended to perceive the pupils' learning in long-term objectives and spoke about the pupils' continuing progression in both building a body of skills and a body of knowledge as a solid foundation for future language learning:

T: If I can just get them talking, I've got them...once they know how to ask questions and respond, they can build on that.
T: They'll have a firm grasp of the basics by the time they leave me....

In comparison, the generalist teachers spoke on occasions of their isolation in teaching French; in all other subjects they gathered ideas from their colleagues and could rely on their help with any difficulties. The project co-ordinator was very helpful and visited schools periodically, offering advice and practical help, but these visits were relatively rare because of the pressures of time and the generalist teachers were more or less self-reliant, which gave greater 'weighting' to the resources. The opportunities for bridging the gap between the primary and secondary phase were informal and the transfer of information haphazard, as one secondary MFL teacher said:

T: I meet John in the supermarket (*the head teacher of a feeder primary school*) sometimes and tell him how the children are getting on, and hear any news about those that are on their way.

The generalist teachers rarely spoke of the need for long-term planning in French which set the subject firmly outside of the National Curriculum; progression of learning tended to be viewed in relation to additional vocabulary and phrases rather than a development of communication skills:

T: Every word they learn now it'll be one less word they have to learn at secondary school when they've so much more to think about.

Pupils' learning tended to be seen as more cyclical, resting on the assumption that pupils would revisit most of the subject matter in secondary school:

T: It doesn't really matter if they don't remember it, they'll do it again in secondary school, but it's always easier the second time round.

The generalist teachers highlighted the importance of pupils' confidence and enjoyment rather than their linguistic competence and planned the lessons accordingly:

T: They're getting so confident, that's what they'll take (*with them to secondary school*)...and the fun... they know learning a language is fun.

All the generalist teachers spoke of the importance of planning a weekly slot for French to ensure that even when it was 'dropped' from the teaching programme, for instance during the run up to the SATs testing, it was always reinstated and sometimes additional time was allocated to compensate for the lessons that had been missed.

The generalist teachers exercised greater freedom to put on hold any planning and responded spontaneously to any unpredictable events. For instance, one extremely hot summer day, the pupils, too lethargic to respond effectively to the video, were led onto the field to play a vocabulary game of 'fruit salad'. The change in the pupils' mood was electric, they became animated and active for the rest of the lesson. The specialists tended to stick to a predictable format to maintain a sense of discipline, order and quietness.

The comparatively rapid pace of work in the specialist classes, and the fact that a proportion of the work was written meant there was a greater range of performance amongst the pupils. The pace in the generalist lessons was much slower, pupils returned again and again to the same vocabulary and phrases, in different games and activities and from the early stages of the study it was noticeable that the lower ability pupils were confident, enjoyed French and 'felt on a par with the others'.

Assessment

All the teachers carried out continuous, informal assessment integrated into their teaching. In addition, the specialist teachers monitored the pupils' progress through regular marking of their exercise books, discussion with individual pupils about their difficulties and through regular testing focused on the learning goals. On occasion, the testing was particularly rigorous. Some of the pupils found rote learning for the tests rather difficult, particularly when this had been set for homework and, on a number of occasions pupils showed signs of demotivation, whether they achieved high marks or not. The following extract from the field notes illustrates the testing procedures of one teacher.

T: Now what have I told you about your number test? (*the pupils had repeated the same test more than once*)
P: Seventy-five per cent of us have to get 75 per cent of the numbers right.
T: Bien, alors j'espère qu'on va réussir cette fois. (*the teacher reads out numbers in French and the pupils have to write them down numerically*)
P: Miss, could you repeat it? (*the number*)
T: J'ai déjà repété deux fois...you should be listening, I only repeat twice. (*the children exchanged their test sheets for marking. 18 pupils achieved over 75 per cent, which was not a good enough average and so the test was re-scheduled for the following week*)

The generalist teachers' attitude to assessment was quite different. It became clear from conversations with them that they believed that, because of the fun nature of the programme, formal assessment procedures were unnecessary. In contrast, the specialist teachers frequently spoke about the high level of pupil performance to the classroom teacher or head teacher. Their approach to assessment may to some degree be influenced by the demands of accountability; the visiting specialist is usually employed for this particular purpose and is therefore likely to be judged to some extent on measurable learning outcomes, which raises an important question about the relationship between the pupils' measurable performance outcomes, the teacher's expertise and their vested interest in terms of future employment.

Social relationships which influence the conditions of learning

The relationship between the teacher and the pupils is an important factor in the quality of learning in any classroom but particularly in the language classroom. Language learning is based on communication, much of which is oral, and part of the teacher's expertise is to create a friendly environment which fosters a positive attitude to work and one where pupils feel supported and encouraged in 'trying out' the bits of language they know in a variety of situations using a 'foreign'-sounding accent. If the conditions are too restrictive, the pupils may choose not to play an active part, MFL communication will breakdown and learning will be impaired. On the other hand, if the dialogues and activities are not underpinned with acceptable codes of behaviour the teacher's attention may be diverted away from the management of learning and towards the management of behaviour (Bennett *et al.*, 1984).

Teacher–pupil relationships

The interactions between teachers and pupils in the two programmes were very different. A dominant factor in this difference was the classroom teachers' broader knowledge and understanding of their pupils and greater insight into their abilities, interests and strengths. The specialist teachers' knowledge of the pupils was limited to the pupils' language learning within the confines of the subject and the lesson.

The generalist teachers tended to see events more from the pupils' point of view and would adapt their teaching accordingly. The teacher tuned into the pupils' concerns and mood, shared in their understanding of events and used this knowledge to promote and facilitate learning. There were a number of occasions during the two-year research period when I arrived at the school for an observation session to find that the teacher had changed the planned activities or even the subject to be taught, for example, one morning in January I arrived, having battled against the snow and the wind and the teacher said:

T: I'm sorry we're not doing French this morning, they're all over the place, sorry...first day of the snow...they need some quiet time, maybe we could do something (*she meant French*) just before lunch...they can run it off in the playground.

The specialist teachers, by comparison, did not have this freedom or capacity to alter the context and were forced sometimes to battle against negative conditions. They also did not have this detailed knowledge of the pupils as individuals or as learners in a variety of contexts; as a consequence, they tended only to speak about the pupils in terms of their linguistic achievement and linguistic prowess.

T: He's a very good listener….,I taught his brother, he had a good ear too…, he works at it but finds it so hard to remember…, he's developing quite a good accent.

In contrast, the generalist teachers tended to speak with more warmth about the pupils as individual characters, having a whole range of the achievements, friendships, difficulties and triumphs. For example:

T: He's a clever lad, look he did that painting on the wall…. Holly's a bit of a chatterbox, but she'll have a go at anything…, he helps his Dad with the milking in the morning, so by lunch time he's ready for a nap.

It is an essential part of the teacher's repertoire to be able to manage relationships in the classroom and to achieve a 'working consensus' (Pollard, 1985). Pollard discusses the process by which teachers and pupils develop a shared understanding of each other's interests based on a concept of fairness and a recognition of what constitutes acceptable behaviour in a variety of situations. This enables teachers and pupils to work out ways to accommodate each other's interests, so that all parties retain their dignity and self-image. He argues that, although the teacher initially has the power, pupils can undermine the teacher's authority and it is through a negotiated process that teachers and pupils find ways of coping with the classroom dynamics in ways that avoid overt conflict so that learning can take place. A good relationship is negotiated over time and assumes shared expectations of the conventions which are based on a understanding of overt and tacit rules, to which both the teacher and pupils conform. There are many widely accepted norms of behaviour, common to most classrooms, but there are also tacit rules which are often difficult for those outside the group to detect and which bind the individuals in the classroom into a community (Pollard and Tann, 1987). The specialist teachers had to negotiate their own working consensus with each class they encountered but this had to be grafted onto the consensus already established by the classroom teacher and of which they had only limited grasp.

Classroom management

Classroom management is a vital component of any teacher's knowledge and the generalist teachers used more invisible management strategies, embedded and underpinned by their relationship with the pupils. The pupils tended to be more compliant and prepared to co-operate and the classroom management tended to be a cheerful, good humoured affair, as illustrated by such comments as 'I know it's football tonight George, but if you don't sit still and listen the team may have to be a member short next week.'

The nature of the social relationship between classroom teachers and pupils is illustrated by the following anecdote. As I walked into a classroom one day, the teacher was speaking to the pupils in a hushed and very disappointed tone, the children were silent, neither twiddling nor rocking nor rooting in their desks; they were still, respectful and repentant. I sat in the corner wondering what terrible event had occurred. From the faces of both the teacher and the pupils I realised that this was private discourse, which involved the teacher in a 'performance', the main feature of which was the expression of her grave disappointment. When the teacher had finished speaking, the pupils were told to read silently. She told me that she had planned to take the children outside to the playground for French, but she thought it better for them to work inside for the first part of the morning. It turned out that the pupils had failed to turn off the computers after they had finished 'playing' with them at lunch time, a privilege they were allowed as the 'biggest' pupils in the school. The teacher's quiet disappointment and the pupils' repentant mood were an indication of the shared understanding of the transgression and mutual acceptance of the agreed expectations. The teacher spoke to the whole class about the importance of their responsibility to themselves, to her and to each other, interweaving constantly the case of the single class identity in the school and the importance of the behaviour of every member of the group.

The specialist teachers often spoke of the difficulties of classroom management and incidents where the teacher stopped the lesson to police the pupils' behaviour seemed more dramatic than those initiated by the classroom teachers. It was sometimes apparent that the specialist teachers were uninformed of the conduct procedures in the school and because they needed to move on to the next school, were unable to administer any sanctions after the lessons, and had instead to pass on the problem to the classroom teacher or head teacher. On issues of more severe discipline the teacher excluded the pupils from the class, by sending them to their classroom teacher or to stand outside the head teacher's office. Similarly, the teachers were often unaware of the reward procedures and tended to ask the pupils.

T: That is really good work...Do you do stars here or house points?

It was extremely difficult in some cases for the specialist teacher to penetrate the culture in the classroom and gain recognition as a significant member of the group. In some schools the specialist teachers received insights into the daily events or predominant concerns of the pupils in the brief asides as the classroom teacher 'handed over' the class; this tended to help with the daily handling of the pupils. Some classroom teachers were friendly and included the specialist teacher as a competent and valid member of the group which appeared to reassure the pupils. The comment below, illustrates this.

T: Ah Mme, Bonjour, we were just chatting about the netball last night, the girls have got through to the semi-final.

However, this was not always the case, there were indications of professional tensions in the relationship between the classroom teachers and the specialist teachers which may to an extent stem from differences in pedagogical beliefs and values. On occasions the specialist teachers were greeted with a 'little joke', for example:

T: OK, everyone, the franglai woman's here.
T: Time for franglai...
T: Bon juwer tutti li mondi. (*in an exaggerated 'un-French' type accent*)

The specialist teacher had to establish her own rules and acceptable norms of behaviour and lack of support from the classroom teacher made it more difficult to access information about the pupils or events in the school. For example, the specialist teacher might not know about a visit by the school photographer or an extra choir practice, so would arrive to find no class to teach.

On many other occasions, the classroom teacher had already left the classroom before the specialist arrived but the tacit understanding established between the classroom teacher and her pupils continued; it was based on trust that the pupils would be on their best behaviour so, although the teacher had left the classroom, it was still under her management rules. In this situation, the specialist teacher on occasion had to struggle to capture the pupils' attention, impose her presence and take ownership of the class. The use of the target language tended to be a handicap; it compounded the difficulty of 'making contact' with the pupils. Not only was she an outsider but she didn't even speak to them in a way they could understand, so the teachers often reverted to English in the early stages of the lesson for the purposes of behaviour management. The following extract is one example of these occasions:

(*The specialist enters the class speaking French, recounting in a lively manner a story about Easter. Some children look at the teacher, others carry on colouring their books. The teacher finishes her story and tries to signal to the children that the lesson has started.*)

T: Bon, très bien, on va commencer, posez tes crayons s.v.p. et regardez le tableaux. (*Most children stop colouring in their books, put down their pencils, and look at the board. In a more forceful voice the teacher asks again*)

T: Posez tes crayons maintenant, s.v.p. je vous attends! (*Another few children put down their pens, the teacher waits....Two boys at the back start to swing on their chairs, one boy drops a ruler, two girls start whispering, a small ball of paper is thrown across the room, the teacher calls for order in English.*)

T:'   Shh, Shh, you boys at the back, pay attention please! (*Some children start colouring in their books again. The teacher produces some flash cards and asks the children to repeat the words in chorus after her...not all the children co-operate in the activity.*)

If the class teacher remained in the classroom as an authority figure, pupils were notably more co-operative, and incidences of rudeness or ridicule of their classmates' attempts to speak with a French accent minimal. As visitors to the school, the specialist teachers were more restricted in their ownership of the space and resources and consequently the lessons rarely took place outside the classroom. Inside the classroom the specialist teacher had relative autonomy, however, a common occurrence, during the initial encounter at the beginning of the lesson was for the teacher to seek permission from the pupils to rub out some other work on the board. On occasion the pupils refused permission because they claimed the work was still needed, so frequently the specialist teacher had to write in a small corner of the board. This sort of incident underscored the idea of the specialist teacher as an outsider and appeared to affect the power relations in the classroom; in the absence of their 'own teacher' the pupils tended to take greater collective ownership of 'their classroom, and their resources'. This augmentation of the pupils' power in the classroom was not apparent if their own teacher remained in the classroom as an authority figure during the lesson, as has been noted in other studies (Low *et al.*, 1993).

Conclusion

By contrasting the diverse practice of the two cases in different LEAs I have attempted to shed light on the nature of knowledge and expertise needed by teachers of primary MFL to create a quality experience for the pupils, which engenders future learning. The question of which approach is best depends on how the aims are conceptualised which in turn depends on a whole range of other factors such as the expertise and experience of those involved. The teacher's expertise is a key factor in determining the nature of provision so we need to be clear about the relative strengths and drawbacks of the approaches contrasted here.

The specialist model clearly has the advantage of the teacher himself or herself being a resource in the classroom. Their own proficiency, the quality of their pronunciation, their fluency, accuracy and range of language use is the major resource. The specialist teachers' rich knowledge of the target culture and, perhaps more importantly their intercultural understanding are also a great advantage. Their greater subject knowledge informs their pedagogy which tends to result in better sequencing, scaffolding and representation of the subject matter. They can also respond more productively to pupil error and build on pupils' comprehension and oral performance. The specialist teacher has a much clearer view of the language learning journey as a whole and is therefore able to see where each child is along that journey. This long-term perspective informs both planning and assessment strategies and tends to bring a certain pace to the lessons. The specialist teachers' relentless pursuit of linguistic excellence is a crucial part of their professional identity which, although it is to be celebrated, is not without its difficulties.

The specialist model would appear to have some significant drawbacks which can all be related to the teacher's focus on linguistic performance and their position as an outsider. The visiting teacher is clearly at a disadvantage when it comes to the management of classroom relationships and has to depend on the authority of the regular classroom teacher. The specialist teacher's expectation of pupils' high standards of linguistic achievement means they tend not to recognise as clearly as the generalist teacher the impact of the language learning experience on some pupils. They also find it difficult to 'tune in' in a number of other respects, for example being able to take account of the pupils' cognitive development and their attainment in other aspects of the curriculum. One of the results of this lack of empathy and understanding is that the lessons proceed at a pace which disenfranchises a significant number of pupils.

The generalist model also has a number of significant advantages most of which are derived from the teacher's position as a classroom teacher and their experience and expertise as a primary practitioner. The generalist is able to draw upon a thorough working knowledge of the pupils' cognitive development and their attainment in a range of subjects. They also know about the pupils' personalities and their patterns of behaviour. As a language learner they are more able to understand the difficulties the children may encounter on the learning curve and to work with them. They are able to adapt to the vicissitudes of school life and local conditions partly because of their insider knowledge but also because they have some control of structures such as the timetable. Their position in the school also means that they can draw upon other resources available within the school and have opportunities to integrate the language learning into the rest of the curriculum. The generalist teacher's background and professional expertise are far more focused on the needs of pupils and are relatively untrammelled by such taken for granted pedagogic strategies as the extensive use of the target language as the medium of instruction. They draw upon a wealth of experience in teaching nine other National Curriculum subjects, are trained in the ways of literacy and motivation, and can adapt some of these strategies for teaching MFL. Their priority is to facilitate the children's comprehension without them being under pressure to perform and to use the target language at the children's level. In the generalist model the pupils experience a continuity in classroom ethos; there is no disruption of the friendly learning environment which has been established over time. The generalist teachers in the study, some of whom had studied MFL at school for a limited time only, could effectively conduct regular classroom routines in a foreign language, provide opportunities for pupils to acquire a body of knowledge and skills and exploit a limited amount of activities in other curriculum subjects.

The drawbacks of the generalist model are predictable. The generalist teacher does not have the linguistic knowledge, fluency or confidence to code switch spontaneously in order to respond to events throughout the day in two languages. They also tend to have limited access to resources to support integration – they are well placed to reinforce language learning in other parts of the curriculum but, in the absence of good linguistic knowledge, need published material to help them exploit these opportunities. They tend to have limited intercultural awareness and limited first-hand knowledge of the target culture. This has significant implications for resources but fundamentally there is a question about the attitudes and beliefs of teachers. If both pupils and their teachers are to expand their cultural horizons, they need access to high quality relevant materials which will convey the cultures of other countries without resorting to stereotypes.

So in responding to the challenge to develop primary MFL, we need to take a fresh look at the whole notion of teacher expertise. The official view, that the generalist primary teacher is not 'equipped' to teach a foreign language has, I hope, been dispelled in this chapter. It is clear to me that there is considerable scope to explore models of implementation which deploy the expertise of the dwindling numbers of language specialists most effectively within a framework of generalist primary practice

It is highly likely, however, given the acute shortage of language specialists for secondary schools, that in the future generalist teachers will, in the main, be asked to teach foreign languages in primary schools around the country. There are advantages to both specialist and generalist approaches; the languages teacher is a specialist because of the years of personal involvement and professional commitment which shapes the way they see the language and culture, which in turn affects their beliefs and attitudes about the subject and informs the way they teach. A specialist's pedagogic strategies are derived to a large extent from the depth of their knowledge about language and culture and I believe it cannot be synthesised and served to non-specialists in palatable bite-size competences.

Teachers are pivotal in the development of successful MFL programmes in primary schools, and to begin with the notion that primary teachers around the country are in some way deficient is not a helpful start. Of course, it is reasonable to expect specialist teachers experienced in teaching older learners to extend their pedagogic strategies to include approaches more appropriate for teaching young learners, but it is far from reasonable to expect the generalist teacher to become a kind of *ersatz* specialist particularly when they may have experienced disenchantment and perhaps even failure with foreign languages within the present educational system. Rather, we need to be clear about the essential ingredients of the primary practitioner's knowledge and pedagogic expertise and to view these as positive assets in teaching a foreign language.

This is not to say that linguistic knowledge and skill, cultural awareness and positive attitudes towards other cultures are not essential for effective teaching, but we need to approach those generalist teachers who are prepared to incorporate foreign languages into their repertoire as experts in their own right, who are experienced in teaching all manner of complex processes and concepts in mathematics, science and language. We need to address the question of what type of language and cultural competence is the most valuable for the generalist teacher, taking into account that many of their attitudes and beliefs about the subject are likely to be different from those of the specialist teacher. We also need to clarify our aims and our views of what realistically can be achieved in offering foreign languages to children in the primary context in the light of a greater awareness of the extent and nature of the generalist teachers' expertise. We clearly need to pay careful attention to questions of planning, progression and strategies for monitoring progress so that generalist teachers can incorporate MFL into their practice in a way which not only ensures quality but will also lead to successful implementation which can be sustained over time. I have no doubt that there already exists a range of excellent practice from which we can learn valuable lessons and from which can be drawn principles to underpin the development of MFL in British primary schools.

References

Alexander, R., Rose, J. and Woodhead C. (1992) *Curriculum Organisation and Classroom Practice in Primary Schools: A Discussion Paper*, London: Department for Education.

Bennett, N., Deforges, C., Cockburn, A. and Wilkinson, B. (1984) *The Quality of Pupil Learning Experience*, London: Lawrence Erlbaum.

Brumfitt, C. (1995) *Language Education in the National Curriculum*, Oxford: Blackwell Publishers.

Dearing, R. (1993) *The National Curriculum and its Assessment*, London: SCAA.

DES (1990) *Modern Foreign Languages for Ages 11 to 16, Proposals of the Secretary of State for Education and Science and the Secretary of State for Wales*, London: HMSO.

Doyé, P. (1995) 'Report of Group 6: Teacher Education', in *Language Learning for European Citizenship – Report on Workshop 8B*, Strasbourg: Council of Europe.

Doyé, P. and Hurrell, A. (1997) *Foreign Language Learning in Primary Schools*, Strasbourg: Council of Europe.

Low, L., Duffield, J., Brown, S. and Johnstone, R. (1993) *Evaluating Foreign Languages in Primary Schools*, Stirling: Scottish CILT.

Macaro, E. (1997) *Target Language Collaborative Learning and Autonomy*, Clevedon: Multilingual Matters.

Pollard, A. (1985) *The Social World of the Primary School*, London: Holt, Rinehart and Winston.

Pollard, A. and Tann, S. (1987) *Reflective Teaching in the Primary School*, London: Cassell.

Sharpe, K. (1991) 'Primary French: More Phoenix Than Dodo Now', *Education 3–13*, March.

——(1992) 'Communication, Culture, Context, Confidence: The Four "Cs" in Primary Modern Language Teaching', *ALL Language Learning Journal*, 6.

Shulman, L. S. (1986) 'Those Who Understand: Knowledge Growth in Teaching', *Educational Researcher*, 15, 2.

——(1987) 'Knowledge and Teaching: Foundations of the New Reform', *Harvard Educational Review*, 57, 1, pp. 1–22.

3

Policy issues for primary modern languages

Lesley Low

The resurgence of interest in teaching foreign languages in primary schools, which took place in the late 1980s and early 1990s among educational policy-makers at national level in a number of European countries, can largely be attributed to the opportunities which an emerging new Europe presented. For some countries, such as Scotland, the main impetus was the advent of the single market in 1992 and the economic benefits which it was anticipated would ensue to those able to do business in more than one European language. For others, such as France and Italy, there was the added incentive of developing and promoting a growing sense of European identity based on cultural and linguistic diversity. For countries from the former Soviet bloc in eastern Europe such as Hungary and Croatia there was the desire to look westwards in both a cultural and economic sense.

In seeking to capitalise on the perceived opportunities of a new Europe, policy-makers opted for an expansion of foreign languages teaching in their schools. Starting the process in primary schools would ensure extra time for pupils to develop competence in a first foreign language or allow a second or even third foreign language to be taught to many more pupils throughout their school careers. The means chosen to expand foreign languages teaching into primary schools varied considerably across the countries concerned. Some such as France, Italy and Scotland have implemented national policies which, over time, should deliver foreign languages teaching to all pupils in the chosen age ranges. Others, for example Croatia, have adopted experimental approaches in a limited number of schools to test out theories and evaluate their success. In the absence of national policies for Modern Languages in Primary School (MLPS), there are a number of thriving initiatives at regional and local level such as those in Kent, East Sussex and the Isle of Man in the UK and in many of the federal states of Germany, such as Sachsen-Anhalt, where educational policy is devolved to state ministries.

Whether operating at a national, regional or local level, policy-makers for MLPS have to address the same sorts of issue. Failure to resolve some of these issues led to the demise of the first wave of MLPS experimentation during the 1960s and 1970s, especially in the UK. For example, we have to ask whether current initiatives are achieving success in tackling the challenge of devising an appropriate curriculum and teaching methodology for younger learners and for teachers who are not foreign language specialists. Is there evidence of strategies being put in place to ensure the continuity of foreign language learning once pupils move on to secondary school? These two issues still give rise to problems and are symptomatic of circumstances where expertise in foreign languages teaching has largely been the domain of secondary specialist teachers (whether working in the classroom or beyond it in an inspection, support or development capacity), who have little experience and perhaps only meagre understanding of the primary school, its curriculum, pedagogy and learners.

This chapter will identify the kinds of policy decisions which have to be made in relation to MLPS and use the current policy approach in Scotland to illustrate the associated issues and draw comparisons with the situation in the rest of the UK. It will argue that the long-term success of MLPS initiatives is largely dependent on how well they articulate with past and current developments in educational policy and practice, not just within the field of modern languages but also across the broader sweep of innovation and change in education as a whole.

MLPS strategy in Scotland

The first consideration for educational policy-makers is whether or not to put a national strategy for MLPS in place. In Scotland, a programme has been underway since 1989 when the pilot phase for MLPS was begun, whereas in other parts of the UK, the same British government preferred not to pursue such a policy. Why this difference of approach? First, the autonomy of a separate system of education for Scotland has to be appreciated. While there are broad features of UK educational policy which are applied across all parts of the country, the relative autonomy of the Scottish system allows a considerable measure of freedom of decision to ministers at the Scottish Office. The later move to secondary education in Scotland following seven years in primary school rather than six as in England, had allowed historically for only two years of compulsory foreign language study in Secondary One (S1) and Secondary Two (S2) prior to pupils making their subject choices for Standard Grade (previously O Grade) of the Scottish Certificate of Education. In January 1989, therefore, when the then Scottish Conservative Minister for Education, Michael Forsyth, published Scottish Education Department Circular 1178, a large number of Scottish pupils experienced only two years of foreign language learning. This circular, which proposed a 'languages for all' policy for pupils up to Secondary Four (the end of compulsory schooling in Scotland) and advocated the piloting of a foreign language in primary schools, offered the potential for expansion of foreign language learning from two to six years for all Scottish pupils.

The motivation behind this expansion of foreign languages teaching was not exclusively an educational one, although its implementation was placed in the hands of Her Majesty's Inspectorate (HMI) for Scotland and their national development officers. There was an economic consideration, as the Minister wanted Scotland to be well placed to take advantage of the opportunities for business and mobility which the single market of 1992 would bring. There is also evidence to suggest that political capital could also be made from an initiative which was considered likely to be very popular with parents. For example, several of the first six pilot projects (secondary schools and their associated primaries) were to be found in the relatively small number of constituencies with Scottish Conservative MPs. The MLPS pilots proved to be very popular with pupils, teachers, local authority personnel and parents alike and it was not surprising that the same Conservative government made a pledge in its 1992 election manifesto to introduce a foreign language into all Scottish primary schools by 1997. In January 1993, the Minister for Education duly announced a national training programme which would aim to meet this commitment by training one teacher in every primary school to introduce a foreign language. This was a departure from the model of delivery for the MLPS pilot which relied on a partnership between visiting teachers from the modern languages department of the receiving secondary school and primary class teachers in the associated primary schools. The secondary teachers brought their linguistic expertise and the primary class teachers brought their knowledge of appropriate strategies and content for primary age pupils. The model for the national extension of MLPS would combine these specialist skills in one teacher through a specially designed training course for primary teachers.

Notwithstanding the political advantages of the MLPS initiative in Scotland, there was widespread support at regional level both for the pilot model with its partnership between visiting secondary teachers and primary class teachers and for the switch to a primary-led model in order to achieve a national extension of MLPS. Large regions such as Strathclyde, Lothian and Fife had run their own pilot projects using the partnership model and other regional educational authorities had provided additional support and resources to the national pilot projects operating in their areas. Officers from the regions worked alongside HMI and national development officers in the design and implementation of the national training programme for MLPS and there appeared to be an unprecedented consensus among educational policy-makers at national and regional level about the aims and approaches for the new MLPS delivery model.

MLPS developments in England

The same political imperatives were not perceived to be operating in England and the resource implications of implementing a similar policy to a much larger school population may have been too large to contemplate. A further consideration was the educational climate of the early 1990s with its concerns about the rigid specification of, and legal requirement to conform to, the National Curriculum, the national testing agenda for primary schools and changes to the role and staffing of the Inspectorate. None of these factors was operating to such a degree in Scotland. Although a national curriculum does exist, it is in the form of Guidelines for the 5–14 age range and the arrangements for Standard Grade, which are followed through consensus rather than requirement and do allow for some flexibility. National testing of primary age children has made much less headway in Scotland as a result of parental objections as well as teacher resistance, and HMI have extended their national role beyond inspection to the development and implementation of educational policy.

In England itself, the formulation of a national policy for MLPS has been undertaken by other bodies such as the Association for Language Learning (ALL) and the Centre for Information on Languages Teaching and Research (CILT). Both organisations have developed comprehensive policy documents which present a detailed case for the inclusion of a foreign language in the National Curriculum of England, Wales and Northern Ireland at the primary stages. They argue for the educational, cultural, linguistic and social benefits of an early start to foreign language learning and outline the political and economic advantages of such a policy. The policies draw on Council of Europe and European Commission documentation as well as evidence and experience from the numerous MLPS projects operating at school and local authority level across the UK. ALL has had access to such projects through its Early Languages Learning Panel and CILT through the Primary Languages Network. As well as offering support to existing projects, both organisations have promoted the cause of MLPS through their conferences and publications and the lobbying of the Department for Education and Employment and other government bodies.

One such body, the Schools Curriculum and Assessment Authority (SCAA), now incorporated into Qualifications and Curriculum Authority (QCA), in line with its remit to keep the National Curriculum under review, organised a conference in October 1996 entitled 'Modern Foreign Languages in the Primary Curriculum' which drew on international evidence and experience of MLPS, including that from Scotland, and sought to identify the implications of opting for a national policy for primary modern languages across the rest of the UK. The report of the proceedings of the conference offered two very tentative ways forward for SCAA: that in the short term it should co-ordinate discussions between key players and in the long term 'consider the desirability of a full consultation on the possible introduction of modern foreign languages in all primary schools' (SCAA, 1997, p.4). The caution emanating from this 'policy' statement is understandable in the light of the potential 'knock-on effects' which the introduction of a foreign language into the primary curriculum is having in those countries which have been less cautious and pressed ahead. These require policy decisions which extend to virtually every sector from primary through secondary education to the initial and continuing education of teachers themselves.

The nature of MLPS innovations

Most national initiatives in MLPS have adopted a language acquisition model in keeping with an overarching aim to enhance the linguistic attainments of the young people concerned. Programmes based on raising language awareness have been tried out at local level. For example, in Basingstoke foreign language assistants were employed to introduce primary children to three European languages prior to making their choice of foreign language when moving to secondary schools. This model was found by evaluators to have promoted positive interest in and commitment to the process of language learning and benefited intercultural awareness (Mitchell *et al.*, 1992). Some national MLPS programmes, such as the ones in Italy and Croatia, have encompassed both language competence and language awareness, by building on children's first language concepts and using first and foreign languages to reinforce one another.

The main policy implication of opting for a language competence model is the need to ensure an adequate supply of linguistically competent teachers. In the pilot phase of MLPS in Scotland, secondary teachers of foreign languages were deployed in primary in order to get the scheme up and running quickly. In France, a similar strategy was used which drew on a wider range of competent linguists. These were not always trained teachers and included native speakers of the foreign language concerned. Both countries decided to abandon this visiting specialist approach in the early 1990s, however, because the supply of such teachers was not sufficient to deliver the nationwide extension of MLPS to which their national governments had become committed. Both moved to a model of foreign language teaching which would be self-contained within the primary sector by giving primary class teachers the responsibility for pupils' foreign language learning.

In France, a specially designed video course was produced at national level and was distributed to all primary schools to allow class teachers to introduce a foreign language to their pupils using very little of the language themselves. The video provided the model for the foreign language and the teacher had the responsibility of managing the children's viewing so that they had as much access to the foreign language as possible, and of setting up activities which allowed the children to use the foreign language (Brun and Panosetti, 1997). By contrast, Scotland's educational policy-makers opted to make the primary class teacher the model for the foreign language and devised a 27-day training course which, over one year, was designed to give primary teachers the necessary linguistic competence and teaching methodology to introduce a foreign language to their pupils.

Scotland's ambitious in-service programme, which has been running since the school session 1993–94, will have trained in the region of 3500 primary teachers by the start of the school session 1998–99, with the result that 75 per cent of Scottish primary schools will have at least one teacher capable of introducing a foreign language into the curriculum for Primary Six (P6) and Primary Seven (P7) pupils, i.e. those aged 10–12 years. At an estimated cost of £4 million for each of the five phases of training, this represents a considerable investment in education. However, more funding will have to be made available if one hundred per cent coverage is to be achieved, not only to bring on stream those schools which have yet to become involved in the MLPS programme but also to plug the gaps in existing provision caused by natural wastage, as primary foreign languages teachers move on or out of post. The staging of the training programme over twelve months means it cannot respond quickly to fill such places, putting in jeopardy the whole foreign language provision within a particular school.

Some local education authorities have demonstrated their commitment to MLPS by providing peripatetic cover in such cases, but for many of the smaller authorities this is not an economic option. Local authorities are also facing the demand for continued support for primary teachers of foreign languages, who, despite the wealth of teaching and other support materials available, often feel isolated. The national decision to continue with a competence model for MLPS means that primary teachers are dependent for their foreign language support on staff operating for the most part outside their own sector. Such colleagues are not as readily available as in the pilot phase for MLPS, particularly at local authority level where the post of dedicated Modern Languages Adviser has all but disappeared since local government reorganisation.

One long-term and sustainable solution to this problem of teacher supply for MLPS would be the inclusion of a foreign language as a mandatory element in the pre-service training of all primary teachers. So far there have been no signs that teacher education institutions in Scotland are willing to go beyond the voluntary courses they currently offer. They argue that such a requirement might affect recruitment to the profession and that the primary teacher education curriculum, like the primary school curriculum itself, has been subject to many other policy initiatives such as the one requiring health promotion in schools, which leave no time for further inclusions. A further disincentive might be the fact that a foreign language does not yet have the status of an accepted subject within the parameters of the 5–14 Guidelines. The existing Guidelines, which relate to the 12–14 secondary age group only, have yet to be amended to take account of the earlier start to foreign language learning in primary.

The place of the foreign language in the primary curriculum

The Scottish Office Education and Industry Department (SOEID) have argued the case for a 'wait and see' policy, preferring to monitor the current national extension of MLPS and see how it develops, before deciding on new curriculum guidelines and identifying the levels of attainment which primary pupils should achieve in a foreign language. There is something of a paradox here. On the one hand, to formalise the place of a foreign language within Scotland's primary curriculum through revised 5–14 Guidelines, inspection and the assessment and reporting of pupils' attainments is perceived by teachers and those who train and support them, as potentially damaging, particularly to the confidence of primary foreign languages teachers who are still getting to grips with a new skill and added responsibility. Yet, on the other hand, to leave the foreign language outside these normal arrangements will make it vulnerable, both in terms of the time devoted to it within the primary curriculum and to any future demands for accountability from government, whether at the national or local level.

The current situation in Scotland illustrates the system-wide changes which the introduction of MLPS as part of national educational policy brings in its wake, and for all the progress that has been made, there are still major policy issues to resolve. Not least, is establishing the place of the foreign language within the primary curriculum itself. Where should the time for the foreign language be taken from? What should disappear from the curriculum to make room for it? SOEID have not yet been able to give a definitive answer to these and similar questions which preoccupy primary head teachers in particular, in their capacity as managers of MLPS within their schools.

The time allocation given to the foreign language during the pilot phase was in the region of 80 minutes a week with visiting teachers from the local secondary school making twice-weekly visits. Any loss of time from other curriculum areas was generally accepted to have been compensated for by the boost in confidence and motivation which learning a foreign language in the final years of primary gave to the children concerned. Furthermore, the approach to MLPS which evolved during the pilot phase and came to be known as 'embedding', was potentially efficient in the use of time as it substituted children's first language with the foreign language in the performance of everyday routines within the primary school day. These include taking the register and dinner numbers, lining up and entering and leaving the classroom and talking about the date, time and weather. It was also used during other aspects of the curriculum, for example, getting the children to do their mental arithmetic, basic PE, art and craft, science and music activities using the foreign language.

When the move from the pilot model of delivery using secondary specialist teachers to the primary-led model was announced, it was argued by policy-makers that, given appropriate training and support, the primary class teacher was the best placed person to embed the foreign language into the primary curriculum in this way (Boyes, 1993; Pignatelli, 1993). The authors of the national training programme for MLPS had been very involved in the pilot phase of the initiative at national or regional level and drew extensively on this experience in identifying a list of ten competencies which primary teachers would need to acquire. These included gaining a confident command of the language needed for daily routines and organising activities in the classroom and of the language required to deliver some basic art, craft, home economics, science, technology, drama and PE activities through the medium of the foreign language (SOED, 1993b).

Missing from this extensive and impressive list is any association with a major curriculum area, namely, English language. The evaluators of the national pilot for MLPS observed the foreign language being used in all the ways identified above, but never to reinforce or to complement the work being done by teachers and pupils in their first language (Low et al., 1995). The decision to opt for a language competence model was argued for very strongly in the setting up of the MLPS pilot and any question of combining this approach with a language awareness or knowledge about language dimension was explicitly rejected (Giovanazzi, 1992). This polarisation has arguably been carried over into the national extension of MLPS, for the national training programme for primary teachers of foreign languages has nothing to say about the role of first language or knowledge about language in developing pupils' foreign language competence, even though these same teachers are the experts in children's first language development.

This omission may have repercussions for the foreign language in terms of finding sufficient time and a natural place within the primary curriculum. The original vision of the trained primary teacher introducing a foreign language to the class and embedding it in the routines and teaching of daily work with the children has proved elusive. In the great majority of cases, the trained primary teacher of foreign languages has become a visiting specialist in their own right, 'dropping in' to the classes of colleagues to teach the foreign language to P6 and P7 classes within the same school. This is the inevitable result of having only one or two trained foreign language teachers in any one primary school, where there may be more than one class learning a foreign language and where head teachers deploy their staff across the full age range of classes, rather than creating upper primary specialists with a foreign language training. All this leaves the embedding approach at best difficult and at worst unrealistic to implement.

The drop-in or swap-over model (as it has variously come to be known) has the advantage of providing guaranteed time for the foreign language within the busy primary curriculum because teachers have to be time-tabled to visit the classes concerned. However, this arrangement has highlighted the time being 'lost' from other aspects of the curriculum and the consequent demand from head teachers to know from where it should be taken. In countries such as Italy and Croatia, the time for foreign language learning comes from that devoted to the general language dimension of the curriculum and teachers foster a strong inter-relationship between first and foreign languages. The exclusion of language awareness from the Scottish model for MLPS has precluded such linkage and has arguably created a separation which has more to do with a secondary school approach to the teaching of English and of foreign languages. If the foreign language is to find a permanent home in the primary curriculum, then these issues will need to be addressed and the impact on other subject areas appreciated and taken into account. In Scotland, it may well be the case that a revision of the 5–14 Guidelines for modern languages alone will not suffice.

Foreign language diversification and transition to secondary school

Two further issues which have implications beyond the confines of the primary classroom, and which educational policy-makers need to address, concern foreign language diversification and the transition from primary to secondary school. In Scotland, strategies for dealing with these issues have been left to local policy-makers, whether at school, cluster or education authority level. No specific guidance has been issued from SOEID or by HMI on how to approach these areas, which depend for their local solutions on good relationships between the receiving secondary school and its associated primaries. Within Scotland, the last big policy push for modern languages prior to the primary pilot was for foreign language diversification in the early secondary stages. Many secondary schools responded by introducing German, Italian or Spanish into S1 or S2 alongside the traditional first foreign language, French. This expansion in the teaching of languages other than French required most secondary teachers of foreign languages to qualify to teach two. Within Scotland this did not just mean having a second language as part of a degree course, because the General Teaching Council for Scotland (which registers all teachers in primary and secondary education) insists on a strict residence qualification in the country whose language(s) the teacher wishes to teach. Secondary teachers of modern languages have therefore invested heavily in the diversification policy over recent years.

Circular 1178, referred to at the start of this chapter, which launched the major expansion of foreign languages teaching in Scotland's schools, expressed a strong commitment to foreign language diversification and the national and regional pilots for MLPS which ran from 1989–95 were diversified across the four foreign languages of French, German, Italian and Spanish. At the time SOEID made it clear that the vast majority of pupils who had begun their foreign language learning in the primary as part of the pilot should continue with the same foreign language on entry to S1. There were some local difficulties in meeting this expectation because most of the pilot secondary schools were diversified. In order to maintain a balance between the two languages on offer, the secondary schools, who argued that MLPS was only a pilot and as such could not be allowed to disrupt existing staffing and other organisational arrangements, tried a number of strategies. These included persuading parents to opt for a new language in S1 on the grounds that pupils would be able to transfer their foreign language skills quite comfortably to a new language, and experimenting with foreign language diversification within the cluster of associated primary schools or actually within the larger primaries themselves.

Both these strategies are still in evidence under the new arrangements for MLPS in a few localities, but there is evidence to suggest that the new policy for primary modern languages is severely undermining the previous policy on language diversification in Scotland. There are a number of reasons for this, the first and most important being that participation in the MLPS training programme is completely voluntary. A survey of primary teachers before the training programme was launched showed that a large majority had taken French up to Higher Grade at school. It was hardly surprising, given the length and nature of the 27-day training programme, that primary teachers opted to be trained in the foreign language with which they were already familiar, which for most was French. Well over three-quarters of the MLPS training places have been for French, with the remainder spread across the other three languages.

A second reason for the dominance of French as the primary foreign language is the strong Scottish parental preference for that language. They themselves probably learnt it at school and therefore associate foreign language learning with French. Parental pressure is responsible in some secondary schools for pupils switching away from their primary foreign language to French on entry to S1. So strong is the tide to French as a result of MLPS that senior management in secondary schools are increasingly considering a move away from foreign language diversification in early secondary. Other pressures in the system, such as impending changes to the curriculum post-16 with Higher Still, are further encouraging school managers to opt for such a 'simplification'. The modern languages teaching community are alarmed at the loss of diversified provision of foreign languages in the mainstream of secondary education in Scotland. The Scottish Association of Languages Teachers (SALT), whilst supporting the policy of MLPS and their new colleagues in primary, have written on behalf of their members to the government (now Labour controlled) and all political parties asking for urgent consideration of the impact which educational policy decisions in modern languages education are having on diversification.

National policy-makers need to be clear which set of priorities should operate: those which support foreign languages diversification or those which mitigate against it. For example, it can be assumed that the desire for pupils to develop competence in languages other than French was broadly in line with the economic imperatives which were perceived to be operating with the advent of the Single European Market in 1992. However, if the over-riding aim is to guarantee extra time for foreign language learning so that pupils can develop a better competence in their first and probably only foreign language, then continuity of language from primary to secondary school is essential. Given parental preference for and existing teacher competence or at least confidence in French, foreign language diversification at that stage of schooling looks to have little future.

There are other issues which have to be addressed with regard to the transition from primary to secondary school if pupils are to make the best of their early start in foreign language learning. These issues arise from whole school management policies as well as approaches to teaching and learning. HMI Isobel McGregor, the current staff inspector for modern languages in Scotland, did not mince her words at the SCAA conference when she talked about these matters: 'intransigent class organisation and timetabling policy could destroy the whole purpose of primary modern foreign languages, hence the need for commitment and a positive attitude at all levels' (SCAA, 1997, p.10). These challenges are not uniquely Scottish, they apply even in countries which have long-standing and successful programmes of early foreign language learning and have to do with the inherent separateness of the primary and secondary schooling experiences both for teachers and learners.

In the pilot phase of MLPS, it was widely assumed that the deployment in primary schools of specialist modern languages teachers from the associated secondary schools would ensure continuity and a smooth transition for pupils in their foreign language learning. The evaluation of the national pilot projects made a specific study of many aspects relating to the transition from primary to secondary and found that these assumptions had proved rather premature (Low et al., 1995). The same teachers operating in primary and secondary classrooms were observed to teach in quite different ways and did not necessarily build on what their pupils had done in primary. There was no specific support or resources given to secondary teachers involved in the national pilot to address the issue of continuity of learning. Their time was initially given over to the provision of materials and lesson planning for primary, then the expansion of MLPS to P6 and younger classes, and finally to preparations for the new model of delivery in their cluster.

Most of the modern languages departments involved in the pilot did, however, experiment with different approaches in S1, but unfortunately, there are few recorded examples of how they coped with the transition from primary to secondary (for one documented case see Low and Wolfe, 1996). As the pilot progressed, time and energies became increasingly focused on the new delivery model for MLPS and how primary teachers could be trained to take over responsibility for the foreign language in primary. As a result, modern languages teachers working in secondary schools with no experience of teaching in the primary have little to draw on as they prepare to receive cohorts of S1 pupils who are no longer foreign language beginners for the most part. Trial and error will be the only approach open to them and the evidence from evaluations of the earlier experiments in the UK and the national pilot in Scotland have shown that failure to take account of pupils' prior language learning can have a demotivating effect on pupils with implications for their subsequent attainments in the foreign language.

Under such circumstances, questions begin to be asked about the purpose and value of beginning the study of a foreign language in primary and, as was demonstrated in the early 1970s, policy-makers can then retreat from such programmes and withdraw funding. It seems almost impossible to contemplate this in Scotland, given the large sums of public money which have been invested in the programme and the commitment which teachers and those who support them have shown. However, one of the consequences of opting for a model which aims to improve pupils' foreign language competence is that such outcomes can be measured and if the anticipated improvements do not ensue, then the whole programme begins to look vulnerable.

The educational imperative for MLPS

This scrutiny of the policy decisions which have been taken and those that remain to be taken in Scotland with regard to a national programme for MLPS demonstrates the complexity of the processes involved and highlights the presence both of policy clashes and policy vacuums. Different policy-makers, albeit operating within the same educational system, put forward and implement changes which may overlook or even undermine developments in another part of the system. The caution which SCAA has expressed with regard to formulating a national policy and strategy for introducing a foreign language into other parts of the UK is quite understandable in the light of such considerations, particularly now the full implications of the initiative in Scotland are becoming understood. ALL's policy statement on an earlier start to foreign language learning argues for a long-term strategic plan for language learning in the UK which should be put in place before a foreign language is formally introduced into the primary curriculum (ALL, 1997). Scotland, in common with the rest of the UK, has no such strategic plan, although calls for such a formulation are being made by SALT and local education authority personnel.

The MLPS schemes which have been operating at local education authority level in other parts of the UK, may well provide the evidence needed to convince national policy-makers that the costs and upheaval which a UK-wide introduction of MLPS would necessarily bring, can be justified. Such schemes, however, must be rigorously and independently evaluated, not least in terms of whether they meet the aims that are set and the claims that are made for them. Many working across the spectrum of modern languages education, from practitioners to policy-makers, actively support an early start to foreign language learning, but hard cash is only likely to follow on the back of hard evidence.

In the case of Scotland, it has to be remembered that the impetus behind the MLPS development was largely political and that educational policy considerations had to be moulded to suit the priorities of ministers at the time. Political intervention has its benefits, most notably in the funding and resources which follow in its wake, but such interest can also wane as governments change and other priorities are identified. If programmes such as MLPS are to survive the whims of political fashion, then they must be underpinned by a strong educational imperative and demonstrate their effectiveness in achieving the goals to which they aspire.

Postscript

Since this chapter was written there have been major developments in national policy for MLPS in two of the countries mentioned. France has abandoned its expansion of foreign languages teaching through the specially designed video course and will put in its place a national programme for the in-service training of primary teachers. In Scotland, the publication in October 1998 of an HMI report into modern languages teaching in primary and secondary schools and the subsequent setting up of an Action Group for Languages by the Scottish Education Minister, Helen Liddell, should in the long term resolve many of the problems identified in this chapter. The HMI report, *Standards and Quality in Primary and Secondary Schools 1994–98: Modern Languages*, contains the first evaluation of attainment in primary schools in the context of the national extension of MLPS. Whilst identifying some key strengths, it concludes that the potential benefits to pupils arising from the study of a foreign language in primary are not yet being fully realised. It recommends, among other things, that: a foreign language should be included in the curriculum of all pupils in P6 and P7; the time allocated to the foreign languages should be consistent within and across schools; appropriate links should be made with other curricular areas particularly English language; teachers should record pupils' attainment; appropriate links should be made with local secondary schools; and appropriate time and support should be provided for teachers to maintain their language skills, prepare work and consult with other teachers. In response to the HMI report, the Scottish Education Minister has set up a national Action Group for Languages drawn from the full range of educational interests, which in collaboration with the Scottish Consultative Council on the Curriculum, will review the Guidelines and secure the place of modern languages in the 5–14 programme, develop exemplar and assessment materials for 5–14 modern languages and advise on attainment targets and the further training of teachers of modern languages at those stages.

References

Association for Language Learning (1997) *Policy Statement on an Earlier Start to Foreign Language Learning*, Rugby: ALL.

Boyes, I. (1993) 'Modern Languages in Primary Schools', in *Scottish CILT Info. 1: Modern Foreign Languages in Primary Schools*, Stirling: Scottish CILT.

Brun, A. and Panosetti, J. B. (1997) 'EILE/EILV: Enseignment d'Initiation aux Langues Étrangères' (Initial Teaching of Foreign Languages) in Bori, A. *et al. Modern Languages at Primary School: Reflections on Monitoring and Evaluation*, ECP Report: Socrates Programme, Stirling: Scottish CILT.

Giovanazzi, A. (1992) *Foreign Languages in Primary Schools, Sense or Sensibility: The Organisational Imperatives*, paper given to the British Council Triangle Conference, Paris, January.

Low, L. *et al.* (1995) *Foreign Languages in Primary Schools: Evaluation of the Scottish Pilot Projects 1993–95: Final Report*, Stirling: Scottish CILT.

Low, L. and Wolfe, L. (1996) 'MLPS: Impact on the Secondary Sector', in A. Hurrell and P. Satchwell (eds) *Reflections on Modern Languages in Primary Education: Six UK Case Studies*, London: CILT.

Mitchell, R. *et al.* (1992) *Evaluation of the Basingstoke Primary Schools Language Awareness Project: 1990/1*, University of Southampton: Centre for Language In Education.

Pignatelli, F. (1993) 'The Strathclyde Primary Foreign Languages Project', in *Scottish CILT Info. 1: Modern Foreign Languages in Primary Schools*, Stirling: Scottish CILT.

Primary Languages Network Working Party (1996) *The Introduction of Foreign Languages into the Primary School Curriculum, Draft 4*, London: CILT.

School Curriculum and Assessment Authority (1997) *Modern Foreign Languages in the Primary Curriculum: An International Conference*, London: SCAA.

Scottish Education Department Circular No. 1178 (1989) *The Teaching of Languages Other than English in Scottish Schools*, Edinburgh: HMSO.

Scottish Office Education Department (1993a) *Curriculum and Assessment in Scotland: National Guidelines, Modern Languages 5–14*, Edinburgh: HMSO.

——(1993b) *Modern Languages in the Primary School, The Training Programme*, Glasgow: Strathclyde University.

II

Classroom issues

4

The four language skills

The whole works!

Alison Hurrell

Understanding

Two children are sitting side by side in the classroom working on number. A pile of buttons is on the table in front of them and each has an old tobacco tin with five glittering stars and the number five on the lid. The following conversation ensues between one of them and a French-speaking visitor:

Visitor:	Alors, tu regardes bien les étoiles sur la boîte. Il faut trouver 5 boutons et les mettre dans la boîte. Tu comprends? Si tu veux, on peut les compter ensemble.
Child:	One.....two...three...four....five. ⎱
Visitor:	Un...deux...trois...quatre...cinq. ⎰
Visitor:	Voilà....très bien...bravo!

The child, with obvious pleasure and a sense of mathematical achievement, punches the air, puts the lid on his box (which now contains the magical five buttons), turns to his friend and says: 'You've to count out five buttons.... she read what was on the lid... and put them in the box.' The second child does so and equally triumphantly places the lid on his tobacco box. At this point, visitor and friend lean forward simultaneously to congratulate the child. I am beaten to it. The friend says, confidently, fluently, with neither inhibition nor any sense of linguistic incongruity, 'très bien...bravo!' Both children are five years old.

Later that morning, after a presumably boisterous playground game, the same child returns to his seat with a grazed knee and a tear-stained face. The visitor points to the child's knee and says sympathetically:

Visitor:	Oh là là, tu t'es fait mal au genou? Qu'est-ce qu'il s'est passé?
Child:	I fell.
Visitor:	Tu veux un pansement?
Child:	Uh huh. Mrs....keeps them in her drawer.

The sore knee is bandaged, the face cleaned, and work resumes.

We might be amazed at this exchange for at least two reasons: because of the child's ability to understand, and interpret for someone else, a flow of foreign language; and because of his desire and ability to reproduce some of that flow in his own interaction with his classmate.

Does this incident illustrate that he *understood* the foreign language in the sense which we normally mean, that of understanding lexis, sentence structure, discourse features? Or was he rather demonstrating that the interaction fitted in with complete appropriateness to the patterns of many interactions? Both he and I understood the situation in the sense that we understood one another's intentions. Language was to a large extent unnecessary and its meaning was highly predictable in the human context of its occurrence. What I *meant* was clear. What the words *meant* could, in principle, be derived from that. It was possible for him to figure out what the words meant because they occurred together with and were embedded within certain non-linguistic events – the sympathetic look, the obvious question in the context of his distress, the obvious solution in the context of his wound.

In Margaret Donaldson's words 'It is the child's ability to interpret situations which makes it possible for him, through active processes of hypothesis-testing and inference, to arrive at a knowledge of the language used.' Children are able to learn language – first and second language – 'precisely because they possess certain skills and have a relatively well-developed capacity for making sense of certain types of situation involving direct and immediate human interaction' (Donaldson, 1978: 37). When a child hears words that refer to a situation which they are at the same time perceiving, their interpretation of the words is influenced by the expectations which they bring to the situation. The child knows that language exists to convey meaning and they are actively engaged in a constant process of constructing meaning, making sense of things and of what people do. This includes what people say. However, there is a considerable distance, and therefore there can be a considerable period of time, between an understanding of the words embedded in a meaningful context, and a separate understanding of those words in other contexts or in isolation.

In the classroom, in the context of foreign language learning, we scaffold the child's understanding of the flow of foreign language – we try to make things easier for the learner so that we might engage in and sustain communication with the learner in the classroom. As well as creating contexts which will provide strong clues as to the meaning of the words within them, we may adopt certain characteristics of what has been described as 'motherese' or 'foreigner-talk':

- exaggerated changes of pitch;
- louder volume;

- 'simpler' grammar;
- a focus on discrete lexis for example, through the use of flash cards, realia, pointing to the article as we talk about it;
- facial expression;
- mime, gesture.

These scaffolding techniques we believe will support the child's foreign language acquisition in the classroom context. However, when a child interprets what we say, their interpretation is influenced by at least three things and the ways in which these interact with each other – their knowledge of the language; their assessment of what we intend (as indicated by our non-linguistic behaviour); and the manner in which they would represent the physical situation to themselves if we were not there at all. These points are made clearly in Margaret Donaldson's seminal work *Children's Minds* (1978). As a young learner of the foreign language the child's foreign language (FL) resource will always be less than that of the teacher and they will give more weight to non-linguistic cues – for example, in teaching terms, to flash cards, visual props, other actions, etc. In addition, they will bring their knowledge of the world and how it works to their active listening and hypothesis-testing. When these are in harmony, a holistic understanding is achieved.

The child tries to 'juggle' all kinds of knowledge and levels of language. When learning, one of these areas can 'take over'; in some cases this will lead to 'error'. If unnoticed, this 'error' can destroy the 'juggling act', and consequently the child's comprehension. If this occurs commonly, the learner may lose motivation, or believe that language learning is a meaningless activity, with little human sense.

I was telling the story of the little elephant (based loosely on the Rudyard Kipling story) to a class of 10 year-olds. The various animals in the story were introduced – le petit éléphant, la girafe, le lion, le singe, le serpent, le crocodile – and the children *seemed* to be following the storyline, evidenced by group chorusing of key repeated structures and phrases, accompanying hand gestures, smiles, and so forth. At the end of the story, one perplexed child asked why all the animals had been phoning each other. It took me some time to realise that for her, *le petit éléphant* had been understood as *le petit téléphone*, and her construction of the story thereafter had been based on that initial misunderstanding. All teachers should take note and beware!

The introduction and development of the four language skills

It is only recently that teachers have started to pay substantial attention to *how* their pupils learn a foreign language. It is well known that since the late 1970s enormous efforts have been made to develop a more communicative approach in schools (Littlewood, 1981), where the language is used creatively for real communication, for real purposes, authentic rather than contrived language, or language used because it exemplifies certain structures. Communication is usually embedded in meaningful contexts, where there are genuine exchanges of information. Children are encouraged to choose for themselves what to say or write; they are enabled to cope with the unpredictable, and develop repair strategies when communication breaks down. But how do young learners reach this stage of communicative competence? What do they bring to their foreign language learning? As stated before, they bring their knowledge of the functions of language, how it works, how it can be built up and they know there is still a lot to be learned. Very often their capacity for acquiring some aspects of the system of rules and strategies underlying communicative language use is intuitive rather than explicit. There can no longer be any doubt that children can assimilate the sound system of a new language and can absorb, reproduce and imaginatively enact quite large chunks of that language without necessarily being able to analyse what it is they have absorbed. An early start to foreign language learning allows for this kind of intuitive knowledge but can, in my experience, be accompanied at times by a more analytical approach, which will enable the children to make more specific links between the FL and their knowledge of L1, building on their concepts about language in particular and on concepts of the world they already possess or that they are learning at school. The foreign language can be overlaid onto these existing concepts, thereby promoting a holistic approach to learning. The grafting of an analytical style is one of the major problems for the teacher. Well handled, it works – but unless the *individual* child can make the connection, it leads to confusion and disenchantment.

For the class teacher with responsibility for delivering the foreign language, questions will arise as to how to teach listening, speaking, reading and writing. I would now like to consider the strategies which we can employ to introduce and develop each of the four language skills. Promoting the four communication skills independently in this way is no contradiction to a holistic approach. All the skills are to some extent interwoven and can very rarely be totally separated and they all involve both social and cognitive processes. On the other hand, to distinguish between them may facilitate an organised presentation and discussion. Most language learning activities currently have as their *main* focus one of the skills.

Listening

Listening is frequently called a *receptive* skill but the term is misleading. Most listening requires a readiness and an active co-operation on the part of the listener. It requires understanding, interpreting and building. It is the skill which the child acquires first in their foreign language learning. A characteristic of the spoken word is its lack of permanence: once something has been said and listened to, it disappears. We are not talking here of pre-recorded text which the child can listen to again and again, but of the most frequent listening input at this stage – the class teacher. What are the implications for the child and for the teacher?

Initially the child will be trying to segment the stream of strange sounds into constituent units and to relate these to the situational context of the utterance so that the whole makes sense. Of course we are helping the child access this flow by the vast repertoire of support mechanisms at our disposal – facial expression, gesture, mime – and most importantly by giving the child *time* to hear, to assimilate, to reflect and to respond where they feel this is appropriate. In early foreign language learning we often lean too heavily on the stimulus-response variety of input even at the earliest stages of the teaching programme. In the area of personal information we ask the child their name, their age, where they live, how old they are, etc. and we look for an immediate response. Paradoxically for many children, this is not appropriate or effective. They have the '*right to silence*', the pupil's right to the Fifth Amendment, as it were, and we should not be troubled by this since they may be actively manifesting their understanding in other ways – or not: they will line up when asked to do so, they will fetch the scissors and cut out their animal masks when directed to do so, they will smile at the FL jokes, they will show their pleasure during storytelling, but they may not wish to commit themselves to speech *at that stage* in their FL learning. Premature insistence on a spoken response can lead to stress, an unwillingness to take risks, 'failure'. This relates well to Cambourne's 'responsibility', where the *child* chooses what to pay attention to, and where *we* provide the scaffold, but do not insist on its use, or its means of use. Initial scaffolding ensures no failure (Cambourne, 1988).

Frequently different learning styles and/or preferences come into play. Not all learners are aural learners. For them (and this includes some adults as well) *the written word is not a peripheral support but an integral, essential part of the learning process*. The written word assists in the segmentation of sound, word, phrase and we should not allow ourselves to deny the child this support on the basis of the oft-quoted belief that they will mispronounce words with which they are not already familiar. This is self-evident and occurs in the child's reading of L1 as well. We have rather to grasp the nettle and provide the child with the means to decode the written word. I can illustrate this by using an example from recent experience. During one particular game with young learners, in order to avoid any physical harm, I said: 'Attention, les enfants! Ne vous bousculez pas...ça peut être dangereux!' This was accompanied by gesture, mime, exaggerated stress on the word *dangereux*, in my mind a word which would be readily accessible to most children of that age on the basis that it sounded like the English word *dangerous*. They did not understand. I started to write the word on the blackboard d-a-n-g-e...and at that point, a chorus of recognition went up. I learned a valuable lesson.

Implications for the teacher

When presenting new language items to the children I believe the sequencing of the activities to be important in the sense that they build progressively on:

- the child's right to silence;
- opportunities to hear and re-hear the new language in a stress-free environment;
- learning through *all* our senses;
- the need some children have to see the written word and decoding strategies this approach implies;
- memorisation skills;
- the holistic involvement (*engagement*) of the child.

Some of the following strategies may be found useful and effective. When presenting concrete items of vocabulary we will want to support the children's understanding by offering visual support, through flash cards or other props.

- Look and listen only: this gives the children the opportunity to relate the sound to the object.
- Listen and point to a variety of visuals placed around the classroom when called out by the teacher: this provides time to assimilate the new sound units.
- Listen and repeat in their heads two or three times the words/phrases the teacher is saying. Silent repeating, like silent reading, is a misnomer: the children sound out the words/phrases in their heads and are thereby gaining confidence and competence in their pronunciation, intonation and rhythm of the foreign language.
- 'Pass the Parcel': the children look very carefully at the teacher's mouth and try to guess what word/phrase is being said. The teacher has to articulate very clearly, exaggerating the position of the lips when making certain sounds. After a few demonstrations by the teacher, the parcel is passed and one of the children in turn has to articulate clearly for the benefit of their classmates. Very often children are either embarrassed or simply not accustomed to articulating, either in L1 or in L2 and prefer to emulate the ventriloquist, speaking through half-clenched teeth. 'Pass the Parcel' is a fun activity and one which the children enjoy enormously and from which they benefit enormously.
- Dessins dans le dos: this involves the children in physically *feeling* the foreign language. Sitting in groups the children pass from one to the other a letter, or a number, or a visual representation, by etching this letter, etc. into their neighbour's back. This can also be done on the children's hands (with their eyes shut). The activity promotes deep

concentration and focus on the new language item — as well as the peripheral and welcome advantage of being an activity that can be conducted in total silence! It is revealing that in English we talk about drawing something *on* someone's back, whereas in French they more aptly and tellingly describe it as drawing *in* someone's back. To complete this phase of non-speaking activities the children might take part in a four-corner game.

Gradually the children can be encouraged to *produce* the foreign language out loud, as it were, through a range of well-known activities, such as:

- repeat if you're wearing something red/black/blue;
- repeat if you've got blue/brown eyes, long/short/straight hair;
- repeat if you like chocolate, maths, *EastEnders*;
- repeat if your name begins with the letter...;
- I'm thinking of an animal which begins with the letter...;
- guess which flash card I'm holding;
- a game of Noughts and Crosses;
- Kim's game.

Storytelling has become recognised as an extremely valuable and effective vehicle for foreign language learning and the arguments for this are well rehearsed. Let us mention here only the following:

- stories develop the imagination and creativity of the child;
- they develop anticipation and prediction;
- they use constant repetition based on language and story structures;
- they reflect a considerably larger context than that which surrounds the 'here and now' interaction alone.

This not only forms part of typical primary practice but also contributes to the child's well-being and sense of security. Stories form part of the universe of childhood. Many exciting and creative pre-, during- and post-storytelling activities have been devised by teacher and child alike and we need not mention these here in detail. However, if the story is well chosen it can elicit much useful work in the area of knowledge about language.

The role of first language

There are arguments for making better use of the process of cognition developed at primary school through L1. Johnstone (1996) has described impressive work being done in Croatia with young children learning French. Here the children's knowledge of grammar in their mother tongue helped them in learning the foreign language. These children were taught French far more regularly than children in the British context but there still seems to be a great deal to learn from this sort of work.

Speaking

Primary class teachers are only too aware of their responsibility in this area of FL acquisition and are anxious at all times that their pronunciation, intonation and rhythm are accurate, if only to ensure that the results of their teaching programmes are validated and approved of by their secondary modern language specialist colleagues. Speaking is demanding of teacher and pupil alike. For the child it means discriminating between different speech sounds and being able to produce them correctly, building up new pronunciation habits and overcoming the bias of the first language, feeling the different stress patterns in the new language, having the confidence to hear themself express their personality in a 'foreign' medium, being content to inhabit a new persona. In their own language they can express emotions, communicate intentions and reactions, explore the language and have fun with it. If we succeed in creating the right ethos and atmosphere, this is what the child will reasonably expect to be able to do in the foreign language as well. However, these expectations can be fulfilled (or thwarted) by the teacher. Constancy of practice, a non-judgemental response to 'errors', and an acceptance of the child's use of the mother tongue will contribute to a more creative, less circumscribed use of the foreign language.

In the foreign language, as in the mother tongue, the child will speak spontaneously only when they perceive the need, what Margaret Donaldson calls the *'intention to-say-so-and-so'* (1978: 74). We can teach formulaic expressions and these will make up a substantial portion of the child's repertoire contributing to their growing sense of achievement. Indeed, their skilful use seems to contribute greatly to communicative success. After all, nothing succeeds like success! These are the child's 'data' which they use to analyse how language works. But how can we help the child go beyond these formulaic, short utterances? How can we scaffold the child's attempts to communicate verbally in the foreign language?

Implications for the teacher

Paradoxically children often assume that there is something unique, other, unconnected to anything else, about learning a foreign language. I would suggest that we remind them of the basic and essential functions of language and that not all communication need be verbal. Non-verbal cues include:

- intonation,
- facial expressions,

- gesture,
- reaction to other's speech.

The sensitive teacher will alert the children to a common feature in speech: we identify a setting, we pause, then we focus, what Cambourne (1988) describes as topic-comment structure. This was clarified for me during a visit to a primary 7 (Year 6 class). The pupils assumed (erroneously) that I was a native French-speaker and that therefore the only access to me was through the foreign language. A group of girls stayed behind after class to engage me in conversation. It ranged from my comments on a particularly attractive sweater (the child concerned nodded vigorously and looked pleased that I had commented on this aspect of her appearance), to the length of a child's hair and how difficult it must be for her to keep it tangle-free. This too was greeted with vigorous head-nodding. After a momentary pause one of the girls said: 'Regarde montre' (setting followed by pause)...'Garçon fille' (focus). After various vain attempts to understand what she was trying to communicate, I confessed to her that I did not understand. In her frustration she tapped me rather forcefully on my arm, and thrust her watch under my eyes, repeating 'Regarde montre' ...Garçon fille.' I finally realised that she was drawing my attention to the fact that the minute hand was a little girl and the hour hand was a little boy. Such perseverance! Such determination to make me focus as she had! The *need* to communicate was occasioned by her excitement, by her determination to transmit a piece of information to someone for whom she felt affection. The major problem confronting teachers is that of identifying 'needful' situations for their pupils.

It is not my brief here to talk about the range of speaking activities which have gained prominence in primary and secondary foreign language learning and teaching. I would like to focus rather on how we can help children go beyond one-word utterances and formulaic expressions (important though they are) and on how we can give them the confidence and the means to engage in extended and original speech. There is a natural tension, of course, between the authentic one-word answer in response to questions such as what's your name? how are you? do you like...? and the fuller utterances which we might wish to encourage. But these fuller utterances, often involving the use of finite sentences, can develop and simultaneously demonstrate the child's growing communicative competence. We all know that to use a language creatively we must be able to operate a system of underlying rules, otherwise we would remain at the level of the phrase book. In order to make a foreign language really work for learners, we have to go beyond lists of vocabulary (nouns, adjectives, etc.) or lists of structures or functions. We have to teach the language as a dynamic system, one that enables the learner to create language rather than reproduce it and provide a learning context which is congenial to risk-taking, uncertainty, problematic situations and a real sense of purpose.

To produce appropriate language effectively, it is necessary to have a certain level of competence in a number of aspects of language use. The Canadian researcher Canale (1983) identified four components of communicative competence:

1   Grammatical competence: knowledge of vocabulary, of sound and of grammar;
2   Sociolinguistic competence: knowledge of how to use the language appropriately in different types of context, for example, deciding whether the situation dictates a formal/casual response, complaining politely, refusing, etc.;
3   Discourse competence: knowing how to begin, develop and close a conversation, how to change the subject, how to take turns, how to intervene, etc.;
4   Strategic/pragmatic competence: knowing how to cope when communication breaks down, asking for clarification, making up words in the foreign language, avoidance tactics, etc.

Competence in these 'higher' levels of language will be attained only if the child has opportunity to hear and use language in situations where these competences are authentically required.

Just as with the mother tongue, a foreign language is acquired through a developmental process that focuses first on language use through meaningful communicative activities (consider the two little boys during their maths lesson), combined with steps along the way that sometimes involve focus on language form with conscious self-editing and refinement of the rules of the language.

What is needed is a consciousness-raising of the rules, a focus on the components of the utterance so that the child can gain more control of their speech. This is not to advocate a return to dry grammar/parsing lessons. It is, rather, helping the child monitor the correctness and/or appropriateness of their utterances, helping them focus on accuracy as well as fluency, on social, discourse and pragmatic features of language use. But this seems far away perhaps from the initial stages of developing speaking in the foreign language. How do we start? By considering the functions of communication through a range of stress-free and fun activities and by moving on to structured opportunities for the child to explore and enjoy this new language.

There is an infinite range of activities − the context, which the teacher, or the teacher and pupils jointly set up, will determine the activity − which will encourage learners to engage emotionally and physically in the language learning process and which will develop techniques to build up a powerful visual and auditory memory and will make them feel able to risk making mistakes. Language is associated with sound, music, movement, colour, drama and thereby impregnated with meaning. There are memory games, songs, rhymes, poems, stories which they will hear and want to adapt, make their own. There will be opportunities for dramatisation which will exploit the child's sense of theatre and appreciation of audience, their awareness of register.

In the context of early foreign language learning the class teacher can do much to promote the above, in simple ways which are consonant with the ways the child will be learning in other areas of the primary curriculum. For example, if we consider length of utterance, the introduction of connectors (*et, mais, qui*) and modifiers (*très, trop, assez*) can be introduced at an early stage in the process during the daily routine slot where the children are talking about the weather. For example:

Aujourd'hui il fait beau.
Aujourd'hui il fait beau et il fait du soleil.
Aujourd'hui il fait beau, il fait du soleil mais il fait assez frais.

Not only does the child have the satisfaction of hearing themself say 'more', but they can also be encouraged to reflect on the change in the intonation pattern occasioned by the introduction of the connectors and modifiers. A pattern can then be established in the child's mind. Equally, there is an expectation set up in their mind that they should be willing to expand on utterances, giving opinions, agreeing, disagreeing – all features of natural conversation in the mother tongue.

We need also to engage the child's creativity in the foreign language within the parameters of their current competence but always with an eye to *expecting* more and *celebrating* more. Where breakdowns in communication occur, as they will inevitably, then the sensitive teacher allows the child to revert to the mother tongue and will translate for the child, thereby setting up a paradigm of foreign language learning which is again consonant with the ways in which the primary class teacher operates in other areas of the curriculum – namely, providing 'knowledge' on a need-to-know basis, personalising the input according to the interests, needs and learning styles of each child. An example is now given, showing how an activity can (a) be connected to an area of the primary curriculum (Maths); (b) allow the children to move gradually from stress-free listening to structured speaking to more open-ended speaking; and (c) encourage the children to develop learning strategies.

Shapes

A fun way of exploring the concepts of colour, shape and size in a foreign language is illustrated in the following graded series of activities around the theme of 'shape'.

1   In groups the children are given a variety of mathematical shapes of different colours, both large and small. These can be cut out paper shapes. The first activity is simply to ask the children to sort the pieces of paper into sets. Interestingly some children will not only sort them into sets (the same colour, the same shape or the same size) but will simultaneously sort them into sub-sets – colour, shape and size.

2   They are then asked on what criteria they sorted the pieces of paper and they are required only to say *selon la taille/la couleur/la forme.*

3   The teacher then asks each group to bring a variety of shape, colours and size, for example, *Apportez-moi trois grands triangles bleus, deux petits carrés rouges et un petit cercle jaune.* At this point normally the children (or adults, as I have done this same activity with primary class teachers during their MLPS training) start to remonstrate that (a) the teacher is talking too fast or (b) there is too much to remember and this provides the teacher with the opportunity to talk about various strategies they might adopt to over-come these perceived difficulties. These might include repeating 'silently' in their heads what the teacher is saying, whilst simultaneously looking for the required shapes, and so on. It might include each child in the group assuming responsibility for a particular shape or colour or size. When the strategies have been discussed in each group and responsibili-ties allocated, the game is played again – this time without a hitch and accompanied by lots of laughter.

4   The children are asked to pick out a given shape, for example *un grand triangle vert.* Thereafter they have to form a line of 10–15 shapes changing *one element* each time, for example *un grand cercle vert* or *un petit triangle vert.* As they choose the next element they say *je change de taille* or *je change de couleur* or *je change de forme.* When they have completed the task they say *Ça y est!*

5   Now they are asked to make a line of 10–15 shapes changing *two elements* each time. On this occasion they would say, for example, *je change de couleur et de taille* or *je change de couleur et de forme* or *je change de taille et de couleur.* This proves quite a demanding task for some children and for some adults – not linguistically, but conceptually, and it is revealing that the foreign language here is servicing development in mathematical concepts and not being used solely as an end in itself! There is much more intensity of motivation in having to access the foreign language in order to come to terms with something that is presented and perceived as being immediately important here and now. *They are acquiring new subject-matter through the medium of the foreign language.*

6   The children then make a picture using some of the shapes they have in front of them – this might be a clown, a house, a street with vehicles – anything! Once the pictures are complete, the children move around the classroom looking at and admiring their classmates' compositions, commenting favourably on what they see – it is a stipulation of the

activity that all comments should be positive and favourable (*c'est beau/joli/amusant*).

7 Finally each group has to present its picture and be prepared to answer any questions which the teacher or other pupils might ask. The degree of fluency, accuracy and range will vary greatly, but it provides the children with the opportunity to recycle and revisit many of the language areas previously presented and practised, for example, name, age, likes and dislikes, colours, habitat, and so on. At this point there is frequently a breakdown in the children's ability to talk: they want to say much more than they have the resource for and this is one of many object-lessons in language acquisition – it is a normal stage in linguistic development and one that we as teachers should neither shirk from acknowledging nor discussing with them. Because motivation is high, because they are *engagés* there is a greater likelihood that they will incorporate some of the coping language which they will undoubtedly have been taught. *How do you say....?*

Finally, in this section on developing the skills of speaking, it would be unwise not to mention the child's love of language and sound *per se* and the role we have as teachers in encouraging this playing with language. I asked a class to tell me what their favourite new French word was – we did this on a weekly basis – and two children came up with the following: *concombre* and *pantoufle*. The first child shared his own pleasure and surprise at liking the word when he hated cucumber! The second child suggested that *pantoufle* would make a wonderful swear word – I had to agree!

Reading

Traditionally in the secondary sector modern languages teachers have made many unfounded assumptions about the reading skills of S1/Year 7 pupils: we have assumed that they are all literate; that they are competent and fluent readers; that because they can read in their mother tongue, they can automatically read in the foreign language. Generations of modern languages teachers were frustrated and incredulous when the child, who confidently and competently asked the question *comment t'appelles-tu?* could not replicate the same sounds when confronted with the written correspondence and would pronounce the phrase as though it were English.

It is salutary for us to remember that a great many children come to primary school not even aware that separate words exist, not aware of the nature of the correspondence between the spoken and the written word. Many modern languages teachers bemoan the early introduction of the written word, focusing on dire mispronunciations, interpreting this phenomenon as an educational premise for delaying introduction of the written word until the children have had intensive listening and speaking practice of all the language which they will see thereafter. It is certainly true that children will mispronounce words they read in the foreign language; they do so in the mother tongue as well, but this can be seen as a natural stage in their language development. Is it therefore an intractable problem for the young foreign language learner? I would suggest that this need not be the case.

Children expect to make mistakes and can see these mistakes as an integral part of the learning process when encouraged to do so. What is needed is a leap of faith on our part, accompanied by a structured introduction to the written word, remembering that the written word is not a peripheral support but an integral, essential part of the learning process for some children. We can provide them with a set of general rules which will enable them to decode, not only language with which they are familiar, but also new, unknown items of language. For every rule there are, of course, many exceptions, and this awareness equally has discouraged teachers from giving children the necessary tools to decode. There is a general belief that children must not be told the truth about the system to begin with, because they could not cope with such complexities. What underlies this, according to Margaret Donaldson is 'a failure to make a crucial distinction, a failure to see the difference between understanding the nature of the system and mastering all the individual patterns of relationship within the system' (Donaldson, 1978: 105). There is no reason to suppose that a child of 8–10 cannot understand a system that contains options. They know very well that if someone is not at school they may either have measles, a cold, or be playing truant. Similarly they know that there exists a set of options in the sound system in English: the letter -c can be pronounced in cake or it can be pronounced as in icing. It will inevitably take the child some time to learn *all* the sets of correspondences. The question is simply whether they will do this better if they are correctly informed about the kind of thing to expect. This way of proceeding would not only appear to offer the best hope of mastering word-decoding skills. It must have the further general advantage of encouraging reflective thought and awareness of the processes of the mind.

I would like to mention three possible activities to assist children in decoding the foreign language: phonic clouds and posters, tracing text and textual features.

Phonic clouds and phonic posters

In French there are many combinations of letters which form particular sounds. For example:

oi   en/an   eu   -in/ain

The teacher, at the earliest stage, can cut out a cloud shape with the phonic grouping written on it and suspend it from the ceiling of the classroom (hence the name phonic cloud). On each occasion that a word containing the particular phonic grouping is encountered, a child writes out the word on another cloud shape cut-out, highlights the phonic grouping as it appears in the word, and hangs it from the stem cloud. So for example, with the phonic grouping -*eu* we could have the clouds as shown in Figure 4.1.

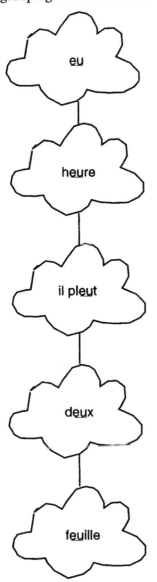

Figure 4.1 Phonic clouds

These phonic clouds are then a permanent aide-mémoire for the children to which they can refer in their reading. When the teacher feels confident that the children have mastered that particular phonic grouping, a poster can be devised for a more permanent classroom display. There is no suggestion that the teacher need systematically present all possible phonic groupings at the one time or indeed throughout the primary teaching programme, but they can none the less make quite explicit the difficulties which the children will encounter and provide them with a strategy for overcoming these difficulties.

Tracing words

I remember as a very young child discovering the wonders of the written word on the page – its permanence, its shape, the spaces between the words – it was for me a truly aesthetic experience. Reading out loud to the teacher involved following each word with a finger. It helped concentration, kept us on task, but had the added value (unknown to me at the time) of helping the reader associate the spoken word with its written equivalence.

In the area of decoding a foreign language we might wish to return to that practice, exploiting all the text (spoken and written) which we offer the children in the rich panoply of activities devised for them. When we ask children to listen to a recorded text and tick boxes, or fill in columns with the appropriate and discrete piece of information we might add as a final activity and as a further way of exploiting a resource, the opportunity for the child to *see* the spoken text and to listen to the text again, this time following the words on the page with their finger. This does many things:

- it reinforces the word-sound connection;
- it reinforces the cadences of the foreign language, the spurts and the pauses, the 'ums' and the 'ems' of natural speech;
- it can reinforce work done previously on phonic groupings;
- it can give the child an enriched source of vocabulary and syntax;
- it can give them models of speech patterns;
- it can allow them to listen and read in security, reflect on word-sound connections at their own speed.

There can be a tension between speed of response and reflective thought. The child who is expected to respond immediately by making the right sound whenever isolated words are shot at them on a piece of paper, will not be considering possibilities of interpretation at all. If they do not know, they will be under pressure to guess wildly, not to pause and reflect and become aware of what they are doing. But reflection takes time. This is undoubtedly true, but laying solid foundations in any area of a child's learning is time-consuming and literacy in, and reflection on, the foreign language are no exceptions. We need to involve as many children as possible in a limited time.

Textual features

We can share textual features with the children, drawing on their knowledge and skills of these in the mother tongue – beginnings, sequencing language, visual support, contextualising clues, the use of the referential pronoun, and so on. We can also encourage them to see links between L1 and L2. Johnstone has listed a sample of linguistic concepts in English language (Johnstone, 1996). The Modern Languages Guidelines at 5–14 (Scotland) make only a small number of references to grammar but these are not specific and refer only to language production. These key concepts include for example:

Verb	Clause
Noun	Apostrophe
Vowel	Punctuation
Consonant	Syllable
Adverb	Root and stem
Pronoun	Prefix and suffix
Conjunction	Simile
Masculine	Metaphor
Feminine	Index
Singular	Dictionary
Plural	Argument
Tense	Conversation
Subject	Discussion
Predicate	Debate
Rhythm	Speech marks

Were the children able to apply these concepts initially introduced through the mother tongue to the FL, pupils might develop a stronger conceptual knowledge of the foreign language than they appear to do at present.

In conclusion, teachers should be aware that, in this context, to deny the children access to the written word until such times as error is avoidable, is to deny them access to a cornucopia and to run counter to pedagogy in mother tongue acquisition.

Writing

Following the same argument, namely that error should be avoided at all costs, many teachers are unwilling to 'allow' the children to write in the foreign language, unless it is at the level of copy-writing, assuming that this sub-skill of writing is the easiest one to master. For many children this is not the case, since frequently we impose a three-dimensional task on them: *distance, angle, elevation*. More often than not children are asked to copy words down from the board or OHP (*distance*); in the normal primary class-room configuration (and increasingly in secondary classrooms) children sit in small groups, some with their back to the board, others sitting side-on (*angle*); we ask them to look at a word/phrase at a distance, retain the shape of the word in their heads, then lower their heads to write the word into their jotter or onto a worksheet (*elevation*). This is a difficult enough task in mother tongue where the children already have an idea of some 'rules' of spelling, for example, that the letter *q* is followed by the letter *u*. They are able to subdivide a larger word into smaller (to them) meaningful chunks, retain these chunks in their head then transpose them onto paper. No such knowledge exists in the children in the early stages of foreign language acquisition and so the copying of a word becomes the copying of all the discrete letters in that word. How often do we see children write down the word *chein* instead of *chien*? Think what they could make of *il fait du brouil-lard*! We have to adopt a more holistic approach to writing, in my opinion, one which includes knowledge of phonic groupings, likely combinations of letters and, above all, an approach which involves the children in making error and having that error dealt with sensitively and reflectively.

What of creative/imaginative writing? There is a creative impulse in all children and they will want to commit this creativity to the permanence of written text. But their emergent linguistic competence will not allow them to express themselves as creatively as they would wish and the sensitive teacher will wish to progress this aspect of foreign language acquisition. This may be illustrated through teaching strategies advocated in *The Foundations of Writing* (CCCC, 1987) and *Breakthrough to Literacy* (Mackay, 1970). The philosophy underpinning these approaches is that the child is given access to language which might be currently outside their repertoire. With *The Foundations of Writing*, for example, the teacher will initially write for the child, leading on to the building of word banks which the child will be able to access to allow them to be able to write on their own. *Breakthrough to Literacy* works in a similar way to encourage children to see that language is something dynamic, something over which they can have independent control, something which is malleable and can be used to express new ideas, new thoughts, new variations on a theme. If we are to introduce children systematically and gradually to the complexities of communicative compe-tence, we need to consider carefully how best to support them in the acquisition of *all* the language skills.

Many foreign language teachers, in good faith, have attempted to circum-scribe the children's writing, to encourage them to write only those items of the foreign language which (a) they had already encountered and (b) they could copy error-free from another source. If we are to take cognisance of

Mary Simpson's observations in her research into differentiation practices in the secondary school (1993), that, for children, the teacher is the key mediator of the child's learning success and that timely interaction with the child is an assured way of working towards that success, then we have to *make the time* for these essential steps in learning and also create flexibility to intervene when useful.

One example of an activity which allows the teacher to mediate in a flexible manner is as follows. Post-storytelling activities can provide the children with the opportunity to create new language for themselves on the basis of the language structures they have encountered in their listening and in their reading. Wordbanks can be created to enable children to *see* how language is structured. As part of an art and craft activity undertaken in the foreign language, the children make a poster illustrating the setting of the story. Underneath the poster there are a range of 'pockets' with headings such as *Prepositions, Where?* and *Verbal Phrases*. In the various 'pockets' language items such as *devant, le village* and *je vois* are placed. The children take one card from each 'pocket', make up a sentence, physically (for example, *derrière la maison il y a un parc grand*) and tangibly lay the sentence out in front of them, have it checked by the teacher, then write it into their jotter with an accompanying illustration if they wish or record themselves onto cassette.

Prepositions prépositions	Where? où	Verbal Phrases phrases verbales	Nouns noms	Adjectives adjectifs
derrière	la maison	il y a	un parc	grand
devant	le village	je vois	une colline	grande
dans	le champs		un cheval	petit
sur	la place		une fontaine	petite
	la rue		un marché	
			un café	

The children take one card from each 'pocket', make up a sentence, physically and tangibly lay the sentence out in front of them, have it checked by the teacher, then write it into their jotter with an accompanying illustration if they wish or record themselves onto cassette. There are important decisions they have to make. What form of the adjective will they choose? Why? Can they change the word-order of the sentence? Why? Why not? Practice and reflection go hand in hand and understanding goes deeper.

The challenge to the learner, pupil and teacher

> Literacy is a word which describes a whole collection of behaviours,
> skills, knowledge, processes and attitudes. It has something to do with
> our ability to use language in our negotiations with the world....Reading
> and writing are two linguistic ways of conducting these negotiations.
> So are talking, listening, thinking, reflecting, and a host of other behaviours
> related to cognition and critical thinking...The more language forms we
> have internalised and can use appropriately, the more successful our
> negotiations with our world will be. This is another way of saying that
> the more control we have over language forms and the more we use
> them and refine them, the more we are empowered
>
> (Cambourne, 1988: 3)

To me, this rather lengthy quotation acts as a signpost for what we as
teachers in primary and secondary are aiming for – in the mother tongue
and in the foreign language. But what might be done in practical terms to
ensure that, as children move from primary to and through secondary, they
are empowered to become effective communicators, effective foreign
language learners? It would seem self-evident that the secondary modern
languages department should have a clear idea of the knowledge, skills and
attitudes which pupils bring with them to the secondary classroom and
many strategies for effective and manageable information-transfer are
currently being explored. What is equally clear is that the secondary modern
languages departments need to create opportunities where they can *acknowledge, validate* and *build upon* the experiences and achievements of the young
learners at primary school.

Understandably many secondary teachers feel overwhelmed at the
prospect of having to 'radically' alter their S1/Year 7 and S2/Year 8 teaching
programmes, yet this need not be their first priority. Children will have
amassed a reservoir of knowledge of words and phrases; some will have been
able to see specific links between their knowledge of their mother tongue
and the foreign language and use this knowledge of language to assist their
comprehension and their production of the foreign language; some will be
able to manipulate their knowledge and skills across a variety of contexts
and may even be on the road to initiating new language for their own
purposes. On the basis of constant interaction with the pupils in the class,
the teacher gradually gains a clearer idea of what the pupils are able to *do*
with the foreign language they have been learning. Interaction, however,
implies observation as well, watching the children as they struggle in 'safety'
to come to terms with new input, observing their achievements and *reflecting*
on them. What questions might the teacher want to ask her/himself?

- Are there different kinds of text (aural and written) that I can ask the children to engage with?
- Are there different, more cognitively demanding tasks that I can ask them to perform?
- Are there support mechanisms that I can put in place to assist them in more open-ended writing, for example?
- Where is it that I want the children to reach in their acquisition of the foreign language?

Such basic questions can often make us feel uncomfortable because they frequently question our own set of beliefs about the teaching and learning process but they are an essential part of this complex job of teaching. As Smith has argued, young learners actually believe they are capable of learning *anything* until they are convinced otherwise (Smith, 1981). As teachers, we are *all* learners.

References

Cambourne, B. (1988) *The Whole Story: Natural Learning and the Acquisition of Literacy in the Classroom*, Auckland: Ashton Scholastic.

Canale, M. (1983) 'From Communicative Competence to Language Pedagogy', in J.C. Richards and R.W. Schmidt, (eds) *Language and Communication*, London: Longman.

Consultative Committee on the Curriculum (CCC) and COPE (1987) *The Foundations of Writing*, Glasgow: Jordanhill College of Education.

Donaldson, M. (1978) *Children's Minds*, London: Collins.

Johnstone, R. (1994) *Teaching Modern Languages at Primary School: Approaches and Implications*, Edinburgh: SCRE Publication.

——(1996) *Conference Report: MLPS in Scotland: Practice and Prospects*, Stirling: Scottish CILT.

Littlewood, W. (1981) *Communicative Language Teaching*, Cambridge: Cambridge University Press.

Mackay, D. (1970) *Breakthrough to Literacy*, London: Longman.

Simpson, M. (1993) *What's the Difference? A Study of Differentiation in Scottish Secondary Schools*, Aberdeen: Northern College.

Smith, F. (1981) 'Research Update: Demonstrations, Engagement, and Sensitivity: A Revised Approach to Language Learning', *Language Arts*, 58, 1, 103–12.

5

Teaching in the target language

Peter Satchwell

The pros and cons of teaching in the target language have been debated in secondary schools for many years, but since 1990 the introduction of the National Curriculum has concentrated the minds of language teachers and examiners alike. In Modern Foreign Languages in the National Curriculum (Department of Education and Science, 1991) the expectation was laid out in print for the first time that language teachers would conduct all, or nearly all, of their lessons in the target language – and 16 year olds are soon to tackle GCSE examinations with all rubrics and instructions in the target language. But the whole issue of teaching in the target language has turned out to be far more complex than anyone anticipated in 1990 and even the most experienced linguists need help in devising strategies to sustain pupil motivation and ensure that pupils use the language regularly in class.

Although there have been helpful publications from the Centre for Information on Language Teaching and Research (CILT) (*Pathfinders* 5, 6, 23 and a video pack: *In Focus*) and from the National Curriculum Council (a video pack: *Target Practice*), all of this material is aimed at secondary teachers. It is only since the completion of the Scottish pilot project that the issue of target language has begun to be tackled from the primary, non-specialist teacher's point of view. While most secondary language teachers are either language graduates and/or native speakers, this is rarely the case in primary schools where the teacher who has volunteered to teach some French, Spanish, Italian or German often has no formal qualifications beyond an A level in the language. This is not a major obstacle, provided that the teacher is confident in the language and has sound methodology and access to in-service training.

It has long been evident in the LEAs where languages are currently being successfully taught in primary schools that the teacher needs first and foremost to be a good primary teacher, not just a 'walking bilingual dictionary'. It is significant also that in 1994 the Scots took a pragmatic approach to the introduction of foreign languages into their primary schools by deciding to retrain existing primary class teachers instead of continuing to 'poach' language graduates from their already hard-pressed secondary schools, as they had at the beginning of the pilot project.

Why should we try to teach in the target language in primary school?

If children's first encounter with a foreign language is to be a positive and rewarding one, their first experience needs to incorporate a sense of real achievement and success. In order for children to come to see the foreign language as a valid and authentic means of communication on a par with their mother tongue, the teacher will need to immerse the class in the new language at every opportunity throughout the week. 'French once a week' is not good enough; the teacher needs to enlist the aid of all their colleagues to help provide opportunities for the children to hear the foreign language spoken as often as possible – ideally every day for at least 15 minutes! This may sound optimistic, but with a little forethought and planning, many of the daily classroom routines can be conducted in the foreign language: the register, collection of dinner money, classroom organisation, PE, games, music, drama, art, craft, cookery and so on. In many primary schools language teachers feel they are working in isolation, but by enlisting the hidden talents, however modest, of their colleagues or pupils' parents, they can begin to find aspects of the curriculum that lend themselves to short modules of foreign language work – what the Scots have called 'embedding' the foreign language in the whole school curriculum, as opposed to one or two rather frantic set-piece language slots in the week (two x 30 minutes still seems to be the norm).

As we pointed out in CILT *Young Pathfinder No. 1: Catching Them Young* (1995), if the foreign language is to have status in the primary curriculum, the teacher will need both the moral and practical support of the head-teacher and the rest of the staff – whether 'drop-in' teacher in a peripatetic scheme or the full-time class teacher. If the staff view work in the foreign language as an important reinforcement of children's general oracy and literacy skills, raising the self-esteem of the slower learners in particular, then the language teacher can embark with confidence on foreign language activities throughout the school year, including classroom display, posters, signs, notices and newspapers in corridors around the school, and of course, special events and performances using the target language in concerts, sketches, poems, fashion shows, and so on. In view of the very small amount of time generally allocated to foreign language learning in the UK, it seems vitally important for the teacher to make the most of every minute of contact time. French or German lessons spent talking in English for most of the time are not really foreign language lessons. Eric Hawkins (1981) talked about the teacher of foreign languages having to 'garden in a gale'; if we estimate that our meagre 60 minutes a week amounts to only 30–40 hours a year of access to the foreign language compared with the 4,000+ hours of waking time our children are exposed to their mother tongue, we can see what he means...we haven't a minute to lose! In mainland Europe children are surrounded every day by gusts of English language and culture in the media, the pop world and the press; by contrast, most of our children are cocooned in a monoglot world and rarely hear foreign languages spoken outside the classroom.

How much can be done through the target language will of course depend on the ability of the class and ultimately on the competence and enthusiasm of the teacher. Lessons in which the teacher constantly switches from French to English and back again are to be avoided at all costs; so it is vital that the teacher sits down to plan the use of the new language in some detail before the school year begins. As most primary language teachers are enthusiasts and volunteers, but rarely language graduates, we cannot expect them to approach native speaker proficiency – indeed, very few secondary teachers achieve this either. But by evaluating their own linguistic refresh-ment needs and seeking contact with a nearby native speaker or secondary languages teacher as a 'consultant', the primary teacher can attempt to update their skills in terms of linguistic and cultural knowledge of the foreign country.

In-service training courses for primary language teachers are, sadly, still thin on the ground, but no-one should embark on a year's language teaching without constant back-up from a good dictionary, both of the walking and the printed variety. Whatever the level of confidence in the language, the primary teacher should plan well ahead and decide:

- what broad topics are going to be covered in the year – five should be enough;
- what resources will be needed;
- what target language phrases are going to be used;
- what target language phrases the children are going to learn to use.

Only by charting their own course through what could become very trou-bled waters can the teacher go into the classroom with confidence and be sure that they can sustain whole lessons in the target language for most of the time. They will need to set clear linguistic aims for every lesson, both for themselves and the pupils. If they know that some children in the class have special needs and will need extra support, this needs to be planned into the programme.

Not every minute of every lesson can be taught in the target language and they may well decide to adopt a strategy used by many teachers of estab-lishing every so often a deliberate mother tongue slot – a ' breather' – in which children who are left behind or have misunderstood have five or ten minutes to ask questions and sort out their individual problems. These sessions can also be used to explain in English aspects of the foreign culture that would be too complex in the foreign language (snails and frogs' legs spring to mind!)

What skills does the primary language teacher need?

As well as a reasonably sound competence in the language, the teacher needs above all the confidence to plan a year's systematic work in the classroom with clear aims and progression for the learners. A useful summary of the competences primary language teachers need has been published in a Scottish Office Education Department (SOED) document, produced as a statement of aims for the extensive retraining programme for primary teachers in Scotland which began in 1994. The primary teacher needs to acquire a sound knowledge of:

- the sound system of the language – accurate pronunciation/intonation;
- the alphabet and the numbers;
- personal language – yourself, your family, where you live;
- descriptive language – people, animals, clothes, houses, town, environment, weather, food and drink;
- affective language – likes/dislikes, feelings, emotions, aches and pains, praise, terms of endearment;
- classroom language – daily routine, greetings, instructions, teacher language for organising pupil activities, pupil language for asking for permission, for help, for solving problems;
- language to cover activities from other curriculum areas such as maths, art, craft, PE, home economics, science, technology, drama;
- language needed to play games; to teach children poems, songs, tongue-twisters; to tell and act out with the children popular stories in the foreign language.

What kinds of language do we need for classroom communication?

These can be listed simply under two headings: teacher talk and pupil talk.

Teacher talk

Much of what the teacher needs to say revolves round classroom routines and organisation of pupil activities. They need to build up a confident command of a relatively small repertoire of questions, instructions and explanations to cover the most common classroom situations – without the embarrassment of having to revert to English.

Publications are now available to help the primary teacher with the phrases necessary for interacting with the pupils when:

- arriving at the classroom;

- entering the room;
- settling children down;
- getting the children's attention;
- taking the register;
- setting out the programme for the day;
- starting the lesson;
- recapping previous work;
- presenting a new topic;
- setting up pupil activities;
- explaining the rules of a game;
- monitoring progress;
- praising and reprimanding individuals;
- changing the activity;
- ending the lesson and packing away.

It will of course take several weeks or months to establish routines which everyone understands, but this is worth working at if the children are to start using the language to interact with the teacher and each other on a regular basis. Primary teachers will find practical help in the comprehensive target language packs recently produced by Miniflashcards Language Games: *Ici on parle français* and *Cartoons for Classroom Communication* (McColl and Thomas, 1997b) and also in the CILT *Young Pathfinder No. 4: Keep Talking* (Satchwell, 1996). The attractive Kent teaching packs in German: *3-2-1...Los!* (Rowe and Killbery, 1996) and in French: *Pilote* (Rumley *et al*, 1992), both provide a sound and supportive foundation for a year's language work. Each pack contains three videos with teacher's notes, including a teacher's audio cassette of target language phrases. These publications emphasise the value of building up a set of visual prompts to help children memorise the new language; classroom display and mobiles play an important part in presenting and practising the key phrases we want the children to learn. Using the humorous cartoon drawings in the Miniflashcards packs, for example, it is easy to devise games to practise the phrases for classroom organisation – such as a game of 'Simon dit' to rehearse:

- Ferme la porte!
- Ouvre la fenêtre!
- Ouvre ton cahier!
- Sors!
- Lève-toi!
- Assieds-toi!
- Écoute la cassette!
- Danse!
- Regarde la télé!
- Compte de 1 à 10!, etc.

Having established some simple classroom routines in the new language the teacher can embark on introducing the special vocabulary areas associated with the main topics for the year. These might be, for example: Where I live, School, Clothes, My friends, Animals. For each topic the teacher would need to have collected, sorted and planned well in advance the introduction of the key phrases she wants the children to retain, using extracts from published course materials, such as *Gaston* (Apicella and Challier, 1996) or *Tamburin* (Büttner *et al.*, 1996), picture dictionaries and any authentic materials she can acquire from the foreign country. Topic Webs are invaluable here!

Pupil talk

In the first few weeks of language learning beginners will produce very little talk themselves – they will be listening hard for meanings, trying to piece together what this new code is all about. New sounds and intonation patterns take some getting used to and the teacher needs to use every visual aid in her repertoire to help convey meaning. But it will soon be possible to build in pupil activities which involve the learners in 'listen and do' tasks that allow them to demonstrate their understanding non-verbally – by total physical response (TPR) to instructions of all kinds from the teacher or from another pupil:

- Stand up!
- Come here!
- Shut your eyes!
- Stick out your tongue!
- Touch your nose!
- Turn to your left!
- Bend down and touch your toes!, etc.

Similarly, many of the teacher's instructions to the class need only a physical response:

- Tim, ramasse les feuilles, stp!
- Rangez vos affaires!
- Mets les scisseuses dans le tiroir!
- Ouvre la fenêtre!

Non-verbal response can gradually be replaced by games where one-word answers are required:

| What colour is | the book? | Brown |
| | the ribbon? | Red |

the hat?	Green
the shirt?	White

The next step might involve short greetings and short phrase answers, for example:

Bonjour! Ça va?
Ça va bien, merci.
Où est le chien?
Dans la cuisine.

and eventually it will be possible to progress to whole sentences. Increasingly the children will want to ask questions in the target language:

Pardon madame, (est-ce que) je peux aller aux toilettes, s'il vous plaît?
Comment dit-on en français...?
Où sont les crayons, s'il vous plaît?

To reach this stage some careful block-building is required, ensuring that the children are fed only a small and digestible number of new phrases each week, accompanied by visuals wherever possible – and they all need constant practice and revision until they are secure! Again, the Miniflashcard packs are invaluable here, as they tackle each situation one at a time, providing plenty of ideas for teaching activities and games.

What else will the pupils want to say? They will of course need the language for basic greetings at different times of the day, to talk about themselves, their family and friends and eventually to tell a visitor something about where they live, their pastimes and interests. It is important to teach children the question forms quite early on. Fortunately, the complications of *Est-ce que?* and *Qu'est-ce que?* in French can often be avoided by teaching the class how to turn a statement into a question simply by changing their intonation:

C'est une tortue > C'est une tortue?
Tu as un animal > Tu as un animal, toi?

Children will only start to talk to the teacher in the foreign language if they are consistent in their own use of it. If the expectation is: *Hier sprechen wir nur deutsch* or *Ici on parle français*, most children will go along with the rule and have a go. They also need to be brought up to the idea that you don't have to be 100 per cent accurate to make yourself understood – arms and legs and the odd English word are also allowed!

As far as possible, we should try to ensure that the pupil tasks we devise cover the notional 'seven intelligences' put forward by Howard Gardner

(1993), so that children can learn the language through using both sides of the brain and by doing tasks that involve not just linguistic but also mathematical thinking, spatial representation, musical/rhythmical activity, use of the body to solve problems and make things, encouraging understanding of others and ourselves. This means bringing into foreign language lessons other aspects of the primary curriculum whenever we can see an opportunity to reinforce the children's conceptual learning. The more activities the teacher can devise to involve the children in using the language for real, the more they will enjoy it and the more they will absorb in a natural way. So every kind of fun – from singing, chanting, clapping in rhythm, reciting rhymes, poems, tongue-twisters, to playing party games, board and card games, going out into the playground to skip, play hopscotch or 'What's the time, Mr Wolf?' in the foreign language – needs to be built into the year's programme.

Groupwork and pairwork are essential if the children are going to make the most of the precious few minutes each week of foreign language talking time. In order to play any kind of game, the ground rules and the instructions need to be clearly understood, otherwise the children immediately revert to their mother tongue. So the teacher will have to demonstrate to the whole class how the game goes, using another pupil or a parent/classroom assistant as her stooge. Key phrases then need intensive rehearsal, before the game can begin. For example:

> Tu commences!
> C'est à toi!
> Vas-y!
> C'est à moi!
> Avance/recule deux cases
> Passe un tour.

This aspect of the language is dealt with in some depth in the CILT *Young Pathfinder No. 2: Games and Fun Activities* (Martin, 1995).

Progression

Planning for linguistic and skills progression over a year or more is no easy task, but the teacher needs to ask: what will the children be able to do in the foreign language by the end of the year? At its simplest level, a beginners' class of, say, 6 or 7 year olds can be given a basic self-assessment sheet like this example devised by an infants teacher, and shown in Figure 5.1, asking them to tick what they can do and how they feel about it.

Even with infants we should expect them within a year to have progressed beyond just one word responses; indeed, many children get so immersed in

Name:-------------------------	Date:------------------------------		
I can say hello	☺	☺	☹
I can say yes and no	☺	☺	☹
I can introduce myself	☺	☺	☹
I can ask how someone is	☺	☺	☹
I can say how I feel	☺	☺	☹
I can count to 10	☺	☺	☹
I can count to 20	☺	☺	☹
I can say the days of the week	☺	☺	☹

Figure 5.1 A self-assessment sheet for infants

the language that they are able after only a few weeks to improvise quite impressive mini-dialogues by themselves:

> Je m'appelle Jane. J'ai six ans. J'habite à XYZ.
> Comment tu t'appelles? Quel âge as-tu? Où habites-tu?
> J'ai un chat et un petit lapin. Ils s'appellent XXX et ZZZ.
> Mon chat aime Whiskas. Mon lapin aime les laitues et les carottes.

If the foreign language is taught for more than one year in the primary school, curriculum planning and pupil profiling will need to go further so that the teacher is able to keep a realistic assessment of what the class has achieved over the year. They may wish to look at progression from other angles:

- How has the pupil's self-confidence in using the target language increased?
- How has the class progressed in the four language skills – Listening, Speaking, Reading and Writing?
- Are any individual pupils beginning to use the language for their own purposes – independently of the teacher?
- Are they able to string whole sentences together with reasonable accuracy?
- How much of the target language can they recognise in print? (Words, phrases, sentences, questions?)

- Do they understand aspects of the foreign culture? (For example, are they aware of the appropriate forms of greeting – *tu/vous; du/Sie?* or of the customs associated with birthdays, name days, Christmas, Easter?)

In the infants school most teachers will expect the emphasis to be solely on listening and speaking skills, but teachers in junior schools can make greater demands on their classes by introducing a modest amount of reading and writing. For example: the days of the week, the numbers and the months can be progressively practised by singing songs, reciting rhymes until they are secure in the children's memory. Then the link between the printed word and the sounds could be reinforced by making a date and weather board which involves individuals in reading and changing the cards and visuals on a daily basis. This could be expanded further to include temperature and wind direction readings, thus bringing in some aspects of science through the foreign language, as in this example:

Das Wetter heute
Datum: 11.9.97
Uhrzeit: 10.30
Temperatur: 20 C
Wind aus: Südwesten
Wetter: Sonnig und warm

Junior schoolchildren can also be encouraged to start reading simple cartoon readers for their own pleasure (e.g. *Bibliobus, Lesekiste, Album des Monstres*) and to start writing their own little stories for a younger class to read. Book making, posters and even a simple class newspaper are all possible, using information technology to assist wherever appropriate. Once children have progressed orally to the point where they can produce a simple profile of themselves and their family/friends, they can be encouraged to start compiling a simple illustrated dossier in the target language, including photographs and drawings of people and the area in which they live. Ultimately this can form the basis both for the transfer of information to the secondary school and also for the beginning of a correspondence with a primary school in the foreign country. A school-to-school link often provides the stimulus for much imaginative and rewarding work, both in and outside the classroom. Children who, before they are 11, have read, written and recorded messages in the foreign language to a real audience of their peers in another country begin to get under the skin of the language and realise the effectiveness of even the very modest repertoire of phrases they have learnt in primary school. They begin to understand what contact with another culture means and that children across the Channel have similar interests to their own, even though they may have some odd customs and eating habits!

Getting the children to this stage in the foreign language by Year 6 should be the ultimate goal of every junior school that teaches a foreign language.

Teachers planning several years of language learning in their school will need to bear in mind that children will stay enthusiastic and motivated only if they see practical outcomes from their language learning. If they see older classes performing in the foreign language, creating interesting displays around the school, or hosting foreign visitors on a school-to-school exchange, they will want to be part of the experience when their turn comes. Teaching in the target language inevitably impinges on all aspects of school life – including making the headteacher perform in French or German in front of the children! French breakfasts, German and Spanish songs and dances at parents' evenings, poetry and drama – all provide unforgettable experiences for the children involved and should be part of their foreign language experience as they get older. With enthusiasm and determination anything is possible!

References

Apicella, M. and Challier, H. (1996) *Gaston*, Reconati, Italy: European Language Institute.

Bevis, R. (1995) *Album des Monstres*, Leamington Spa: Language Centre Publication.

Bromidge, W. and Burch, J. (1994) *In Focus: The Language Classroom* (video pack), London: CILT.

Büttner, S., Kopp, G. and Alberti, J. (1996) *Tamburin*, Ismarning, Germany: Max Hueber Verlag.

Department of Education and Science (1991) *Modern Languages in the National Curriculum* (The Harris Report), London: HMSO.

Gardner, H. (1993) *The Unschooled Mind*, London: HarperCollins.

Halliwell, S. and Jones, B. (1989) *On Target: Pathfinder 5*, London: CILT.

Hawkins, E. (1981) *Modern Languages in the Curriculum*, Cambridge: Cambridge University Press.

Holmes, B. (1990) *Communication Reactivated: Pathfinder 6*, London: CILT.

—— (1995) *Keeping On Target: Pathfinder 23*, London: CILT.

McColl, H. and Thomas, S. (1997a) *Cartoons for Classroom Communication*, London: Miniflashcard Language Games.

——(1997b) *Ici on parle français*, London: Miniflashcard Language Games.

Martin, C. (1995) *Games and Fun Activities: Young Pathfinder 2*, London: CILT.

National Curriculum Council (1993) *Target Practice Video Pack*, York: NCC.

Rowe, I. and Killbery, I. (1996) *3-2-1...Los!*, Kent: Invicta Media Productions Ltd.

Rumley, G., Rowe, I. and Killbery, I. (1992) *Pilote: Kent Primary French Project*, Dover: KCC/KETV.

Satchwell, P. (1997) *Keep Talking – Young Pathfinder 4*, London: CILT.

Satchwell, P. and De Silva, J. (1995) *Catching them Young: Young Pathfinder 1*, London: CILT.

6

Classroom connections

John Muir

Past imperfect?

When I took part in a Scottish pilot project to introduce French to primary children in 1990 I had a distinct sense of *déjà vu*. As a raw recruit to the primary classroom in the mid-1960s I trained to participate in the Modern Languages in the Primary School (MLPS) experiment of that era only to see it abandoned following the publication of a damning report from the Scottish Education Department. The following quotation sums up the views of the inspectorate on the ill-fated project.

> The conditions necessary to ensure success in teaching a foreign language in the primary school are so difficult to create that the enormous effort involved is beyond the resources of all but a limited number of schools. In the majority of schools the results achieved were not commensurate with the amount of time, money and energy that was being expended.
>
> (HM Inspector of Schools, 1969: 18)

The Scottish inspectorate were particularly critical of the 'lifeless presentation of lessons' and of methodology which was 'frequently alien to the spirit of the modern primary school'. In retrospect, I am also of the opinion that one of the greatest drawbacks in those days was the more didactic approach to modern languages, with reading and writing prevailing over the spoken word, which primary pupils encountered in their first year of secondary schooling. In addition, not all primaries in secondary catchment areas were included, resulting in what is commonly called a 'clean slate' approach, where all pupils in their first year received the same teaching, regardless of their previous experience. This inevitably sealed the fate of the project.

Having experienced a sense of *déjà vu*, could I now sigh, *'plus ça change...!'*, as many of my colleagues did at the time? On examination, I have to acknowledge that the climate has changed since the late 1960s. Secondary schools now lay greater emphasis on speaking a foreign language with 50 per cent of the Scottish Standard Grade assessment on speaking skills; lessons are often activity led and there is greater recognition of the importance of curricular continuity between the primary and secondary sectors. Notwithstanding these changes, one of the main reasons for the rebirth of MLPS in the United Kingdom must be the embarrassing inability of the majority of our young people to engage in even the most basic communication in a foreign language, in comparison with their counterparts in other European countries. 'Some sixty to seventy per cent of the world's population are bilingual. Unfortunately, in the United Kingdom, monolingualism is seen as the norm and bilingualism as the problem.' (Johnstone, 1994)

Twelve pilot projects, each comprising a secondary school and its associated primaries, were set up in Scotland; six in 1989 and six in 1990, involving seventy-six primary schools in all. There were important lessons to be learned but the projects were, in general, hailed as a success. Research supported this:

> All those involved in the pilot projects in Scotland have found them to be a very demanding but worthwhile development but the wider implementation of the programme will be based on a different approach, not directly involving secondary teachers.
>
> (Low et al., 1993: 8)

Following this success, political will, backed by considerable public finance, led to an ambitious extension of the programme to the rest of the country in 1992, this time embarking on the training of primary classroom teachers to deliver the programme. In contrast with many parts of England, Wales and Northern Ireland, the decision was made that all areas of Scotland should take part with a view to total coverage in the foreseeable future. Phase Six of the training programme was launched during session 1998–9. Some authorities anticipate that before long a large proportion of pupils in the upper stages of primary schools will have been introduced to a foreign language.

Curricular connections

The aim of the Scottish project is to embed the teaching of a modern language in the primary curriculum. As the Scottish education system is different from that provided in England and Wales, it is helpful to clarify what is meant by the curriculum in this context. The five main areas of the Scottish curriculum, to which I refer later, are: language, mathematics, expressive arts, environmental studies and religious and moral education.

The annual 27-day training programme in Scotland has been very well received by the primary teachers who have participated, not only because it has been an enjoyable personal development experience for them, but also because they have returned to their schools armed with a wealth of ideas and activities to use with their pupils. Given that the primary class teacher has the opportunity to use a cross-curricular approach when teaching any subject, participants are encouraged to foster the use of the foreign language in this way also.

> When the foreign language can be linked to other aspects of the primary curriculum, it enables the children to relate the foreign language to concepts of the world they already possess, to make links between the foreign language and language(s) they already possess, to approach their foreign language holistically.
>
> (Hurrell, 1996: 53)

However, it is important to emphasise that this form of embedding does not mean teaching the core content of other curricular areas through the medium of the foreign language.

In the years following the pilot projects, certain strategies have emerged which are now regarded as indicators of good practice. On visits to schools over the years of my involvement I have been encouraged by the enthusiasm of teachers, despite the self-confessed linguistic shortcomings of a number of them, and can vouch for the variety of ideas which are praised in various reports. As might be expected, however, it is not all sweetness and light in my part of the country nor in Scotland as a whole. Much support is required and it is imperative that we do not let up in our attempts to foster and disseminate good practice.

The following examples, gleaned from the guidelines which were put together for Scottish participants (Scottish Office Education Department 1990) and from the extensive training folders issued to all staff taking part, do not constitute an exhaustive list. Primary teachers are adept at identifying new ways of working and innovative approaches to teaching, which reflect both their experience and the varied needs of their pupils. To illustrate embedding for each curricular area would require a book in its own right so I have selected a few examples in French. The principle of embedding can be applied to any modern language being taught, which it is in many parts of Scotland and elsewhere.

A word of caution is appropriate at this point. There is concern that the use of a modern language across the primary curriculum may be so contrived that it loses its impact with the pupils and may lead to digression from the subject selected. Researchers have noted this and some, like Richard Johnstone of Stirling University, have signalled a warning to guard against it.

> There is the danger that it can lead to a rather fragmented approach – e.g. one week a bit of PE, next week a bit of environmental studies, the week after a bit of mathematics. This raises the problem as to how these

various bits and pieces are to be made to hang together in one coherent system of language that pupils can understand and use. It therefore places heavy responsibility on both teachers and pupils to construct their own progression dynamically as particular areas of the curriculum are exploited.

(Johnstone, 1994: 8)

While paying heed to these concerns, there are, nevertheless, many ways to consolidate the teaching of MLPS across the curriculum which, if done with careful planning, have a positive spin-off.

Heard and not seen?

In the early stages of the pilot there was a debate about whether or not pupils should be given the opportunity to read and write the modern language. There were those who argued that exposure to print would serve to confuse pupils and possibly affect their reading and writing in English. As one who learned to read and write languages at secondary school, with little or no opportunity to speak, I tended to support this viewpoint. It was time to redress the balance, I believed. However, involvement with the MLPS programme soon convinced me that most, if not all, children can be assisted in their learning experience if they are exposed to the written word, even if the emphasis is on the speaking and listening component. That does not mean writing essays or conjugating verbs, but simply using print as a teaching aid.

Creating a climate for learning

My early experience of learning a foreign language in secondary school consisted of revising vocabulary lists and reciting regular and irregular verbs: necessary to pass the exam but not always an enjoyable experience and, more often than not, very stressful indeed. By contrast, we now encourage teachers to introduce pupils to language for pleasure and to enable them to interact and communicate with others. As soon as possible children should be given the opportunity to use the language in a variety of realistic situations. For example, in the Scottish guidelines, we encourage teachers to use the language with pupils to do the following:

- to exchange information;
- to realise a task;
- to express feelings and needs;
- to have fun;
- to relate events and incidents;
- to give classroom commands;
- to take the class register.

Greetings, instructions, words of encouragement and organisation of activities can all be spoken in the foreign language (for example, *Sors tes affaires*; *je fais le rappel....qui est absent aujourd'hui?*; *Tout le monde est prêt*, etc.). Areas of the classroom can be labelled and exhibitions of pupils' work displayed. It is valuable also if illustrations of these activities spill out into the corridor for others to see and discover the language for themselves.

It is an interesting and valuable educational experience for pupils to meet a native speaker, who may be a visitor to the community or a secondary language assistant. Pupils can also take part in exchanges with schools abroad or classes may organise trips to other European countries. Playing music and singing songs from the country also help to create an atmosphere which can serve to make the language alive to the children. The most obvious ones in French, for example, are: 'Frère Jacques'; 'Sur le pont....' etc. but translations of well-known English songs such as 'Le fermier dans son champ' (The farmer's in his den) make interesting and enjoyable comparisons.

Reinforcement

Reinforcement through language skills

Having studied a language to an advanced level at school, I recall with embarrassment going abroad on a camping holiday and being asked to spell my surname at the reception office. I could read and write in the subjunctive mode but no one had taught me my ABC! It is not surprising, therefore, that one of the most common aspects of language first covered is the alphabet, which has similarities but, surprisingly to most children, many tricky differences. Memorising skills and strategies are an important feature of the child's first language acquisition. There is any amount of games and songs which can be used to help children remember (see also Chapter 7).

Games and drama techniques can be used to create situations which give rise to communicative language use, for example:

- role playing;
- commands and requests;
- instruction, explanation, organisation;
- encouragement;
- creating or memorising a script, produced by teacher/pupil.

Stories and rhymes may be used effectively:

- to introduce new foreign language items;
- to provide easy (and fun) ways to memorise words already learned;
- to develop listening skills;
- to perform pupils' work;

- to link with themes current in class;
- to re-enact a story already known by the pupils;
- to illustrate the linguistic stress patterns of the foreign language.

A teacher reading, for example, *Little House on the Prairie* (by Laura Ingles Wilder), was able to revise language relating to the family, the house and clothes. One group made up a family tree for the Ingles, drew and labelled a plan of the house and described the clothes which Laura wore.

Simple translations of short passages from popular children's fiction have been used in many classes as have familiar English fairy stories, with pictures as illustrations of the text. It has been shown that, contrary to many teachers' fears, older children are not put off by looking at the foreign language version of Little Red Riding Hood or The Old Woman Who Swallowed a Fly. If anything, they tend to be keen to hear more and may participate in telling the familiar story-lines. Repetition of key phrases mean that they can predict and join in.

Listening skills can be developed through a 'listen-and-do' or a 'listen-and-draw' activity. When something is being read to a class, pupils may be asked to tune their ear to listen for a particular piece of information. 'Simon Says'-type games (Jacques a dit: touche la tête; touche le nez) may be used to encourage the language used for understanding specific commands. For some pupils, such practice has led to improvements in these skills in the native tongue.

Reading skills can be reinforced in a variety of ways through opportunities to see print in the foreign language, including labels and signs. Children may read to follow directions or to act on information given by the teacher or another pupil. They may also be able to follow the written text which is being read by the teacher or another pupil.

Word searches, made by pupils or teacher, can also be a fun way of improving word recognition.

Reinforcement through mathematics

Apart from the obvious reinforcement of basic *number*, given time, children can cope with higher numbers in some languages as well as terms such as 'add', 'subtract', 'multiply' and 'divide'. Pupils of all ages continue to enjoy simple number *games*, such as Snakes and Ladders, with a move only allowed when the number is given in the foreign language. *Money*, either in our own currency or that of another European country, can be used to reinforce skills, including the recording of the decimal point (watch out for the use of the comma in place of the decimal point in some countries) and place value.

Understanding the vocabulary of *measurement*, in the classroom or further afield, may be hampered by our society's failure fully to adopt the metric system outside school, but it is easily translated to another language. Children can very quickly pick up phrases such as 'How tall are you?' or 'How far is it to...?' *Shape*, either in the context of everyday mathematics in the classroom, or within the environment, may be referred to in the modern language being introduced. Words of comparison, such as 'larger', 'smaller', may be used across mathematical areas.

Reinforcement through the expressive arts

In the school curriculum, expressive arts are: art and craft; home economics; drama; music; physical education. When doing *art and craft* activities pupils can be given the opportunity to recall colours, shapes, the names of various materials (scissors, paper, pen, paint, etc.). Where activities necessitate following simple instructions to make an object, these can be given orally or in writing.

If we wish to include *home economics* activities, instructions and recipes may be followed in the foreign language or they may relate to a theme being covered in class. A good example within a Christmas theme is shown in Figure 6.

La Bûche de Noël

If faut
    un gâteau roulé; un grand bol;
    un cuillère en bois
    une spatule; une fourchette;
    100 grammes de sucre glace;
    100 grammes de beurre bien ramolli
    une cuillerée de cacao en poudre

Pour fair le glaçage:
    Mélangez le beurre, le sucre et le cacao, et
    battez bien avec la cuillére pour faire une crème épaisse.
    Nappez la fourchette et striez le glaçage pour faire ressembler
    le gâteau à une vraie bûche de sucre glace et décorez avec feuilles
    de houx (vraie ou en sucre) ou des bonbons.

BON APPÉTIT ET JOYEUX NOËL

Figure 6.1 A Christmas recipe

The particular value of crafts and cooking activities is the reinforcement of the language of instruction and command; it is in this way that language can be most successfully embedded across the curriculum. By identifying this language at the end of primary school, it should be possible for secondary teachers to continue when pupils transfer.

In the language section I referred to activities within *drama* which may be exploited to good use. In *music*, songs can be sung, memorised or listened to, with words duplicated for the class. Rhymes and raps to reinforce language, made up by pupils or teachers, are good fun.

In *physical education* the activity can be conducted using instructions in the foreign language particularly related to the subject, or to reinforce foreign language already introduced in the classroom context, e.g.:

> Alors, mettez-vous en cercle ici.
> Oui, c'est ça, mais serrez-vous un peu.
> Écoutez bien. Je vais vous lancer la balle.

Reinforcement through religious and moral education

The most obvious use of a modern language here is with themes of Christmas and Easter which may also involve art and craft activities as well as songs and poems. The latter might include prayers and graces before meals or a verse of a familiar hymn. Some teachers may wish to include topics from other world religions. Depending on the composition of the community in which they live, others may feel they are unable to link this area to the foreign language. However, times and seasons throughout the year, as they relate to RE, can provide ideal opportunities to revise language skills, as might themes of caring and sharing.

Within the specific area of *moral education*, class or school rules (if not the Ten Commandments!) may be listed in another language and displayed.

Reinforcement through environmental studies

I should make it clear here that, in the context of the Scottish 5–14 curriculum, 'Environmental Studies' covers specifically: Science, Technology, Information Technology, Health Education and Social Subjects (including History and Geography). Many of the skills in *language and mathematics* can be reinforced as a matter of course across the curricular areas mentioned and there will be places where the use of a foreign language may be appropriate, particularly related to the skills I have noted so far.

At the beginning of this section I referred to the danger of lessons being so contrived that the impact is lost. The main purpose for teaching a topic within environmental studies may not always be served by including modern language teaching. Having said that, some examples of good practice have emerged.

In *science*, particularly where aspects relate to the modern language topic generally covered in the teaching programme, it is not difficult to identify areas for reinforcement. Areas which teachers have found most useful include elementary biology, the weather, the seasons, water, air, sounds, colour or simple gardening activities. Some teachers have related work to topics on space (even if only the names of the sun, moon and their links with names of days of the week) and energy (e.g. electrical appliances; sources of energy).

A simple activity at the start of a day may be to discuss the weather (*la météo*) which can be presented on a chart (*un tableau d'observation*) to include vocabulary such as:

> Quel temps fait-il aujourd'hui?
> Il fait beau.
> Le ciel est bleu.
> Le soleil règne sans partage.

or, more likely in the UK: *Le ciel est gris mais sans pluie. Il pleut!*

Simple instructions for investigations may be written down or read to the class/group. Anything already successful in English can be translated, although some teachers may wish to have the sentence construction checked by a linguist to ensure accuracy with unfamiliar terminology.

Similar ideas could be developed in relation to *technology* but the main way to include language here may be through simple instructions for designing and constructing.

Information technology may provide opportunities for children who are at the stage of writing the foreign language in simple form on the word processor to make labels, put together a class information sheet (for example, names, hair, eye colour, and so on of pupils). Computer programmes are becoming available which are more attractive and educationally sound than some of the earlier ones which relied so much on drill and practice that pupils were in danger of being put off by the experience. As more and more schools become involved in MLPS, software is bound to become more abundant so teachers will need to investigate what is available before purchasing an expensive resource which may do no more than teachers can just as well do themselves.

A number of good modern language activities have been developed within the general topic of *health education*, albeit reinforcing some simple language. The most obvious of these are parts of the body, personal descriptions, the senses, common ailments, food and drink, hobbies, exercise, sport, and so on.

Even if loosely connected to health education, children may also be introduced to affective language to express likes/dislikes; feelings/emotions/reactions; talking about aches and pains; terms of endearment, etc. For example:

J'aime bien regarder la télé.
J'adore me promener.
Je n'aime pas tellement lire.
J'ai horreur du sport.
Je m'intéresse beaucoup à la musique.

Social subjects can be a good medium and a list of activities could be lengthy. A few examples are outlined. Local studies can be used to develop language on 'then and now'; houses and homes; local buildings and centres. A model village or street could highlight for example: *l'école*; *le boulanger*; *l'église*, etc. Vocabulary such as: *à gauche*; *à droite*; *à côté de*; *en face de*; *au coin de*, might be reinforced in this context.

Studies of other countries allow work on flags; capitals; holidays; tourism; travel, including phrases to cope with everyday life (tickets, food, train and bus timetables, directions, etc.); currency/exchange; shopping; customs (e.g. birthdays, saints days); costumes; etc.

Vocabulary related to climate/weather abroad might be included. Conservation may give opportunities to explore the foreign language associated with rain forest; animals, weather, food and drink packaging.

Periods of history, such as the Romans, Vikings, Tudors and Stuarts, the Victorians or the Second World War are examples of popular topics covered by many primary schools. Certain areas of study may allow the teacher to look at language 'then and now' as they consider homes, families, school, clothes, methods of travel, pastimes.

Sharing good practice

The cross-curricular connections in all that I have mentioned above are evident. As I pointed out early in the chapter, with care, the imaginative primary teacher can reinforce the foreign language being introduced in so many ways and can simultaneously complement and reinforce skills and concepts in other areas of the primary curriculum. Sharing good practice is essential if developments are to take place and if the cautious or sceptical among us are to be reassured. An effective way for classes, schools or clusters of primaries linked to secondaries, to do this is to hold open days or festivals of language when teachers and pupils are given the opportunity to perform or display work they have been doing in class. This is not only a worthwhile inter-school activity but it also allows pupils to reach out to parents and the wider community.

Matters of quality

There is no doubt that, this time round, the introduction of modern languages has been a more enjoyable experience for teachers and pupils than it was over thirty years ago, for all the reasons I have already mentioned. But enjoyment, while it may be conducive to success, is not the be all and end all of education. Learning a language was not, initially at least, a fun experience for me and exams had to be passed if success was to be achieved.

I once read of an old Scottish headmaster who said, of Scottish education, 'If you can't mark it, you shouldn't do it!' This sentiment has tended to dominate education for centuries. Teachers, wise parents, but sadly few politicians, realise that in some subject areas it is hard to be objective when assessing quality and there are others where it is almost impossible; aspects of speaking and listening, personal search in RE, inventiveness, or works of art are examples which spring to mind. The result has often meant that the more easily assessed areas of the curriculum (those which can be written down) dominate and determine an individual's record of achievement.

When it comes to modern languages in the primary school, then, with its important emphasis on enjoyment through various activities related to the four language skills, how can we ensure quality, particularly when non-linguists are involved in the delivery? With expenditure amounting to millions of pounds since its introduction, we can be assured that politicians and taxpayers will be looking for answers.

Much discussion and research on assessment of MLPS will have to be done before expectations of achievement can be written down, which they surely will. Before I embark on a few pointers which may be considered – a word of caution. The status of MLPS within the National Curriculum (England, Wales and N. Ireland) and the 5–14 Guidelines (Scotland) has yet to be clarified. Schools are being encouraged (some would say compelled) to take part; teachers, whatever their level of ability/qualification, are being trained to deliver a language. In many quarters, even where everyone is positive and enjoys the introduction of the language, there is a climate of concern that someone, sometime will ask them to grade the pupils or, worse still, come to assess their own foreign language competence after only twenty-seven days training.

If local authorities, the inspectorate, OFSTED or any national bodies involved in quality assurance, rush into a system of assessment before the profession is ready, we may suddenly find, perhaps without warning, that MLPS is seen as the 'straw' which will finally break their backs and MLPS may die a dusty death. Since we cannot afford for that to happen, let us proceed with caution. Matters of quality assurance should, I believe, be addressed in the following 'user friendly' ways.

In-service training

If we aim to ensure that delivery in the classroom is effective, it is essential at the outset that the quality of training is high. Courses must be enjoyable, related directly to the primary curriculum (not a watered-down secondary course) and backed by good resources. The Scottish experience has been positive on these counts to date, with twenty-seven days delivered by a modern linguist alongside, in the majority of courses, a native speaker, both of whom attend induction days. The challenge of any course is whether differentiation can be achieved, particularly to allow for the absolute beginner who has a long way to go to feel able to deliver a language and who almost always lacks initial confidence. One way to avoid this challenge would be to insist that applicants, prior to training, have achieved a minimum standard of linguistic competence. In my experience this has not been possible and is unlikely to be so in the near future. In the circumstances, therefore, it would be helpful, perhaps even essential, for some form of introductory course to be available for the 'linguistically challenged' on top of the normal training days. In addition, for that group in particular, strategies and resources must be given to allow them to deliver the language more effectively in the classroom. Tapes, videos, CD-ROMs and links with more competent teachers are but a few examples which might be considered.

The challenge is to sustain support for trained staff in the years ahead. Arguably this pertains to any subject area but I consider it particularly important for non-specialist primary teachers who are expected to deliver MLPS. Schools, local authorities and ultimately governments must provide the means to realise this.

Quality in the classroom

Having established the importance of good training and the need for ongoing support for the teacher, we must also consider how best to measure effectiveness in the classroom. The teacher has the initial responsibility here to construct a teaching programme which will ensure continuity, coherence and progression; to plan appropriate use of the teaching materials provided; to organise resources and consider classroom organisation and to record when and how topics were taught. In addition, there is a need for a systematic approach to the monitoring of pupil progress.

Remembering the aphorism 'weighing doesn't fatten the pig', any system should not be so time-consuming that it impinges on teaching time, and records kept must have a clear purpose and an identified audience. Put simply, we must ask: who will want to read them and why? In larger schools it is the responsibility of promoted staff to assess the quality of provision within the framework of an agreed policy for MLPS. To do this effectively, they must be aware of the expectations of teachers and pupils by becoming familiar with the content of the course and know the breadth of activities that are essential to create a climate for learning. I mention this because I firmly believe that the promoted staff in general and the head teacher in particular play a key role in the organisation and monitoring of the effectiveness of MLPS in their school. It should not be left to the trained teacher to take on this responsibility alone.

Assessing pupil progress

To assess pupil progress, we must consider what it means in the context of learning a foreign language. Richard Johnstone (1994) points out that there are some very obvious ways in which to think about progression. For example, we can expect learners to become more fluent, more accurate and more wide-ranging in their use of language. We can also expect them to deal with increasingly lengthy and complex language and be able progressively to under-take tasks which are cognitively at a higher level; for example, beginning with simple conversations, then later telling stories, reporting, interviewing, etc. by which time of course pupils have moved well beyond primary school.

Until the aforementioned national expectations are determined, it is to be hoped, after lengthy discussions and a consensus with all concerned, one can only consider what aspects within these parameters may be included. However, after some time, as teachers gain confidence, it may be possible for schools to embark on assessment at least of fluency, accuracy and range. With support, teachers may also take into account length and complexity. These are consid-ered at length by Alison Hurrell in Chapter 4 with progression exemplified in the following:

> Aujourd'hui il fait beau.
> Aujourd'hui il fait beau et il fait du soleil.
> Aujourd'hui il fait beau, il fait du soleil et il fait assez chaud.

However, given the range of training and the diversity of types of delivery across the country, it may not be possible for many teachers to go beyond a basic exposure of pupils to the foreign language.

It is certain that the debate will continue, for there are as many questions being raised about assessment of MLPS at this stage as there are answers.

Future perfect?

If MLPS is to succeed in the future there are a number of important key issues which have to be addressed locally and nationally. I suggest that these are: initial teacher training, in-service support, continuity within the primary school, continuity from primary to secondary school and leadership.

Ideally, teaching of MLPS should become an integral part of the initial training of most, if not all, primary teachers, as it is in other countries. Only in this way, I believe, can we begin to meet demands to extend effective delivery beyond 2000. There are implications for entry qualifications and inevitably for recruitment of secondary pupils. In Scotland at least, there are signs that more student teachers are electing to study MLPS, if only to add another 'string to the bow' which may be attractive to potential employers in a competitive market. However, if this is not taken up nationally, we must rely on the training of existing staff.

I have already summarised the components of a good training course for existing staff in the primary school. However, it is recognised that twenty-seven days training, particularly for absolute beginners, is not enough. They and other teachers need to continue to be motivated in order to maintain the momentum which a successful course will engender. A variety of opportunities to do this might arise, for example, through a network of self-help groups; links with teacher training institutions; links with teachers and classes in European member states through writing and exchanging books and magazines; making use of information technology (Internet and video conferencing for example); short visits abroad; 'refresher' courses and supportive links with secondary colleagues.

Until such times as we reach the position where all, or even the majority, of qualified primary teachers are able to deliver MLPS, the greatest challenge will be coping with retirals; maternity leave; illness, etc. of trained teachers. It is also accepted that there will be movement of staff within and between schools, resulting in gaps which may not be easy to fill.

While I believe that a modern language should be taught in primary school for its own educational worth, there is need for good liaison and continuity with the secondary sector. Finding time and money to establish effective links in any subject area is an continuing challenge. Perhaps a special effort is required with modern languages, if only because, with few exceptions, it is not an issue with which secondary languages teachers have had to be concerned until now.

In the Scottish MLPS programme there is an expectation that pupils will be able to continue through to fourth year secondary with the language to which they have been introduced in primary. In some secondary schools this may challenge a policy of diversification in Sl. However, in Scotland at least, Her Majesty's Inspectorate have stressed that pupils should not be allowed to switch to another language at the start of their secondary schooling, even if it presents a timetabling problem to departments. Not surprisingly, this has engendered considerable debate among secondary modern linguists.

Each secondary school should adapt their programme to take MLPS into account by increasing expectations of pupils' achievements and ensuring differentiation when planning class work. Languages departments should find ways to establish links with primary schools in their cluster. Examples of good practice which I have identified include:

- secondary linguists joining the primary training programme for a day or two to familiarise themselves with the content;
- mutual observation of teaching;
- visits by primary teachers to ML departments to view course materials;
- a bridging topic commenced in primary and progressed in secondary.

No training programme will succeed, whatever the good intentions of head teachers or local authorities, if national political support is not forthcoming. Laying aside the issue of the amount of money invested to date, no government can be complacent while other countries in Europe promote language training for their young people. An article in the *Scotsman* newspaper (27 June 1997) entitled 'Bottom of the Class' makes this point.

> The British lack motivation to learn a foreign language and tend to assume that everyone else will understand basic English. An internal poll conducted among EU officials last year showed that even highly educated Britons are lagging far behind their multi-lingual colleagues.

Reflecting the views of many other politicians, Brian Wilson, when Secretary of State for Scotland, expressed concern that only a small percentage of secondary pupils were studying a European language to an advanced level. He was keen to emphasise that, notwithstanding the apparent universality of our native tongue, dogged reliance on 'they all speak English anyway' has no place in the modern world of education. However, actions will speak louder than the well-meaning words of politicians, particularly in these formative years of MLPS when financial commitment is crucial.

References

HMI (1969) *French in the Primary School*, Report by HM Inspectors of Schools, Edinburgh: HMSO.

Hurrell, A. (1996) *The Teacher as Traveller: Keynote Address*, in L. Low (ed.) *MLPS in Scotland: Practice and Prospects*, proceedings of two conferences on modern languages in primary and early secondary education, Stirling: Scottish CILT.

Johnstone, R. (1994) *Teaching Modern Languages at Primary School: Approaches and Implications*, Edinburgh: Scottish Council for Research in Education.

Low, L. (ed.) (1996) *MLPS in Scotland: Practice and Prospects*, proceedings of two conferences on modern languages in primary and early secondary education, Stirling: Scottish CILT.

Low, L. *et al.* (1993) *Interchange No 19*, Edinburgh: Scottish Council for Research in Education.

Scottish Office Education Department (SOED) (1990) *National Pilot: Modern Languages in the Primary School*, Edinburgh: HMSO.

——(1993) *Modern Languages in the Primary School: The Training Programme*, Glasgow: Strathclyde University.

7

Games and songs for teaching modern foreign languages to young children

Glynis Rumley

In March 1990 I was appointed as the 'Primary French Co-ordinator' following the decision of Kent County Council to fund a pilot project to introduce French into a small number of primary schools. From the twenty-one pilot schools grouped around Folkestone, Sandwich and Dover it has now spread to over 400 schools throughout the county. The Kent experience is important because it has involved a large number of schools, teachers and pupils and has been sustained over eight years. It is delivered by class teachers whose linguistic skills are limited but who are skilled in teaching all other aspects of the curriculum. They attend the county's in-service training programme which is designed to provide the teachers with easy but effective strategies to introduce modern languages into their classrooms.

Rationale behind the Kent project

The rationale of the Kent project is, above all, to sensitise children to the existence of languages other than English and to make them aware that they can be used for real purposes. The project was developed in collaboration with Canterbury Christ Church College where Keith Sharpe was developing the theory of using ordinary classroom situations and routines as opportunities to speak other languages (Sharpe, 1991a, 1991b, 1992, 1995). We have concentrated on helping primary generalists to develop the necessary skills to enable them to introduce languages into their own classrooms. The training programme provides the teachers with a repertoire of songs and games which experience tells us the children will enjoy. It is important that language learners feel motivated and the success they experience in participating in the activities contributes to the development of positive attitudes which they take with them to their secondary schools. The content of the curriculum is necessarily very limited but targeted at key vocabulary and skills.

Who teaches modern languages in primary schools?

Given the shortage of teachers with specialist linguistic knowledge, skills and abilities (SCAA 1997), it was clear from the outset that it would be impossible to put a specialist modern languages teacher into every primary classroom. This influenced the way the project was conceived and implemented. The lack of specialists was, paradoxically, seen as a strength because we believed that the generalist primary teacher is the best person to take this initiative forward. Young children spend the majority of the school day with one teacher who is a very significant person in their lives so, if that person were to exhibit interest and enthusiasm for language learning, this could stimulate and engender positive attitudes within the children in their care. The generalist teacher is also in the best position to be aware of the myriad opportunities to exploit, teach and reinforce other languages. Classroom teachers are also best placed to be able to match the maturational stages and needs of the learners to the objectives of the languages curriculum. Where language is used naturally and reinforced in everyday contexts it develops subconsciously (Krashen, 1981, 1982, 1985; Carroll, 1981).

Content

The emphasis in the Kent approach is on simple language such as greetings, number and transactional situations including *politesse* which complement the primary curriculum and are within the competence of a primary teacher. As the content of the project is so limited and specific it is not very important which language is being practised although we have used French as the training language.

Given that the primary curriculum is now heavily prescribed, there is very little time for formal lessons so the opportunities for exposure to other languages have to be created within the boundaries of the National Curriculum. The emphasis on numeracy and literacy is self-evidently important. This is a pragmatic approach to the introduction of modern foreign languages learning which is based on a recognition that it is an important factor in educating the whole child.

It is important that teachers feel comfortable using other languages. The majority of non-specialist teachers will be less than fluent in the language being taught so the emphasis has to be on individual words and phrases. However, some of the games and activities outlined below lead naturally to opportunities for sustained use of the language even for the least confident teacher because they rely on simple repetition, often with only minimal variation.

Being non-specialists, the Kent teachers needed a clear framework. This has been presented in a variety of ways. There is a teaching pack, *Pilote*, which includes models for pronunciation, a scheme of work and teaching ideas

(Rumley *et al.*, 1991). Table 7.1 shows the minimal contents reflecting the key competencies of the Kent scheme. The training programme is designed to make the teaching pack more accessible and helps the teachers to identify possibilities for integrating language learning into the established curriculum.

It is clear how important mathematical and number-related work is. Primary teachers are dealing with skills such as direction, time, currency and all other measurements but other cross-curricular applications are readily identifiable.

Languages can be taught both through incidental language use and specific teaching which needs to be planned. Initially, even incidental language needs to be taught and practised but as it is very limited it does not take long for it to become a natural part of the life of the classroom or even the school.

Table 7.1 The 'PILOTE' scheme

Units	Objectives	Mathematics
1 Moi	greetings	numbers
	name	age
	where I live	01–16 20 30
	siblings	1st
	pets	months days date birthday
2 En Ville	Where? (nouns)	1–12 hours
	please thank you	40 50
	There!	digital time
	left/right/straight on	2nd 3rd 4th, etc.
3 Faison Les Courses	Want!	60
	There you are!	100
	Transactional languages (e.g. ordering in a café)	1000
		measurement of money/distance/weight, etc. mathematical calculations (as appropriate)

Source: Rumley et al. (1991).

Incidental language use

There are three main areas of use to be considered: greetings, routines and 'politesse' and I shall now explore each of these in turn.

Greetings are an obvious starting-point for even the least confident or competent of teachers. They have been encouraged to use *bonjour* and *au revoir* as often as they can. Taking the attendance register can be as simple as the child replying *oui, Madame/Monsieur*. Some teachers use a variety of languages to register their children. In one class I observed, the children used French numbers in one term, Spanish the next and Italian in the last. No time is lost through this activity, but the children's understanding of the world was expanded to the extent that they realised that, for this purpose, English is just one of many possibilities.

Routines: apart from the attendance register as outlined above, any class-room routines provide the opportunity for daily repetition. For example, the dinner register can be taken as *déjeuner, sandwichs/pique-nique, chez moi*. This takes no time out of the school day and enriches the experience because the children are speaking and listening with enhanced purpose.

Children readily learn instructions because they are short, often heard and used in supportive contexts often with physical clues, for example:

écoutez	hand to ear
silence	finger to lips
regardez	point to eyes and object
asseyez-vous	teacher sits and indicates
levez-vous	teacher stands and gestures.

One Year 1 class created the following verse which they used with great enthusiasm: 'Taisez-vous, merci beaucoup!'

Politesse: for non-specialists, using polite language is another way into using foreign languages. Whenever there is a request or a need to thank, the target language can be used. All ancillary staff and parents can be encouraged to use this language too in the normal course of events. By remembering to take these opportunities, the teachers are using incidental moments to reinforce the idea that languages can be used at any time as appropriate.

Specific teaching

This section deals with directions, number, nouns and phrases taught through games and through songs.

Directions

Knowing about direction is key to understanding the concept of space and place and is an important primary school objective, included in the National Curriculum for Mathematics, Geography and Physical Education and it can be exploited for language teaching. A teacher of a Year 3 class had been working on directions by playing 'Simon Says' and decided to try it in French (*Jacques a Dit*). The pupils directed one another around the maze painted onto the tarmac of the playground. As in the computer activity LOGO, they could turn left or right 90 degrees by being told *à gauche* or *à droite*. They could then go forward by being told *tout droit* and a number to represent how many steps to take.

In the same way, any mathematical or ICT games which use LOGO can be similarly adapted. 'Going Dotty' is a variant of the playground game which involves using a 5 x 5 grid marked out on graph paper. The teacher tells the children which points to join without showing them the shape. The paper needs to be turned as in LOGO so that the pencil is always going forwards. Eventually everybody should have produced the same image. The children need to have mastered the concept of LOGO to do this task but, as in all these activities, they need practice in order to internalise the concept and doing it in another language makes it enjoyable.

Number

Number is fundamental to the primary school curriculum and any opportunities for counting can be used to reinforce the children's ability to memorise numbers in order. However, they must also be able to identify the numbers out of sequence. The following are ideas to help teachers exploit equipment readily available in the primary classroom and which relate to activities which would be normal for the children.

Dice

Playing with dice provides a good context for using and practising numbers. A large foam die can be thrown into the air and the children can be asked to call out the number on the face that the teacher turns to them. This has the benefit of enabling all children to feel involved in the activity. Those who do not yet know can listen to the others and they will eventually join in with the rest. The teacher should always repeat the correct answer to reinforce it. As it is so simple it can result in target language interactions for quite a sustained period even for someone whose language skills are limited. The children themselves can be asked to throw and catch the die or to throw it to the teacher. When children are able to play dice games they can be encouraged to say the numbers and to count round the board in other languages. The die can be used for demonstrating *politesse*: passing it on, the children say *voilà* and on receiving it, they say *merci*.

The song 'Bleu, blanc, rouge' from the cassette, *OK Chantez* (Finnie, 1993), is very well received by children from the reception class onwards. If a cube is painted with the colours mentioned in the song it enables the children to learn the names of the colours as separate words, out of the sequence in the song as they call out the colour which comes up as the die is thrown. If this die is then used with an ordinary die the number–colour game can be played. The number and colour are thrown and the teacher asks the children to identify them in the target language. An extension of this is to ask a child to write the number, in the correct colour, on the board.

Any board games which use dice can be played by saying the numbers 1 to 6 in another language. Games which use two or more dice increase the numbers which can be practised. From the age that they can play co-operatively children find it amusing to count from 1 to 6 in any language.

In one Kent classroom I saw children taking it in turns to throw two dice and then asking the rest of the class to write out the sum of the two numbers by adding, subtracting, multiplying or dividing them. The teacher asked the rest of the class for the answer, checked if it was correct with the child who had said it and then wrote it on the board as a sum, repeating it in French. Any mathematical sentence can be used from $1 - 1 = 0$ to $6 \times 6 = 36$. Adding one more die will hugely increase the number of possible permutations from $1 + 1 - 2 = 0$ to $6 \times 6 \times 6 = 216$.

In another school the children play a game to practise mental arithmetic. Two pupils stand back to back at the front of the class; the teacher calls out two numbers and the first to call out the answer is the winner. The winner stays at the front and another challenger takes his/her place.

Dominoes

With dominoes we can introduce the word zero and practise numbers up to 6. A set of dominoes on large cards can be used for a wide variety of whole class activities designed to develop the children's computational skills and to enable them to practise other languages at the same time.

Children engage in these activities as part of their normal mathematical education and by doing these computations they are simply and naturally reinforcing age-appropriate skills. Many children can count in sequence but are unable to manipulate the mathematics and need a great deal of practice. It is sometimes not appreciated by specialist languages teachers that, for the majority of children, honing of their mathematical skills is still very important. This does not need to be explained to a primary generalist. With practice, children can calculate as quickly in L2 as in L1.

The clock

The clock face can also be used. The two hands point to a combination of numbers and so a variety of activities can be devised to reinforce number skills whilst also developing language learning.

Birthday games

To be successful in these activities the children must know the months in their first language, have the concept of month order well established in their minds, understand that each month is divided up into days and know their own birthday. The teacher can first go through the numbers – from the first to the thirty-first – and the pupils can be asked to stand up when their birth date is mentioned. This provides an opportunity to practise listening and speaking in relation to the dates and the months. A variant is to have them standing at the start and sitting down when their birthday is said until everyone is seated. The children can then be asked to get into number order according to the date of their birthday. When everyone is in place, the class can be asked to call out the dates in order to see whether or not they have negotiated correctly.

Games to teach nouns and phrases

Games can be used to help reinforce learning of nouns and phrases and can be justified in a number of ways (Sharpe and Rumley, 1993). First, the format is known to the children and can be adapted for a variety of situations; second, there is a reason to be using the language in playing the game because it provides a context. Third, playing the game is motivating; it is a real challenge and they want to win. Finally, a game provides an opportunity and a context for repetition which is otherwise tedious.

Games can also be used to bring the children together before lunch or at the end of the day. Children can be encouraged to use some of the games during break or lunch times. When these games are being learned, it is best to use them with the whole class. Later on some of them can be transferred to group or pair situations. If children understand the principles involved in L1 they can transfer them to L2. These games can be played in short bursts and children enjoy them because they understand the format and are happy to take part. They reinforce speaking and listening because all the children must concentrate for the duration of the activity. In addition, because the language is so limited, it is possible to sustain quite long exchanges in the target language.

The following are quick games which use familiar classroom objects to help children to reinforce language learning.

Fruit salad

Children love this game but it can get very boisterous. It needs to be played in an open space such as a hall. Its aim is to teach between four and six words. Variations on this theme could be numbers, days, months, places in a town, fruit or whatever vocabulary needs to be practised. The children sit in a circle on chairs and the teacher stands in the middle. The teacher chooses the words to be practised (e.g. *bleu, blanc, rouge, noir, jaune, vert*). Everybody, including the teacher, is allocated a word which stays with them all through the game. The teacher nominates a word such as *rouge*, all the children who are *rouge* must change places and the teacher must try to sit down too.

The person left standing must now call the next item. As the seats are changed that person must attempt to find a seat too. It is possible to use more than one element as in *bleu et vert* or *noir et jaune*. It can be a great deal of fun to change all the colours by shouting *couleurs*.

Lotto/bingo

This game enables the children to practise listening and identifying words or phrases. It is played in the same way as conventional bingo but instead of just numbers, the cards can contain images which indicate the words to be practised, for example: colours. The teacher calls out the words which relate to the images on the cards and the children cross them out as they appear. The winner is the first to make a line across, down or diagonally or who fills the card. As a reward the winner can become the next caller. The activity could be developed by using the written words on the card, rather than pictures.

Kim's game

This is another well-known game which can be adapted for teaching languages. A collection of items is shown and identified to the children. These are then covered and one item is removed. The pupils are asked to say what is missing using the target language of course.

Hide it

This game enables the children to practise their vocabulary through listening and speaking. The teacher shows the children pictures which represent the vocabulary being practised. The teacher then selects one of the pictures and asks the children to guess which one has been removed. The child who guesses correctly has the next turn. Later on written words can be substituted for the pictures.

At one school a teacher with a Year 3 class plays the following hiding game. Two or three children go out of the room while a teddy bear called Tom (nobody in the class is called Tom) is hidden in one of the other children's desks. The three children come back in and ask the other children their names. All the children reply with their correct name except the child who is hiding Tom who says, 'Je m'appelle Tom'.

Hunt the thimble

In this simple game one child is asked to leave the room and an item is hidden. When the child returns, they are directed towards the hidden item by being told whether they are near it or not by the other children shouting out *froid* (cold) or *tiède* (warm) or *chaud* (hot).

Noughts and crosses

This game is helpful in learning and practising vocabulary. The words to be practised are represented by images drawn in the boxes on the noughts and crosses grid. The children win a nought or a cross by naming the item and the first child to join a row of three noughts or crosses vertically, horizontally or diagonally is the winner. Before playing the game the children can be asked to identify the items which are to be included in the grid. The teacher can say a word and ask the children to volunteer to come out to the front of the class and point out the corresponding item. Correct answers can be rewarded with applause. Once the children are secure with this activity, the teacher can ask a child to nominate an item and choose another pupil to identify the word. The volunteer can then select the next word and the next pupil. Possible items for the squares can be any nouns such as animals, numbers, colours or numbers drawn in different colours. Arithmetical exercises can also be put in the boxes. Eventually nouns can be presented as written words with the correct gender.

The Ball

This game demonstrates how, in conversation, we take turns in questioning and answering. It also provides an opportunity to practise basic phrases. The children stand in a circle with the teacher in the middle. The teacher asks a question and throws the ball to someone around the circle who throws the ball back with the answer. This continues all the way around. The questions can remain the same or vary.

In a variant of this activity, the children stand in a number of lines facing the teacher. The first child in the line holds a ball. The teacher asks a question. The first child answers and passes the ball with a question to the next child who accepts the ball and answers the question. They then ask the next question of the next child. The first team to pass the question to the end is the winner. This game can be varied by the last child running to the front and the game continuing until every child has been at the front and the first child is back in the original position.

Word games

At an appropriate stage, children need to see the written word. These can be presented as *word searches* which simply require the children to identify given words in a grid of random letters. *Odd one out* also requires simple identification. *Continue the sequence* requires research unless it is supported by a bank of words which contain the correct answer. *Anagrams* need the child to have access to a correct model of the spelling of the word. *Crosswords* can have the clues supplied as pictures or symbols; children who have been learning L2 for some time can see the word in English and find it in the other language.

Songs to teach nouns and phrases

Young children can readily imitate sounds and they enjoy singing and rhythm in general. The tunes help them to internalise structures and words and the repetition is tolerated because of the fact that it is part of a song. Incorporating songs in other languages into their everyday activities is very easy as they accept them as normal. Songs give an immediate context which justifies using another language. It is possible to use foreign versions of familiar songs and rhymes and original age-appropriate materials from other cultures and languages. Fawkes (1996) advocates inventing songs and rhymes using any of the above, or similar tunes to practise familiar, or to introduce new, vocabulary.

Familiar songs include 'Old MacDonald had a Farm', 'The Farmer's in his Den' and 'Ten Little Indians' which exist in other languages, or can be adapted quite easily. Traditional songs and rhymes can be used such as 'Frère Jacques', 'Quand Trois Poules Vont aux Champs', 'Sur le Pont d'Avignon', 'Au Clair de la Lune', 'Le Coq Est Mort' or 'Meunier Tu Dors'. These songs are widely available commercially.

The days of the week can be sung to the tune of 'Frère Jacques' – 'lundi mardi, lundi mardi' and so on. The months of the year can be sung to the tune of 'The Farmer's in his Den' – 'janvier février mars, janvier février mars, les mois les mois janvier février mars', and so on in groups of three.

A simple but effective method of teaching numbers is to sing them to a well-known tune. For example, the numbers one to five can be taught by counting to the tune of 'One, two, three, four, five, once I caught a fish alive'. Variation can be introduced by singing the numbers backwards or by starting with a number other than 1 and counting on to fit into the tune. A clock face is a useful resource when singing numbers. The numbers 1 to 12 can then be sung (forwards or backwards) to such tunes as 'Frère Jacques', 'Three Blind Mice', 'Ten Green Bottles', 'London's Burning', or any other familiar tunes.

The children can create their own personal songs and illustrate them with pictures of the people, pets, or places they are singing about. For example, or, to the tune of 'Frère Jacques' they might sing:

J'ai une sœur, j'ai une sœur, et deux frères et deux frères...
Je m'appelle, je m'appelle, Glynis Rumley Glynis Rumley, J'ai une sœur, j'ai une sœur, et deux frères, et deux frères.

Un Kilo de Chansons (Kay, 1978) and *OK Chantez* (Finnie, 1993) are recorded collections of songs widely used in Kent schools. The front cover of *Un Kilo de Chansons* recommends some useful activities to accompany the songs and these can just as easily be applied to the *OK Chantez* tape too.

Conclusion

The Kent primary modern languages project has taken as its starting point the assumption that the teacher in the classroom is the person best placed to introduce children to languages before secondary school. Its objectives are to enable the children to enjoy speaking and not to be afraid to have a go. It seeks to exploit a limited language content in the greatest possible number of ways. The limited content is reassuring for the non-specialist teachers who are able to acquire a useful repertoire to use with their children in the normal course of their work (Rumley, 1996, 1997).

Games and songs help children to learn because they provide a safe, non-threatening context within which to play with language. They provide excellent opportunities for repetition and practice which would otherwise be tedious. This repetition helps learning and this in turn leads to familiarity so that children feel comfortable with a language other than their mother tongue. By exposing children to other languages from an early age it is hoped that they will become aware that it is possible to function in another cultural and linguistic environment and will understand how this can be achieved.

For me the most significant and encouraging response to modern languages is that children find French 'light relief'. This indicates that they are happy and confident; ready to continue to try to deepen and widen their knowledge secure in their feeling that they are successful learners and will continue to be so.

References

Canadian Modern Languages Review Vol 37, No. 3, pp 462–74.
Carroll, J. B. (1981) 'Conscious and Automatic Processes in Language Learning',
Fawkes, S. (1996) *With a Song in My Scheme of Work: Pathfinder No. 25*, London: CILT.
Finnie, S. (1993) *OK Chantez* (song cassette), Cheltenham: Stanley Thornes.
Kay, J. (1978) *Un Kilo de Chansons* (song cassette), Cheltenham: Mary Glasgow Publications.
Krashen, S. D. (1981) *Second Language Acquisition and Second Language Learning*, Oxford: Pergamon.

——(1982) *Principles and Practice in Second Language Acquisition*, Oxford: Pergamon.

——(1985) *The Input Hypothesis: Issues and Implications*, London: Longman.

Rumley, G. (1996 and 1997) 'The Kent Primary Modern Languages Project', *Kent Curriculum Services Agency Newsletter*.

Rumley, G., Rowe, I. and Killbery, I. (1991) *Pilote Series 3* (teachers' video packs and INSET video), Maidstone: Kent County Council.

School Curriculum and Assessment Authority (1997) *Modern Foreign Languages in the Primary Curriculum: An International Conference Held by SCAA*, London: SCAA.

Sharpe, K. (1991a) 'Primary French: More Phoenix than Dodo Now', *Education 3–13*, March.

——(1991b) 'Deutsch Dès le Début, se faz favor', *Language Learning Journal*, 3, March.

——(1992) 'Communication, Culture, Context, Confidence: The 4 "Cs" of Primary Modern Languages Teaching', *Language Learning Journal*, 6, September.

——(1995) 'The Primacy of Pedagogy in the Early Teaching of Modern Languages', *Language Learning Journal*, 12, September.

Sharpe, K. and Rumley. G. (1993) 'Generalisable Game Activities in Primary Modern Language Teaching', *Language Learning Journal*, 8, September.

8

Resources for the teaching of modern foreign languages in the primary school

Shelagh Rixon

As is clear from other chapters, the picture across the UK is one in which many schools are trying to introduce an MFL to primary school pupils. However, there is great variation in regional or local policy and financial decisions which will affect resources. At one extreme teachers may be well supported with in-service training, advice as to suitable teaching programmes and access to locally devised and distributed tailor-made packages of MFL resources. At the other, they may be left very much to their own devices to create their own course plans and find or make their own teaching resources.

The teacher is the most important learning resource a class can have, but different teachers will feel comfortable with different ways of fulfilling this role as regards MFL. Those who are very fluent in the target language will more confidently act as the language model and informant; but others may prefer to act more as orchestrators of learning, making more use of audiovisual means of bringing the authentic native speaker model of the language to the children. Of course both types of teacher will carry out both roles to some extent.

Range of resources surveyed

Besides the more obvious area of teaching and learning materials for pupils, it is worthwhile investigating sources of support for teachers themselves in relation to both language and methodology.

Learning resources come in very many forms, from complete learning packages based on video or textbooks, to supplementary teaching aids such as flash cards and posters, to materials for children to use independently in their own time. I have paid particular attention to supplementary teaching aids and resources for more independent work by pupils, since these are more feasibly affordable by most schools, are flexible and therefore are a better investment in terms of the numbers of children who can benefit.

The Resources List in Appendix I gives current (1998) information on obtaining all material resources discussed, as well as ones not directly mentioned. However, information like this quickly goes out of date. Therefore, I have been selective in this chapter and have concentrated on resources that have the most interesting implications for methodology now and for the future.

I have occasionally referred to English as a Foreign Language (EFL) materials, rather than MFL materials. The reason for this is that EFL for young children (EYL) is a worldwide and very profitable enterprise, and thus a great amount of research effort and financial backing goes into publishing resources for English. Many of the learning resources for EYL are highly developed in their methodology and presentation. Many materials developers, especially at the 'high tech' end of the market, have established themselves in EYL resources, and have taken the next step to see how their materials could be adapted for MFL use at primary school level. I hope for more cross-fertilisation of ideas in times to come, so it is worthwhile checking if more such 'cross-over' resources will come on to the market.

The Resources List is organised under headings which describe the type of resource. In many cases resources are part of a series with the same basic design for each of the languages covered. An example is the Friendly English/French/Spanish CD-ROM materials. Other resources can be used for several different languages. For example, several multi-media resources, such as the Vektor 'Muzzy' CD-ROM materials allow switching between several languages on the same disk, and many games kits can be used for any language.

The principles of methodology built into a set of materials must be understood when evaluating them. Comments on a set of materials available for just one or two languages could therefore be useful when evaluating similar materials that may become available in the future for other languages.

Keeping up to date

Section 1 Useful Addresses and Points of Reference in Appendix I indicates how to find more information. The linked CILT/NCET pages on the Internet are a superb source, with many links to other pages nationally and worldwide. For teachers without these facilities, a request to CILT (The Centre for Information on Language Teaching) will bring information sheets on resources for different languages at primary level. The CILT Reference Library in London is open to the public and has a large collection of materials.

The Association for Language Learning (ALL) publishes a general newssheet and journal and members have a choice of two of the ALL journals covering specific languages. The reviews sections of ALL journals are an excellent source of information on new materials.

Reasons for teaching MFL at primary level

There is some debate about appropriate goals for primary MFL. The cultural awareness goal is perhaps the most commonly accepted, but there is much more discussion about the type of language experience and about the type and level of language achievement that is appropriate.

The discussion of resources below raises some of the issues and gives preliminary suggestions about materials and resources that most obviously fit these particular goals. However, many resources are flexible enough to overlap these categories.

Cultural awareness

The widening of children's cultural horizons, the stimulation and satisfaction of curiosity, and the development of positive, open-minded attitudes to other societies and cultures should be fostered from an early age. Geography, History and Personal and Social Development strands in the curriculum can carry these aims, but most proponents of MFL learning at the primary school would agree that MFL presents a major additional opportunity to do all these things in a very specific way.

Channel 4, in its *Eurokids* television broadcasts, made a major contribution to this 'language and cultural awareness' strand of teaching. The aim of the 10 short programmes (15 minutes) was to invite children of the 9–14 age band to see themselves, culturally and linguistically, as Europeans. The programmes were designed for use in class by teachers not necessarily proficient in an additional European language and covered authentic events in Italy, France, Spain and Germany, with tasters of the languages for both children and their teachers, in a rich context of visual and cultural information. Sadly, Channel 4 tells me that the programmes will not be rebroadcast and the video versions and Teachers' Notes are out of stock with no reprint envisaged. Schools which video-recorded the programmes under an Education Recording Agency licence should make the most of their foresight, and perhaps offer to share the programmes with others.

There are a few non-broadcast video materials which focus on general cultural background (e.g. Video-France from the European Language Institute, ELI) but many of the language teaching packages with a video component also help to meet cultural awareness aims, even though learning of useful language items by the pupils is the main purpose. There are also supplementary pictorial materials that give interesting cultural insights, as well as providing a stimulus for language input and practice. ELI 'Flip-Posters France' are a good example. They consist of 30 large photographic posters of French life and scenes, which could be used by a teacher in culture-based lessons, incorporating as much or as little of the target language as is thought appropriate. There is also a separately purchasable Teacher's Guide, and a Pupil's Book, which teaches language through cultural themes, and an audio cassette of songs and spoken texts. These go rather beyond the language level aimed at in most primary schools, but the posters and Teacher's Guide would be a good flexible resource for many classes. There are Flip-Posters for other levels and for other languages, but so far, no equivalent of the French photographic scenes for Spanish, German or Italian.

Culture learning of a different sort is also involved when using traditional songs and stories on video or audio tape, although perhaps their main role is to provide a memorable and motivating context for language learning.

Magazines in the target language for subscription over a school year are a wonderful resource for both culture and language, although this is an expensive option. One important aspect is that their readership is not confined to the UK and letter pages and offers of pen friend contacts with children from all over the world learning the same language give a double benefit. The addresses of the ELI and of Mary Glasgow Ltd, a magazine publisher, are given in Appendix I.

Language competence

In Scotland there is a strong commitment to the development of a considerable level of competence in the languages offered in primary schools. Giovanazzi, writing when the Scottish MFL initiative was still in its pilot stage, stated clearly:

> The purpose of our teaching languages in primary school is language competence *not* awareness...nor is our pilot project seen as simply being a preparation for the 'more serious' work of secondary school. The primary school may be the beginning of language learning, but it is no mere 'softening up' process..
>
> (Giovanazzi, 1991)

Resources which support this aim include full teaching packages such as the Scope video-based materials, available for French and German, which not only successfully integrate 'culture learning' with systematic language practice, but also create interest and motivation through allowing the children to see and hear the language from seeing and hearing the target language used by native speakers in genuine or very realistic situations. The kits include Teacher's Notes and photocopy masters for activities in class, which makes them a very cost-effective resource.

A different style of video-based resource is the 'Muzzy' animated cartoon video, which has been produced in French, German, Italian and Spanish. This is an example of successful EFL material which has been adapted for other languages. In English, it follows a careful structurally based syllabus which makes the step-by-step learning of English a seemingly effortless process, but the grammar of the other languages will not necessarily fit into such a smooth progression, since the strong story-line dictates what new language is needed for each episode. It is set in a never-never-land, where a friendly green space-monster helps to rescue a beautiful princess in a kingdom where helicopters and computers are the weapons of the wicked court magician. Cultural awareness development can hardly be expected as a bonus here but the videos are so amusing that even reluctant learners will be motivated. Most of the teaching happens 'on screen' and the accompanying print materials are rarely needed.

The following are some examples of textbook-based 'full packages' with which the teacher committed to language competence development could work. The 'Gaston' 3-level textbook-based course for French, published by the Italian company ELI, has had excellent reviews from UK MFL specialists. This company also produces materials for German, Spanish and Italian, as well as lesser-taught languages. All of these, however, need careful inspection for the 'match' in scope and levels aimed at, since they were not tailor-made for the UK market. Purchasing a textbook package is beyond the budget of many schools, since this means the purchase of a book for each pupil in a group. Print-based materials produced for Local Education Authorities in the UK such as 'Salut La France!' (East Sussex County Council, 1989) will be more affordable and more likely to be in tune with local needs and ambitions.

Language awareness

The rationale for the language awareness approach, widely adopted outside Scotland, includes two significant points. First, it is important for children to have experience of other languages and some insight into how they 'work differently' from the native language. This helps the development of insights into the native language, as well as providing a useful 'softening up' for the future experience of tackling an MFL at secondary level. Second, until the school system is organised in a way that allows better co-ordination and continuity of language learning from primary to secondary levels, it is better to limit the language learning aims to a knowledge that will not be seen as an interference or even an irritant upon transfer to secondary school.

Teachers with this aim will appreciate materials that support or extend their own use of the target language, and can be used many times during the school year. For example, audio-taped song and story materials provide good models of the language for pronunciation and also promote listening comprehension. They are also relatively cheap and certainly cost-effective in that they provide the type of experience that is aesthetically appealing, fun and popular enough to be used again and again with the same group of children and are not too age- or level-sensitive. Because of their rhythmic element they are highly memorable, and could become part of a child's mental 'data bank' of language, unanalysed at the time but available to be drawn on at a later stage when more formal learning begins. How many of us have shored up a shaky memory of an aspect of grammar in later life by 'running through' the words of a song remembered from primary school days? Resources like these are of course also valuable to teachers working towards language competence, but for a teacher who wants to provide a decent and motivating 'language awareness' introduction to MFL with minimal outlay of funds, and using limited time to the best advantage, they can provide a good 'backbone' around which to structure a whole course.

Another approach is to select materials such as games and role-play kits which do not supply a language model in themselves, but which can support many different activities. Teachers will need to be confident in their own language use, since vocabulary and structures needed for the activities have to be introduced and practised. Games and role play kits can be used at many levels, and although it is rare to find a primary school in which several languages are actually offered, these materials can act as a resource for any language, including English as a Second Language. The Miniflashcards Language Games kits offer this type of flexibility and inspiration. Some of the cards are developed for specific languages but most of the kits can be used for several languages.

Some education authorities have a policy of introducing MFL modestly but still systematically in all schools and have therefore found funds for teacher support and especially for developing custom-made packages of resources. An example is the Invicta Media French and German video-based materials (*Pilote*, and *3, 2, 1... Los!*). These were originally developed for use in Kent primary schools. They are similar in design to the Scope video packages in that they use lively 'vox pop' authentic materials, which bring the native speaker's voice into class and also integrate rich cultural content, filmed in the target language environment. There is a wealth of photocopiable worksheets and communicative game-type activities for class use. The reason why they fit more into the language awareness category is that the inventory of language items aimed at is deliberately quite restricted, and the type of productive language practice done using the video is more 'open' and with a definite focus on developing confidence in listening comprehension. This type of material would be highly appropriate in other places where teachers want to promote solid and systematic learning, but are constrained by a lack of time and their own language confidence.

Different learning modes

Whatever the overall goals, teachers of MFL need to follow principled steps in their teaching, moving from clearly contextualised and easy to understand introduction of new items to support for pupils while they come to grips with and practise the new items, and finally to the provision of opportunities to experiment more freely with the new language within a comfortable framework, so that children can 'have a go' by themselves and make the new learning their own. These three stages can be summarised as follows:

1   presentation of new language;
2   controlled practice of the new language;
3   freer communicative use of the new language.

Most of the materials mentioned above will provide resources for one or more of these essential stages. The 'full teaching packages' aim to be useful particularly for presentation and controlled practice, and the better ones also give ideas and resources for free stage activities such as role play and problem-solving communication games in pairs or groups.

Supplementary materials, such as song tapes or games kits may focus on just one or two stages in this process. Songs are attractive and thus very useful for presentation, but they need contextual clues to be added for children to work out exactly what is meant. They are also great for very motivational controlled practice (loud and enjoyable singing) but the teacher may need to find another activity to follow up with, to allow the children to 'try out' the language in a communicative context.

Games kits are often one answer to allowing pupils to 'try out' recently presented and practised new language in a communicative way (e.g. 'Tell your partner about your picture, so that he/she can draw it') but many games are suitable for a type of 'pleasant drill' in controlled practice mode (see Chapter 7 and Rixon, 1981).

Story-telling is an excellent way of engaging children's interest, and helping them to develop comprehension skills on longer spoken texts. If the story contains a lot of repetition and easily predicted 'next steps', they will also be encouraged to 'join in' and respond, which is a good communicative reason for repeating phrases and sentences from the story. There are kits of stories on tape, often with accompanying visuals, but the best story-teller is 'live' on stage. In fact many teachers use the tapes to help them 'rehearse' their own live version rather than as the main means of presentation.

Simple picture story books can be used as presentation aids in the class, as well as being good for private reading by the children later. For example *Where's Spot?* from the 'Spot the Dog' fold-up-the-flap book series, published by Puffin, was originally intended for very young native-speaking children, but has become a staple for teaching prepositions and expressions of location to older primary children learning English as a Foreign Language. The children tend to accept the 'babyish' look, because of the language challenge, and the fun of predicting and calling out who they think is hiding behind the different flaps in the book 'in the piano', 'under the stairs', and so on. The French version *Où est Spot mon petit chien?* (published by Nathan) should be just as popular and useful. The other books in the series are also available from the same publisher, and teachers should keep their eyes open for similar story books in MFL.

Materials for pupils to use independently

Effective class teaching is the bedrock of successful MFL learning, but, if MFL is taken seriously within a school, it is also important to allow children the chance to re-visit some of the resources already used in class, or to explore and find out new things for themselves. The Resources List gives ideas for puzzle books, story books and attractive picture dictionaries and word books that can be added to the school library or class book-corner, to support language or cultural awareness development. Not all children will take up this option, but the provision of attractive MFL resources for independent use can allow enthusiastic children to do more, and also sends the powerful message to everyone in the school that foreign languages are part of normal learning, and not some 'add-on' to the 'real' curriculum.

Few primary schools will, at the moment, have the space or the finances to have a special foreign languages learning area, but good use can be made of existing equipment and 'corners' in classrooms for such activities as looking at books, doing puzzle work and using computer-based material.

The MFL resources should not all be placed on view at once, but gradually 'fed into' the system, after the relevant lessons, with an explanation and demonstration of how to use them being part of the whole class lessons. For example, a card game used first in class can be announced in the lesson as available from that lesson on in the reading or home corner for private use. Many published kits allow photocopying of some elements, and there is also the possibility of creating home-made versions of most card or paper-based games. Song tapes that have been enjoyed in class can be heard again privately if the school has playback equipment with headphones. The same goes for video materials, which could perhaps also be re-scheduled for watching again by a small group if popular. Computer materials that have a thematic link with a lesson can be given a brief demonstration in a lesson, so that children can see how they are relevant. Diskette-based materials can be copied on to the hard disk, but security is more of a problem with CD-ROM materials, where the disk needs to be in the machine. This means that these should only be used under supervision, since the disks are relatively expensive.

Computer-based materials

Much of the more highly developed computer-based MFL material under review is for use on PC or Mackintosh only. However, I am assuming that schools will be gradually moving in that direction away from BBC/Archimedes machines, and it is therefore worth discussing these resources for future reference. (Some of the web sites mentioned in Appendix I in the 'Useful Addresses and Points of Reference section give useful updates on the state of play with regard to computer provision in schools.)

A CD-ROM drive and a sound-card are necessary for the more interactive sound and animation type material. Some of this material also allows the children to record their own voices, so a microphone to connect to the computer is also necessary, but not expensive. My own microphone was under £12.

Schools connected to the Internet can access a wide variety of authentic material at a suitable language level, though this will need setting up by the teacher. Some suitable and fun sites are listed in the Useful Addresses and Points of Reference section. E-mail connections also provide the possibility of 'keyboard/pen-friend' links between your school and schools in the countries where the target language is used.

Methodology issues with computer-based materials

Computers are very good for setting up activities and challenges that require matching, or correct repetition, and many games and activities therefore smack of quite narrow, behaviouristic stimulus/response/reinforcement approaches, with 'match the word to the picture' , 'choose the right answer', 'put the letters/words in the right order' activities predominating. Most of the older diskette-based programmes are of this limited sort, and since they are often slow to react and not very glamorous-looking either, I feel that teachers should be cautious about choosing them, before they have looked at other options. Reinforcement or support can be given in more or less spectacular and motivating ways – dancing and singing characters, reassuring voices giving praise or advice to try again from CD-ROM based materials, or small visual jiggles and irritating whoops or 'hurrah!' type noises in the cheaper programmes provided on 3.5" diskette.

Where there is a 'record your voice' facility, as there is on many CD-ROM materials, the present state of the art does not allow for any checking beyond the pupils listening and comparing their efforts with the spoken model given by the program. That latter feature can be positive, if it promotes careful and critical listening by the children, but in essence it does no more than a language laboratory of the 1960s could do, except that the experience of doing it with a computer is more fun!

This type of limited practice does have its place for establishing items of language such as vocabulary or fixed phrases, and perhaps it should be said in favour of the above type of programs that they make it fairly palatable. However, there can be serious problems. The tendency is for the 'bits' of language on many computer-based programs (CD-ROM included) to be very limited indeed, most often at the word level, occasionally a phrase or a whole sentence, with very little that allows the children to get to grips with continuous text or spoken discourse.

Language analysis issues

Some programs present language in ways that actually distort its use, so teachers are again advised to be cautious and try before they buy. (Most companies offer sampler disks, will send disks on approval, or have web-sites where you can inspect the materials.) For example, some sets of vocabulary games present the nouns with a seemingly random mixture of definite article, indefinite article, 'zero' article or the plural form. An example for English would be 'the girl', 'dog', 'cats', 'the houses'. The designers of one such program justified this by saying that they wanted to 'give variety'. My view is that this is simply bad design since it is very likely to lead to confusion. There is also a common problem with intonation when words or phrases are heard in isolation on the screen. The actors who record the original texts for the audio track of many programs often seem to have adopted the typical 'list' intonation, with the first words that they actually recorded 'going up' and the last item 'going down'. Since the words can later be accessed in a different order by the learner, a very unnatural and confusing set of pronunciation 'models' is often the result.

More recent programs, especially those on CD-ROM, deal with connected language in context through story-lines and dialogues, and this seems a more useful and authentic approach. However, some are more easily accessible to young learners than others. The materials based on the Asterix cartoons (available for several languages) are enjoyable and motivating, but they use the authentic, uncontrolled language of the original cartoons. However, coming to grips with well-loved characters and a possibly familiar story could be a real spur to discovery learning through exposure to a rich input in the FL, even if not all the clever word-play is understood immediately. In addition to being able to choose to see the words of the speech bubbles, to hear them, or to see and hear them together, there is the option to hear any words in a bubble and then record and play back your own voice. (An option for hearing/seeing a translation in the native language is also available as a support.) There are many other options, such as explanations of the more difficult expressions designed for teachers' information, but these would probably be of little appeal to children working alone.

A set of materials that is in the same spirit as the Asterix materials, but with deliberately learner-friendly activities designed by teaching experts, is the Muzzy CD-ROM materials, 'starring' the same characters as in the video course discussed above. The language is designed to be accessible without the need for an explanation option, although, since the disk is multi-lingual, translation is an option. The language can be presented as text on the screen and/or in audio form according to choice, and it is always part of continuous discourse. Images have amusing animation in each scene that is presented. The same CD-ROM allows access to the story in several languages including British and American varieties of English, European, Latin American Spanish, French, German and Italian, and so represents very good value for money.

For teachers prepared to work on their own materials I would recommend the 'authoring' materials originally designed for teaching English as a Foreign Language. These allow teachers to write and save their own short texts to be used as the basis for several types of puzzle-solving involving reconstructing the original text. For example, the user can be challenged to guess the words in a text 'from scratch' given only the title and a set of blobs representing the letters. Successfully guessed words will pop on to the screen in a satisfying way. You can play against the computer or with a friend, and this latter type of interaction is splendid for encouraging language accuracy, language awareness and the capacity for making inspired guesses from context. You get a score and an encouraging message at the end of each activity and the fact that the texts are 'tailor-made' by the teacher for the particular pupils is very motivating and ensures relevance. The presentation is modest and plain, with no sound track and no images on screen but the sheer challenge of 'playing with' the text of a story told in class or of a well-loved song could be more engaging for many pupils than the more apparently fun-providing but less intelligent activities offered by some of the programs described earlier. The teacher could provide cue sheets with visual clues, or hints about vocabulary to support the pupils. There are several sets of programs of this type but, in particular, the Wida Software Authoring suite is available on diskette or CD-ROM and has recently become available in versions for French, German, Spanish and Italian. The catalogue of the KELTIC Bookshop is a good source of information on this type of material, as well as other 'ex-ELT' programs.

Support for teachers

The Central Bureau for Educational Visits and Exchanges (CBEVE) has produced a very useful video 'European Awareness in Primary Schools' giving suggestions and examples of good practice in this area. The Goethe Institut produces videos on the methodology of teaching German to young learners.

The French publisher Didier publishes the video and print materials for a project supported by European Community (Lingua) funding for materials to provide language-development support for teachers of French, German and Spanish, as well as English as a Foreign Language. The distributor in this country (as for much of the overseas-published material) is European Schoolbooks Ltd.

The Modern Languages Adviser is the first port of call and probably has a 'watching brief' for Primary MFL. He or she should know what is available in each area, and whom to contact, since conditions vary greatly. My local MFL Adviser (see acknowledgements) gave me a very clear path to organisations that I would never have traced without his advice.

The Training and Enterprise Council in each region of England and Wales sub-contracts the local Education Business Partnership (See Useful

Addresses in Appendix I for the national headquarters of the EBP) to make links between schools and local industries.

It could be that a local industry with its headquarters in a target language country (e.g., Peugeot in Coventry for French) has an interest in promoting the primary learning of their 'home-base' language, and you may be able to access funds for providing cultural, methodological training or a target language experience in the target language country. For example, a primary French teacher from Coventry along with secondary colleagues gained sponsorship from Peugeot for a Cultural Awareness Course in Paris in 1998. During my enquiries, it was made plain to me that some EBPs have their own direct funding from local industry and other sources, and that others have precisely nothing or very little in terms of funding. It is worthwhile enquiring, and seeing what could be made available for your local needs.

The local Modern Languages Advisor should know about EC-funded schemes, such as Socrates, with LINGUA and Comenius being the relevant sub-programmes. Both of these could benefit primary schools in a number of ways, including school links, in service courses, exchange visits by teachers and finding assistant teachers from EU countries. The co-ordinating body in Britain is the Centre for Educational Visits and Exchanges, which will send full details on request. It should be remembered that the CBEVE also offers a pen-friend service.

Appendix I includes Useful Addresses and Reference Points, and Select List of Resources which give more specific details of what there is to choose from, and how to keep up to date with the latest information.

Acknowledgements

In carrying out my survey, I was very much helped by the advice and insights of many very helpful professionals. I should like to mention in particular, here, my local informants in the Elm Bank Teachers' Centre, Coventry and in particular, Mr Mike Bench, Modern Languages Adviser for the Coventry area who drew my attention to sources of funding and support from national and international organisations and schemes, and also gave me a number of concrete examples of imaginative use of such resources at the primary level in the West Midlands. The many people I spoke to in Education Business Partnership organisations (see Appendix I) around the country were also extremely helpful and informative.

References

Giovanazzi, A. (1991), 'The Scottish Project', *JET Magazine*, 1: 3.
Rixon, S. (1981) *How to Use Games in Language Teaching*, London: Macmillan.

9

Intercultural competence and foreign language learning in the primary school

Michael Byram and Peter Doyé

The purpose of this chapter is to argue for and explain the need to ensure that language learning in the primary school has a 'cultural dimension', which is to say that a foreign language is not just learnt as an encoding of children's first language but as a language in its own right embodying other cultural beliefs, behaviours and meanings. This 'cultural dimension' has been variously called 'cultural awareness', 'cultural studies' and in France and Germany *civilisation* and *Landeskunde*, respectively. Here we shall refer to 'intercultural competence' as the key concept.

We shall assume that the basic rationale for early language learning has been accepted and shall not consider the advantages and disadvantages of early experience in the acquisition of linguistic competence. On the other hand, the question of cultural learning in the primary school and the acquisition of intercultural competence has been very little debated and this chapter will only attempt to outline the parameters and identify the unresolved questions. It will none the less take a strong view of the need to include a cultural dimension, i.e. that language learning in the primary school must have such a dimension. It will also propose an approach to language learning which is likely to lay the foundations for intercultural competence in early language learners even if there remain some unanswered questions. For it is clear that early language learning is developing quickly and could become too narrow in its aims and scope if the cultural dimension is not taken seriously.

The chapter will therefore include both a rationale for the cultural dimension and a discussion of the implications for teacher education and for curriculum and materials development.

Language teaching in context

It is easy to forget, in the activities of daily routine in the school and classroom, that all education functions in a given society at a given time, that the choice of what is taught and how it is taught is partly determined by the social, political and economic position of the society which the education system serves. Language teaching is no exception. In the UK and Germany, the pressure from parents to introduce language teaching in the primary school is a reflection of their awareness of how society is changing, how the position of these countries in Europe is developing, how their children's future is likely to have an international context quite different from their own adult lives. At another level, in European politics, there is an awareness of the need for greater linguistic and cultural competence in citizens of Europe – Western, Central and Eastern – if the desire for greater integration is to meet with success. In Western Europe, this is articulated most clearly in the European Union's White Paper *The Learning Society* and the argument that all citizens of a future Europe should speak three languages. The effect of such pressures from below and above on the policies national governments will make, and the British government in particular, remains to be seen, but will be impossible to resist.

What, then, does this mean for the content and methodology of language teaching in general? Since future citizens of Europe will be able and willing to continue the already visible trends to greater mobility for purposes of work as well as leisure, they will need increased linguistic and cultural competence. Such mobility will be to the advantage of individuals seeking richer opportunities but also a necessity for a Europe competing with other countries and continents and depending on a mobile and flexible workforce to do so. But the linguistic and cultural competence required for work and residence in another country is quite different from that required for leisure and tourism. The theories and methods which have provided the guidelines for language teaching hitherto are inadequate for the new task and require refining and developing.

For we must also bear in mind that, in addition to the social, political and economic context, there is another: the disciplinary context which determines what happens in the classroom on a day-to-day basis. It is theories of language (of what a language is and how it works), of language learning (of how people of different ages acquire a foreign language), of social interaction (of how people of different language origins relate to each other when they meet), which determine classroom methods. Even though such theories often seem distant from practice, even a cursory analysis of the history of language teaching in the last hundred years would reveal how changes in theory have visible effects on classroom practice.

The most recent theory, usually labelled 'communicative language teaching', has stressed that when a foreign language is used for verbal communication between living individuals in real time, linguistic competence (knowledge of the grammar and of the dictionary meanings of vocabulary) is insufficient. Learners need both linguistic competence in order to produce grammatically correct and meaningful speech and also the ability to speak appropriately, to choose the language which suits the occasion, the topic, and the person with whom one is speaking. Thus the aims of language teaching have become more complex, but not complex enough. There still remains the problem that this description of 'communicative competence' is based on an analysis of how native speakers interact with each other (Hymes, 1971) but does not take into consideration the special nature of speaking in a foreign language, either to a native speaker of that language or to another foreign speaker with whom the only common means of communication is the foreign language – the lingua franca situation. Thus the theory of communicative competence has to be changed and developed to take into consideration what happens when people move to and reside in another country with a different language and different ways of behaving, different beliefs and different shared understanding of the world, in other words, different cultures.

Thus both the macro-context of social, political and economic conditions is changing and the micro-context of defining what is involved in language and culture learning are being developed. Both have significance at school and classroom level and the second will determine what and how teachers should teach a foreign language. It is to the second therefore that we turn in more detail in the following section.

Describing intercultural communicative competence

The description of communicative competence has been refined for foreign language teaching in two well-known publications (Canale and Swain, 1980; van Ek, 1986) and in both cases the underlying comparison with native speakers was enriched by emphasising that foreign speakers of a language need to acquire means of overcoming difficulties of communication caused by incomplete knowledge of the language. This was called 'strategic competence'. However, it was still implied that learners should strive to acquire a native speaker's understanding of the vocabulary and of the cultural environment in which the language is usually used, in order to be able to converse success-fully with a native speaker.

There are two major problems with all this. First, there is the difficulty of 'the native speaker'. Which native speaker should the learner strive to imitate? Should it be the highly educated or the one with basic schooling only – perhaps not entirely literate in the language? The native speaker in country X or country Y, both of whom have the language as their national language – German in Germany and Austria, or English in the UK, Australia and the USA, for example – should they strive to acquire the same cultural knowledge, the same accent, the same grammatical accuracy – and for which country? In fact, the native speaker as a model for language learners has been much debated in recent years (Kramsch, 1998; Davies, 1991) and the whole debate becomes even more complicated when the language is a lingua franca, an international language which learners do not see as linked to a specific country and, second, when the language is considered to be a means of imposing neo-colonial power structures on developing countries – as is the case for English (Phillipson, 1992; Pennycook, 1994).

The second problem is related to the first. When it becomes evident that learners cannot and should not attempt to become native or 'near-native' speakers, it is still necessary to ask how a 'foreign speaker' of a language interacts with native speakers or other foreign speakers and what special abilities are needed. The strategic competence of knowing how to get round gaps in one's knowledge or lapses of memory is certainly necessary but is it sufficient? When one reflects that foreign speakers need to adapt to an intercultural communication by changes in attitudes – abandoning prejudice and intolerance, for example; by changes in presentation of self; not assuming that one's interlocutor shares the same cultural beliefs and behaviours; and by being able to notice what the other takes for granted and to find out what their assumptions are, then it becomes evident that the foreign speaker needs more than good linguistic competence. They need the ability to see how different cultural assumptions are similar and different, to anticipate and overcome misunderstandings and conflicting interpretations of 'the same' phenomenon, to act as interpreter or mediator between two cultures. Rather than attempting to be a native speaker, the learner needs to acquire the skills, knowledge and attitudes of an 'intercultural speaker' (Byram and Zarate, 1997).

The abilities of the intercultural speaker involve both communicative competence and intercultural competence and can be briefly described as follows (Byram, 1997b):

- linguistic competence: ability to produce and understand language which follows the standard grammar;
- sociolinguistic competence: the ability to understand the meaning of language in a specific context, including what is taken for granted and left unsaid;
- discourse competence: the ability to overcome difficulties of production and understanding, especially by clarifying and negotiating with an interlocutor.

These are the competences specific to language.

The intercultural speaker also requires the components of intercultural competence:

- attitudes: curiosity and openness, a willingness to accept the other person's perspective as normal and one's own as strange, when seen from the other's perspective;
- knowledge: of different social groups in one's own society and that of one's foreign interlocutor, of their cultural practices and products and of

the social processes involved when people of different groups or different
societies meet and interact;

- skills of interpreting: the ability to use knowledge of one's own and the
  other society to interpret a foreign text or any other kind of document
  in ways which explain it in one's own society;
- skills of discovery and interaction: the ability to acquire new knowledge
  about one's interlocutor and to interact with them under real time pressures.

The skills, attitudes and knowledge of intercultural competence are known
as the four *savoirs*, because the French version is particularly elegant. The
four *savoirs* are:

1 attitudes = *savoir être*; for example, the kind of learner who notices and
   asks questions, who expresses wonder and interest in other people's
   behaviours and beliefs, rather than rejection and disgust;
2 knowledge = *savoirs*: for example, knowledge of different eating habits
   or work practices and how the difference can lead to misunderstanding
   and rejection;
3 skills of interpreting = *savoir comprendre*: for example, the ability to take
   a person's school report and not just translate it but explain the significance of what is written, how it relates to the education system;
4 skills of discovery and interaction = *savoir apprendre/faire*: for example,
   knowing how to ask questions which elicit information which one's
   interlocutor does not mention because it is too 'self-evident': the fact
   that boys and girls are taught separately in many Islamic societies is
   seldom mentioned in a discussion of education in such societies.

A closer examination of these four *savoirs* will show that they are relevant to
any kind of interaction with someone from another social and/or ethnic
group, even within one's own society and when the language is essentially
the same, with 'only' differences of dialect and accent. Acquiring intercultural competence is thus part of general education and learning to live in a
complex society. It can and should be developed in all aspects of the school
curriculum.

The special contribution of foreign language teaching comes when intercultural competence is linked to communicative competence in a foreign
language. This is not just an addition, however, because it changes the
nature of the experience. Language is intimately bound up with personality
and social identity and the shift into another language means more than just
a change of code. Speaking (and writing) a foreign language are not like
changing what one says or writes into Morse code, or some other one-for-one
representation of words and sentences.

Among other things, shifting into a foreign language and engaging in conversation with a native speaker of that language creates a change in social identity. Whether one likes it or not, one becomes a representative of one's nation, an American, a Spaniard, a Briton, and so on. In other words, one's social identity, what social groups one is seen as belonging to, has to include national identity, however else one would like to be seen. Some people discover their national identity for the first time when they speak a foreign language or go to a foreign country. Thus, if the conversation is going to be successful, one must know something about the other person's country/ nation and about how one's own is seen from the outside (*savoirs*). One must also be able to ask questions to supplement that knowledge (*savoir apprendre*) whilst using the foreign language (*savoir faire*).

A fifth *savoir* (*savoir s'engager*) ensures that the acquisition of intercultural competence has an educational dimension. Foreign language learners compare and evaluate foreign behaviours, beliefs and meanings by contrast with their own. The language teacher should not try to prevent this but should ensure that learners are conscious of the criteria they are using in their evaluation, and are able to turn their critical evaluation on to their own culture as well as that of others. Foreign language teaching thus develops a 'critical cultural awareness' in learners and thereby contributes in a major fashion to learners' ability to decentre, to take other perspectives, to challenge what they have hitherto taken for granted, to see that what they thought was 'natural' in their own way of life is in fact cultural and subject to change. This critical cultural awareness is also applied to other cultures. Rather than the 'tolerance' often expected of language learning, learners should develop a critical/analytical understanding of other cultures.

These, then, are the qualities and competences of the intercultural speaker. They are not attained quickly or easily. They depend upon complex learning opportunities, in the classroom and beyond, and upon the educational philosophy which encourages challenge and critical analysis. The question which now arises is whether and to what extent learners in primary schools can become intercultural speakers.

Learning foreign languages and culture in primary education

The general condition and context for language learning described in earlier sections also apply to young learners. They too find themselves in a world of close-knit internationalism and of increasing mobility. They meet people of other cultures and origins in their own environment and they are as mobile as their parents. So the encounter with otherness is not simply somewhere in their future but also in their present. Thus, the initial tendency of language teaching in primary schools which puts emphasis on language skills is inadequate. It is also misleading because it encourages learners to think that there is a simple one-to-one relationship between the elements of their own language and elements of the foreign language, and hence between their culturally determined understanding of their own world and that of others, and this clearly is not the case.

There is therefore an evident need to revise the aims of primary foreign language teaching and to include intercultural competence. However, there is also the widespread fear that such an inclusion might go beyond the capacities of most primary schoolchildren.

Whether such a fear is justified has to be thoroughly discussed. On the one hand, the attainment of intercultural competence presupposes cognitive and moral dispositions that many young learners will not acquire during primary school. Melde (1987) has shown the close links between the language learning process and the moral and cognitive development of young people and Wiegand (1992) has demonstrated the dependence of children's intercultural competence on their knowledge and understanding of places, countries and nations. Other authors, like Kramsch (1993), have stressed the importance of the abilities to analyse, to evaluate and to take a new perspective on one's own taken-for-granted reality, abilities that are indispensable for the attainment of intercultural competence. All these age-related statements have one hypothesis in common: learners must have reached a certain stage in their development before they can be confronted with tasks that might lead them to intercultural competence.

Yet it is logically as justified to propose the opposite hypothesis. In his famous *Process of Education*, Bruner maintains that any subject can be taught effectively in some intellectually honest form to any child at any stage of development (1960). Bruner agrees that it is a bold hypothesis, but also emphasises that no evidence has been presented so far to contradict it. He argues that in most school subjects, learners and teachers are concerned with rather wide fields of learning and that in any case the selection and gradation of the concrete contents and objectives have to be carried out according to the capacities of the learners. 'Learner appropriateness' is the key concept. For the intercultural education of primary schoolchildren, this means that the tasks given and the experiences offered must be selected in accordance with the learners' stage of development. They may be cognitively demanding as long as they are concrete; they may be emotionally complex as long as they are experiential; they may be practically exacting as long as they are systematically arranged, i.e. they permit the progression from simple to difficult. A number of other requirements could be mentioned, but these conditions can be fulfilled.

Several primary school theorists have dedicated themselves to the interaction of language and culture learning precisely from the aspect of an integration of linguistic and intercultural competence, and have convincingly shown how the integration can be achieved in a learner-appropriate manner. Curtain and Pesola (1994) have identified seven cultural goals for primary foreign language teaching and given excellent 'child-appropriate' examples for each of these goals. They also make valuable proposals for the identification of cultural contents in an integrated curriculum. The common characteristic of these proposals is the fact that they locate the representations of other cultures in the environment of the children and use them as starting points for intercultural information and experience. The representations are grouped in three categories: *Cultural symbols* (such as flags and insignia), *cultural products* (stories and songs, coins and stamps) and *cultural practices* (habitual forms of greeting, gestures, eating and drinking practices). Similar suggestions come from Skender (1995). What she proposes for the teaching of French in Croatia in particular is none the less applicable to primary foreign language teaching in general. She suggests four groups of techniques:

1   repérage des éléments de la culture étrangère dans l'environnement des enfants;
2   utilisation des images types;
3   accent sur l'aspect ludique de l'apprentissage à travers les chansons, les jeux, les comptines, les histoires;
4   création d'une atmosphère 'française'.

As it is not our aim here to discuss methods, we cannot go into further details; such details will be dealt with in a separate publication (Doyé, forthcoming). We can, however, summarise the ideas presented by relating them to the *savoirs* mentioned in our previous section. There are aspects of intercultural competence which seem to be very appropriately pursued with children of primary school age. *Savoir être*, the attitude of openness and curiosity, is obviously more easily encouraged in primary school than later, partly because children have not yet been socialised fully into the assumptions of their own cultural environment, and do not yet perceive the cultural as natural. This is, too, a *savoir* which is best developed through experiential learning where immersion in experience is followed by reflection upon it, under the guidance of the teacher. Young children also have already some knowledge (*savoirs*) of the practices of their own social groups, how to behave in specific situations, what is considered polite and what not. They can be introduced to related practices in another language and culture and invited to think about similarities and differences, and what might be the problems and dysfunctions arising from one set of practices being inappropriately used in another language and environment. In the framework of primary education, where one of the tasks is to convey the fundamental techniques of learning (*savoir apprendre*), it is possible also to promote the basic tools needed for intercultural competence. Primary schoolchildren can learn to ask relevant questions, analyse cultural phenomena, and carry out their own investigations. Realistic foreign language teachers who declare intercultural competence to be one of their central aims do so even though they are aware of the complexity of the task. They know that the road is long and strenuous. Intercultural competence is certainly not attainable in all its dimensions at the end of primary schooling, but the foundation for this important competence can be laid.

In the following we shall deal with the consequences of our acceptance of the aim of intercultural competence in three areas: teacher education, curriculum development, and the production of teaching materials.

Teachers of language and culture in primary education

Language teaching with an intercultural competence dimension presupposes that teachers themselves will have acquired intercultural communicative competence to a reasonable level. It is tempting to argue that the level need not be very advanced since the learners will not advance to complex levels of competence themselves. This temptation is all the stronger if the teacher is also to be responsible for other subjects in the curriculum, as is the case in the UK and many other countries. For it is clear that there will be many demands on the inevitably limited time for primary teachers' education and training. To some extent, the time constraints are eased if a more comprehensive view is taken and integrated education and training at pre-service and in-service levels are planned. It could for example be argued that teachers of languages should be trained through in-service courses with a minimum of pre-service training; the right to teach languages only being attained after in-service training. This is, however, in the UK at least, a medium-term option.

In the short term, training is likely to be in-service, but it is important to resist the temptation to suggest that language teachers in primary education need only a limited degree of intercultural communicative competence. For it is clear from our previous section that teachers have to make complex decisions about how and when to develop intercultural competence in their learners. In order to make these decisions they need a rich personal experience of the acquisition of intercultural competence themselves – the five *savoirs* – and a knowledge of developmental and social psychology.

These abilities can hardly be acquired by in-service training alone. Therefore, in the long term, primary foreign language teachers will have to gain their qualifications through a combination of initial studies and in-service training. As the final report of the Council of Europe Workshop 8B states:

> The need is for teachers who are specialists both in primary education and foreign language pedagogy. As primary school experts they will be familiar with the conditions and the framework into which, as foreign language experts, they can integrate the language and culture of other

countries. They have to gain their qualifications through initial studies at universities and colleges and through in-service studies. Although we realise that in the near future quite a lot of the teachers needed will have to receive in-service training only, we are convinced that in the long run this procedure cannot replace or serve as a substitute for a full range of teacher education consisting of studies at universities and colleges and subsequent in-service courses.

(Felberbauer and Heindler, 1995: 134)

We are arguing therefore that the acquisition of advanced levels of intercultural competence has to include both classroom work and experience in another country, which we have described elsewhere as 'fieldwork' (Byram, 1997a). It has long been recognised in British higher education that communicative competence at an advanced level is only attainable through fieldwork and this applies all the more to intercultural competence. Thus it is important that primary school language teachers should have an obligatory 'year abroad' as do future secondary school language teachers. This necessitates a proper attention to preparation and debriefing as well as appropriate tutoring, face to face or at a distance, during fieldwork to ensure that students develop and reflect upon their intercultural competence as much as possible during this unique experience.

The second dimension of teacher training involves the acquisition of methods and techniques for the classroom and fieldwork. The latter is particularly relevant where the geographical distance is not too great and even young children can be taken to another country to experience a foreign reality for themselves. Choice of methods and techniques is in turn dependent on knowledge of developmental and social psychology as well as theory of language and language learning. The former will be part of the primary teacher's general training and need only be linked explicitly with discussion of intercultural competence. Language learning theory too can be linked with the teacher's training in first language acquisition theory and with training in the teaching of literacy in the first language. It is thus evident that training for foreign language teaching can be integrated with other aspects of primary education with respect to general pedagogy.

The degree of integration of training in methods will depend on decisions about the place of foreign language learning in the curriculum. A full discussion of the question of 'integration' or 'separate subject' would take us beyond the limits of this chapter and is discussed elsewhere in this volume (see also Tost Planet, 1997) but it will have significance for the methods of developing intercultural as well as linguistic competence. We shall return to this issue in the next section.

It is clear that the education and training of foreign language teachers for the primary school will appear problematic in the English education system where languages are not considered to be a core subject, unlike many other countries. It will appear that as well as being specialists in English, Mathematics and Science, trainee teachers also have to acquire a specialism in a foreign language, and not merely in linguistic but also in intercultural competence. One model proposed in a Council of Europe workshop in Prague (Felberbauer, 1997) would appear to demand a detailed specialisation which would require most of the time usually available for pre-service training, without even including a year abroad. Thus language teachers in primary schools may have to be specialists, because if our argument that language teaching should include intercultural competence, is taken seriously, it will not be possible to cut corners and reduce the time needed for appropriate education and training.

Curriculum planning

In one sense there is no problem about including an intercultural dimension in foreign language learning at primary school level since most curriculum documents refer to the desirability of developing 'cultural awareness' or similar concepts in their introductory statements. In the UK these exist only for secondary education but in other countries, where primary school language teaching is already established, parallel statements can be found for this level too.

In the USA, the intercultural dimension has for a long time been recognised in a number of elementary school foreign language projects. Curtain and Pesola (1994) quote an excellent example of guidelines for the integration of culture instruction into the elementary school curriculum. It comes from Maryland (Montgomery County) and gives detailed recommendations for the introduction of cultural contents into the various subject areas of basic education. In Europe too, such examples can be found. In the curricula of some German *Länder*, the intercultural aspect plays an important role. There is a common consensus that, if culture is to be integrated into the language learning process, it must be planned for as carefully and in as great detail as are the language elements. Therefore the *Didaktisch-methodischen Empfehlungen für das Fremdsprachenlernen in der Grundschule* in Niedersachsen do not only state the necessity for such integration, but also make suggestions for each recommended topic in which ways *interkulturelles Lernen* could be promoted (Niedersächsisches Kultusministerium, 1995).

It is, however, at the level of curriculum planning, where a national or regional curriculum is changed into a scheme of work for a school and a set of lesson plans for a class, that the difficulties arise. The English and Welsh National Curriculum for secondary schools does at least include indications of what might be expected in a course of study.

Pupils should be given opportunities to do the following:

- to work with authentic materials, including newspapers, magazines, books, films, radio and television, from the countries or communities of the target language; to come into contact with native speakers in this country and, where possible, abroad;
- to consider their own culture and compare it with the cultures of the countries and communities where the target language is spoken;
- to identify with the experiences and perspectives of people in these countries and communities;
- to recognise cultural attitudes as expressed in language and learn the use of social conventions.

There are also proposals for classroom techniques for cultural awareness in more recent secondary school textbooks. These may serve as inspiration but will not be directly applicable to primary school classrooms, all the more so because they pay little explicit attention to *savoir être*, which we have argued should be a priority in the primary school. Other chapters in this volume discuss methods in more details. The development of a classification of methods and techniques in terms of the five *savoirs* remains a task for the future.

We mentioned earlier the question of integrated or separate subject teaching. Others in this volume discuss integration as a means of developing linguistic competence. There are also implications for intercultural competence. Given that *savoir être* and *savoir apprendre* are most susceptible of development in the primary school, it is in a comparative methodology that integration might be best achieved. Wherever a topic can be planned to include a foreign perspective – one associated with the particular language being taught – there is potential for arousing children's curiosity and allowing them to see a different perspective (*savoir être*). Older children particularly may be encouraged and provided with the resources for discovering parallel phenomena in another country (*savoir apprendre*) and even discover how other people perceive the children's own society and its practices and products. It is, however, crucial to ensure that children do not over-generalise from their discoveries, assuming that 'all French people do this, believe that...'. They must always have opportunities to discover a range of perspectives and experiences in other countries and one method of doing this is through the direct contacts of visits, exchanges of materials and electronic communication.

Teaching materials

Criteria for the analysis of teaching materials for primary education have been established by Balbi (1997). These are particularly useful where languages are taught as a separate subject. They identify above all the ways in which linguistic competence is served by different kinds of teaching materials. Criteria for the analysis of the cultural dimension of secondary school textbooks have also been established (Doyé, 1991; Byram, 1993). A similar task still needs to be done for primary education materials which takes into consideration the prioritisation of *savoir être* and *savoir apprendre*, identifying materials and techniques which provide a basis for the teacher's work on these *savoirs* in particular.

The criteria will also need to include consideration of developmental psychology. Even more than in secondary school, it is evident that materials for children beginning to learn a language at age 5 will differ radically from those starting at age 8, for example. The complexity of decisions which have to be taken in materials development and selection, as well as in curriculum planning in general, is immense. Adding a requirement of intercultural competence to the decisions about at what age and in what ways to promote linguistic competence, creates a planning problem which individual teachers cannot be expected to resolve alone.

Conclusion

All this is, however, only a continuation of the story of foreign language teaching as it has grown and changed over the last hundred years. We have recognised with the help of researchers and teachers that language learning is a complex activity. We have seen how the purposes and nature of that activity have also changed and become more complex in response to societal changes. If foreign language teaching in primary education is to contribute seriously to the international education of young people, it has to recognise the complexity of the task, to include intercultural competence among its aims, to seek relationships with other aspects of the curriculum in systematic ways and to demand properly trained teachers and appropriate teaching materials.

References

Balbi, R. (1997) 'Resources', in P. Doyé and A. Hurrell (eds) *Foreign Language Education in Primary Schools*, Strasbourg: Council of Europe.

Bruner, J. (1960) *The Process of Education*, Cambridge, MA: Harvard University Press.

Byram, M. (ed.) (1993) *Germany: Its Representation in Textbooks for Teaching German in Great Britain*, Frankfurt on Main: Diesterweg.

——(ed.) (1997) *Face to Face. Learning 'Language-and-Culture' through Visits and Exchanges*, London: CILT,

——(1997) *Teaching and Assessing Intercultural Communicative Competence*, Clevedon: Multilingual Matters.

Byram, M. and Zarate, G. (1997) 'Definitions, Objectives and Assessment of Socio-cultural Competence', in *Sociocultural Competence in Language Learning and Teaching*, Strasbourg: Council of Europe.

Canale, M. and Swain, M. (1980) 'Theoretical Bases of Communicative Approaches to Second Language Teaching and Testing', in *Applied Linguistics*, 1, 1, 1–47.

Curtain, H. and Pesola, C.A. (1994) *Languages and Children: Making the Match*, New York: Longman.

Davies, A. (1991) *The Native Speaker in Applied Linguistics*, Edinburgh: Edinburgh University Press.

Doyé, P. (ed.) (1991) *Großbritannien. Seine Darstellung in deutschen Schulbüchern für den Englischunterricht*, Frankfurt on Main: Diesterweg.

——(1993) 'Fremdsprachenerziehung in der Grundschule', *Zeitschrift für Fremdsprachenforschung*, 4, 1, 48–90.

——(forthcoming) *The Intercultural Dimension of Foreign Language Education in the Primary School*, Berlin: Cornelsen.

Doyé, P. and Hurrell, A. (eds) (1997) *Foreign Language Education in Primary Schools*, Strasbourg: Council of Europe.

Felberbauer, M. (1997) 'Teacher Education' in P. Doyé and A. Hurrell, (eds) (1997) *Foreign Language Education in Primary Schools*, Strasbourg: Council of Europe.

Felberbauer, M. and Heindler, D. (1995) *Foreign Language Education in Primary Schools. Report on Workshop 8B*, Strasbourg: Council of Europe.

Hymes, D. (1971) 'On Communicative Competence', in J.B. Pride and J. Holmes (eds) *Sociolinguistics*, Harmondsworth: Penguin.

Kramsch, C. (1993) *Context and Culture in Language Teaching*, Oxford: Oxford University Press.

——(1998) 'The Privilege of the Intercultural Speaker', in M. Byram and M. Fleming (eds) *Language Learning in Intercultural Perspective*, Cambridge: Cambridge University Press.

Melde, W. (1987) *Zur Integration von Landeskunde und Kommunikation im Fremdsprachenunterricht*, Tübingen: Gunter Narr Verlag.

Niedersächsisches Kultusministerium, (1995) *Didaktisch-methodischen Empfehlungen für das Fremdsprachenlernen in der Grundschule*, Hanover: Schroedel Schulbuchverlag.

Pennycook, A. (1994) *The Cultural Politics of English as an International Language*, London: Longman.

Phillipson, R. (1992) *Linguistic Imperialism*, Oxford: Oxford University Press.

Skender, I. (1995) 'Éléments culturels dans l'apprentissage/l'enseignement des langues étrangères', in M. Vilke (ed.) *Children and Foreign Languages*, Zagreb: University of Zagreb, Faculty of Philosophy.

Tost Planet, M. (1997) 'Objectives and Contents', in P. Doyé and A. Hurrell (eds) *Foreign Language Education in Primary Schools*, Strasbourg: Council of Europe.

van Ek, J. (1986) *Objectives for Foreign Language Learning. Volume I: Scope*, Strasbourg: Council of Europe.

Wiegand, P. (1992) *Places in the Primary School*, London: Falmer Press.

10

European school links as a vehicle for promoting languages in the UK

Michael Evans

If one is to hold the generally accepted view that learning a foreign language should not be done without reference to the people who speak it, then the value of cross-national collaborative projects between UK schools and those in other European countries bears some consideration. Whilst different attempts have been made to define the relationship between 'cultural contact' and language learning, these remain largely vague, prescriptive or partial in that they fail to situate the relationship within the broad spectrum of priorities and objectives of language learning. Even the National Curriculum for England and Wales is elliptical on the subject. The Modern Foreign Languages programme of study states that all pupils should be given opportunities to 'come into contact with native speakers in this country and, where possible, abroad' (DFE, 1995: 3) but there is no explanation as to why this is important. It is therefore not surprising that whilst the value of this relationship is generally accepted, its purpose, in the minds of many people, pupils and language teachers included, remains blurred or confused.

Broadly, there are two main perspectives: one where the purpose is linguistic (contact improves linguistic performance); and one where the purpose is cultural (learning the language helps the process of mutual understanding, co-operation or social integration).

It has been argued that 'acculturated learners' (i.e. those who are 'socially integrated with' and 'psychologically open towards' the target group) are likely to be more successful at learning the language in question. If direct contact with the target group is the main way in which the process of acculturation can be promoted, then a school which is involved in a programme with partner schools from other European countries might be said to be providing opportunities for its pupils to develop their competence in the foreign language.

However, Schuman's theory of acculturation, discussed in Krashen (1982) and Johnstone (1994) amongst others, is principally set in the context of second language learning: in other words, the situation is one in which the desire for social integration with the host country is usually very strong and has almost unlimited opportunities for fulfilment. In the case of children, the likelihood is that they will be going to schools, making friends, and continually interacting in an environment in which the use of the target language will be an indispensable means of communication. The same, of course, cannot be said of foreign language learners: in other words, those who are not living in the target country. In this situation, the drive for learning and integration (European integration in this case) is provided externally by schools or society as a whole. There is no parallel desire for assimilation.

A further difference between the second and foreign language learning situations is that the amount of direct contact in the latter case is likely to be very limited. Research indicates that a year's residence abroad during a modern languages degree course does have a beneficial impact on the students' linguistic performance in the target language, though not seemingly on their grammatical competence (Coleman, 1996). The most reliable variable in the influence of residence on language learning is the length of stay in the target country. Those students who stayed longest abroad scored highest in proficiency tests in Coleman's research study. However, at pre-university level, direct contact with the target country is normally confined to holidays or school visits. The role of 'acculturation', by Schuman's definition, in motivating pupils to learn a foreign language is therefore, in most cases, insignificant.

The alternative perspective referred to earlier sees the role of language learning as subsidiary to a wider intercultural purpose. Some writers on the subject, such as Colin Wringe, have argued that 'the effort to learn and speak something of each other's languages is one of the ways in which' the aspiration towards closer European union 'at an affective as well as a merely instrumental and commercial level' can be expressed (Wringe, 1996: 73). However, whilst it is logical to assume that learning French (at least, learning it successfully) can lead to an enhanced sympathetic attitude towards France and French people, it is less clear that learning French (or any other one European language) will lead to a greater sense of solidarity with Europe as a whole. The latter case depends on the principle of metonymy (part for whole) in the shaping of cultural attitudes which seems unreliable in this context since, first, European countries and peoples differ culturally and socially and, secondly, language learners, including children, often express strong differences of views towards different European countries.

In this perspective, schools are encouraged to give their pupils opportunities to travel and to meet counterparts from other European countries so that they can develop a better understanding of the people and their culture. This process in turn can be underpinned by at least one of two purposes: to encourage comparison, competition and collaboration between teachers and pupils in different European countries; or to encourage a closer bonding or identification on a transnational scale. One could argue that Schuman's notion of 'acculturation' is still relevant here since these attitudes could be described as different points along a continuum; namely that of 'social distance' between the language learner and the community he or she is relating to. Clearly assimilation or identification would be one end of such a continuum.

However, the model needs further clarification in its application to the current educational setting in the UK if it is to provide a useful account of the relationship between language learning and cultural contact. It may be that economic, ethnic or political factors in certain countries can lead to strongly felt expressions of assimilation which in turn provide the driving force behind foreign language learning at school level. There may well be a correlation between the foreign language competence (especially in the English language) of people in northern European countries and their desire to relate closely to neighbouring countries. Surveys have consistently shown, for instance, that children and adults in The Netherlands place great importance in foreign language learning and international relations. In 1994 90.4 per cent of Dutch 14–16 year olds participating in a research study said they thought of themselves as 'totally European' compared with 18.6 per cent of English pupils of the same age (Convery et al., 1997).

Therefore, one could argue that there is a similar process of acculturation at work in that socio-economic interests in, for example, The Netherlands and in Scandinavian countries, are providing the backdrop for motivation in foreign language learning. The same, however, cannot be said, at the moment, for the majority of children in the UK. Foreign language learners at secondary and primary level in this country are located at a much earlier point on the continuum of 'social distance' from the foreign country. The rest of this chapter will attempt to define what that point is and what the pedagogical implications may be for the connection between target language learning and target culture contact in the light of a recent study of UK schools involved in European partnership programmes.

Comenius Action I funded projects

The main source of funding for school European links in this country is through the Central Bureau for school visits and exchanges. This is the government-funded body which also acts as the agency for the European Commission with regard to Brussels-led initiatives relating to educational links across Europe. The European Union Education Programme, known as SOCRATES, adopted in March 1995 for a five-year period, includes two 'chapters', or programmes, which relate to inter-school links. LINGUA is specifically concerned with the promotion of language learning throughout the EU. Its five strands or 'Actions' are primarily concerned with promoting in-service training of languages teachers (Actions A and B), or with the development and exchange of language teaching materials and tools for assessing acquired skills (Action D).

An example of an Action D project involving primary schools is the project entitled 'The use of multimedia for foreign language learning at primary and lower secondary school level'. Funding was awarded to pay for teacher trainers, teachers and student teachers from Cambridge, Paris, Alicante and Klagenfurt to meet and produce multimedia programs in English, French, German and Spanish suitable for language learning at beginner level. Funding was also granted to pay for computers for each of the participating schools so that pupils' use of the programs could be monitored and results compared between the different countries. Such a project is inevitably heavily dependent on the training institutions because of the technology involved although the final year of the project is scheduled to provide the schools with the authoring means to produce their own programs independently in the future.

Action E which supports joint educational projects for groups of students from two EU/EEA countries to work collaboratively over a period of time and take part in an exchange visit to a partner establishment has a minimum age stipulation of 14. Therefore, whilst valuable projects involving primary schools can and have been funded through LINGUA, the focus has been on the work of teachers rather than on facilitating direct contact between pupils from different countries.

The alternative source of funding in SOCRATES is through the Comenius Action 1 programme which aims:

> [to] promote co-operation between schools; to encourage contacts among pupils in different countries and promote the European dimension of their education; to encourage the mobility of school teachers; and to promote an improvement in the knowledge of the cultures and languages of European countries.
>
> (European Commission, 1996: 42)

The guidelines for applicants states that projects

> should be designed in such a way as to contribute understanding among participants of the languages and cultures of other participating countries and should therefore provide some opportunity for the pupils (and) teachers to develop competence in one or more other European languages.
>
> (European Commission, 1996: 44)

Nevertheless, proposals for projects with a language learning focus are supposed to be directed to LINGUA Action E and therefore to the exclusion of primary-aged children.

The Cambridge study

The evaluation was conducted with the co-operation of those UK schools named by the Central Bureau for Exchanges and Visits as co-ordinating institutions involved in Comenius Action 1 European partnership projects starting in January 1996. The total number of UK co-ordinating institutions contracted by the Central Bureau for this period was 48, consisting of three colleges of further education, 28 secondary schools and 17 primary schools. From this cohort 26 schools agreed to participate in the evaluation, 17 secondary and nine primary schools. In total, 483 pupil questionnaires were completed as well as 67 teacher questionnaires. Follow-up interviews were held with teachers at 12 schools later in the year.

One of the most striking aspects of school involvement in international links is the fluidity of the development of the work. To some extent, Comenius-funded links form no more than a part of a wider network of existing links with schools established through heterogeneous factors such as personal contact between teachers, town twinning, and so on. As a result, the system is prone to instability through change and unpredictability. In most cases the success of the links depends on the motivation and hard work of the school co-ordinator responsible for the projects, with the strong moral support of the headteacher. In weaker links, the departure of this key member of staff from the school leads to the collapse of the entire initiative. In other cases, whilst frequent changes are made in the identity of the foreign schools involved in the links, continuity and a tradition of European school collaboration are maintained through successive years of similar experience. However, aside from the financial benefits of the Comenius scheme (funding is provided only for travel and subsistence costs related to preparatory visits by teachers), the discipline of working to a set of centrally endorsed aims and objectives as well as having to account for the success of the projects on completion can give shape and direction to the work.

Given the non-linguistic focus of most Comenius projects, there was little difference between the thematic content of the projects in the primary and secondary schools participating in the Cambridge survey. As the project titles indicate, the focus was mainly either cross-curricular or intercultural. The project titles at primary schools were:

- Development of European awareness
- Europe écoles
- Houses and homes
- Water in our lives
- European landscapes and culture
- Health
- Channel Tunnel

In most cases, the specified aims of the project were set on a broad cultural awareness level. The project aims were:

- to promote European citizenship via educational projects;
- to promote greater awareness and understanding of European countries and to work in curriculum areas that promote a real sense of understanding of similarities between countries;
- to provide pupils with an understanding that all people have similar needs, but different ways of satisfying those needs. 'No way is better than another, just different.'
- to develop an understanding of similarities and differences between different cultures within the European Community and to develop an awareness of environments beyond their immediate locality;
- for children to become aware of and value the cultural heritage diversity in Europe;
- to compare data from pupils in Italy, Ireland and the UK in order to examine perceptions and actual behaviours focusing on aspects of health and safety.

At one primary school in our survey the aims were narrower and more pragmatic:

- to improve language competence in French/English;
- to work with other schools on a joint project;
- to communicate with two other schools abroad.

At this school, a Church of England primary school in Surrey, the project involved Year Six pupils with counterparts in France and Belgium. The pupils communicated with one another in their own language via letter and fax, exchanging information about their countries and local area. They also worked on a common project about the Channel Tunnel in which they designed and made a vehicle to travel through the tunnel as a problem-solving task regarding transport. In the class teacher's opinion the experience 'inspired children to have penfriends and to learn French'. It 'put French learning into a context'.

On the face of it, this kind of collaborative project which combines cultural contact with foreign language learning largely resembles the pattern of similar projects conducted at secondary school level. Authentic documents, written in the target language and exchanged between schools, can provide examples of meaningful material which the language teacher can exploit for linguistic purposes. In general, if the material is written by the link schools and if, in addition, it is based on a joint project which the pupils are engaged in, pupil motivation in the language learning process should rise. At the same time the language learning task is given added purposefulness by being related to an external cognitive and productive objective.

However, as our survey also revealed, this co-habitation between foreign language teaching and other non-linguistic areas of learning can be less easily facilitated at secondary than at primary school level. The compartmentalisation of subjects at secondary level inhibits cross-curricular initiatives. There is the pressure to abide by the subject-based National Curriculum programmes of study, to 'cover the syllabus' and to prepare for exams. In addition, many language teachers are weaned on an educational diet which focuses on form to the neglect of content so that they feel they lack sufficient knowledge in, for instance, geography or science needed for cross-curricular collaborations. One Head of Humanities interviewed in the study felt that modern languages was the 'least suitable' of subjects for promoting the European dimension because language teachers are 'blinkered with the language agenda'. This view was echoed by a Head of Modern Languages at another school who rather sadly confessed: 'Sometimes I wish I was not a linguist because languages is not the area...I can speak two languages, three languages now very well but I have got nothing to say.'

However, an opposite view would be to suggest that international school projects such as these can stimulate a more flexible approach to interdisciplinary connections within a school and break down barriers between subject departments within the same school. A Head of Science at a school in Hampshire justified his school's decision to engage in a Science/Modern Languages Comenius project as follows:

1   Science is content heavy and modern languages are totally content-free, so you have an ideal partnership because we actually complement each other.
2   Boys at secondary school level tend to be more motivated at science and less motivated in modern languages. For girls it is the exact converse, so put science and modern languages together and you have a situation where girls pick up a greater motivation to look at science as a good activity and the boys pick up the greater motivation to communicate their science ideas in modern languages.

One could argue that both issues raised by the teacher in this quotation are more readily dealt with at primary than at secondary school level. Opportunities for linking different subjects are more prevalent in the primary curriculum, and gender stereotyping of attitudes towards foreign language learning is less acute.

Summary of survey findings

Of all the primary school teachers surveyed, 75 per cent said that their school had benefited 'very much' from participation in the Comenius project.

All of them also said that the European dimension was a worthwhile addition to the curriculum and that schools should promote awareness of opportunities in Europe; awareness of European issues; European citizenship; and a sense of European identity.

At one infant school (where the age range of pupils is 3 to 7) teachers remarked that these topics were appropriate in the context of secondary or upper primary education and that at infant level the aim was 'to help children have a positive attitude to enable this later'. This school was involved in a project entitled 'Water in Our Lives' in collaboration with schools in Belgium and France. The aim of the project was 'to develop an understanding of similarities and differences between different cultures within the European Community and to develop an awareness of environments beyond their immediate locality'. All the pupils in the schools were involved in the activities. There was an exchange of educational materials made by children on the theme of weather and water. The Spanish school had sent paper clothes made for wet weather, such as rainwear, sailor outfits, frogmen, etc. There was a weekly exchange of fax messages between the schools on the same topic as well as more general exchanges of photographs and information about each other's schools.

Whilst the pupils at this school engaged in this project through the medium of English, nevertheless attempts were made by staff to inject some linguistic input to the activities. For instance, pupils read words in Spanish and sang songs with Flemish words inserted. The communication between staff in the schools involved was, on the other hand, through English, Spanish and French. And as constant interaction between the partners is necessary in order to keep the partnership alive, this is likely to encourage and motivate some primary school teachers to update or learn a foreign language which in turn might help in any future attempt to introduce the teaching of foreign language at Key Stage 2.

By far the most commonly quoted area in which primary teachers said their school had benefited from participation was that of developing in pupils a 'broadening of horizons'. This cliché is frequently used to describe the value of language learning or intercultural contact and is often used as a convenient catch phrase in place of a more focused definition of the purpose and value of the enterprise. Nevertheless, the spatial metaphor is an interesting reflection of the way in which teachers and students conceptualise the experience of foreign language learning. First, 'broadening one's horizon' may be interpreted as being in contrast with the state of 'insularism' (Johnstone, 1994) which cuts us off from other cultures, societies and languages. In this sense, it is a heightening of children's awareness of differences and similarities with children in other European countries. Second, the image is most commonly taken to mean that one is put in touch with new experiences and ways of seeing the world; but the wording of the cliché suggests that this new world is no longer 'other'. The new experience may well remain at the edge of one's home territory (both physically and cultur-ally) but the phrase implies that one's horizons have been adapted or stretched in order to encompass the new or the foreign.

In this way, it may be argued that collaborative projects between schools can play a part in developing the process of acculturation discussed at the start of this chapter. There is some evidence that pupils involved in these projects become more psychologically receptive or sympathetic to the target culture. Most teachers in the survey said that there had been a change in pupils' attitudes towards Europe as a result of participation in the project: the most frequently mentioned effect (49 per cent of primary school teachers) was that of increasing pupils' interest in Europe. Two teachers said that the experience led to improved attitudes to language learning. It would seem, therefore, one of the functions (and possibly the main one) of inter-school European partnerships, as far as the pupils involved are concerned, is affective rather than cognitive.

General conclusions

The following conclusions can be drawn from the Cambridge study:

1   European school partnerships (Comenius-funded) tend not to be language-focused. The direct benefit in terms of learning a foreign language is minimal (except where the focus is specifically the foreign language). The direct spin-off, as far as foreign language acquisition is concerned, is likely to be in relation to language awareness rather than language learning.

2   The programmes are media-based (with heavy reliance on communica-tion skills and technologies) rather than sustained personal contact or residence in the foreign country.

3   The programmes can promote an interest in 'minority' European languages (for example, Italian, Finnish, Greek).

4   The programmes can promote an interest in other European cultures and societies and can sow the seeds for motivation in foreign language learning.

5   Whilst secondary school teachers, on the whole, pointed to institutional benefits gained from involvement in the Comenius scheme, primary teachers tended to point to the beneficial effect on the pupils. Most respondents said that pupils became aware of differences and similarities with children in other European countries.

6   Teachers from the secondary schools placed Modern Languages at the top of the list of subjects most appropriate for promoting the European dimension in schools, whereas the primary school teachers ranked the subjects in the following order: Geography, English, Modern Languages, Technology and History.

To some extent the perception of the relative importance of languages departments in developing European awareness is influenced by the fact that the subject is not taught in most primary schools in this country. It is nevertheless interesting to see that what, on the whole, begins as a cross-curricular responsibility in primary schools is largely handed over to Modern Languages in the minds of secondary teachers.

What role, if any, should the Modern Languages teaching community play in this? The relationship between the European dimension and foreign language learning is one of reciprocal support. On the one hand, foreign language teachers can play an important role (both linguistically and through their knowledge and experience of European culture and society) in furthering links and projects with other European schools. On the other hand, it is likely that pupils who are favourably disposed to Europe as a result of fruitful contact with their counterparts in European schools, working collaboratively in other areas of the curriculum, are likely to be more motivated to learn other European languages.

Foreign language syllabuses should be redrawn according to the principle that the starting-point for the language learner is social/personal contact with the target country. This would avoid creating a separation in pupils' minds between foreign language learning and real communication with people living in another European country. Most current languages course books open on the assumption that the learners have no prior experience or knowledge of the target country and present it as a novel encounter with foreignness. As the number of primary schools in this country who enable their pupils to have some direct contact with children in other European countries grows, so too should the pressure for recognition of this experience at Key Stage 3. Equally there is little evidence that visits abroad organised by languages teachers at secondary level are drawn upon during lessons (Buttjes and Byram, 1991).

Secondary Modern Languages teachers should take an interest in partnership projects at feeder primary schools and at their own school. At the very least, languages teachers need to talk to Year 7 pupils about their European links in order to provide continuity between the two types of experience, language learning and contact with the people.

The value of Information and Communication Technology (ICT) as a means of communication at the disposal of languages teachers and pupils cannot be stressed too much. Languages teachers need to adopt the technology as an indispensable bridge for direct contact with other European countries. In many ways ICT (through the use of e-mail, the Internet and video conferencing) is the means by which language learning is tuned in with the development of international understanding and co-operation.

Languages teachers need to adopt the idea of close collaboration with exchange schools, building and maintaining relationships over time, and in particular to organise joint projects in collaboration with other departments at the school. The division of form (i.e. language) and content (i.e. topics which are based in science, geography, art and so on) is artificial. The inter-disciplinary nature of much of the primary curriculum and pedagogy has a lot to offer foreign language teaching at all levels. Before engaging in collaborative work with colleagues in other countries, languages teachers must learn to collaborate with colleagues at their own school.

References

Buttjes, D. and Byram, M. (1991) *Mediating Languages and Cultures*, Clevedon: Multilingual Matters.

Coleman, J. (1996) *Studying Languages: A Survey of British and European Students*, London: CILT.

Convery, A. *et al.* (1997) *Pupils' Perceptions of Europe: Identity and Education*, London: Cassell.

Department for Education (1995) *Modern Foreign Languages in the National Curriculum*, London: HMSO.

European Commission (1996) *Socrates Guidelines for Applicants: Comenius*, Brussels: Socrates and Youth Technical Assistance Office.

Johnstone, R. (1994) *Teaching Modern Languages at Primary School: Approaches and Implications*, Edinburgh: Scottish Council for Research in Education.

Krashen, S. (1983) *Principles and Practice in Second Language Acquisition*, Oxford: Pergamon Press.

Wringe, C. (1996) 'The Role of Foreign Language Learning in Education for European Citizenship', *Evaluation and Research in Education*, 10, 2–3.

III

Future development

Modern foreign languages in the primary school in England

Some implications for initial teacher training

Keith Sharpe

Although over the decades, and particularly in recent years, there has been both in England and other countries a great diversity in the nature of localised projects (Edelenbos and Johnstone, 1966; Hawkins, 1996) aimed at introducing modern foreign languages (MFL) into the primary curriculum, ultimately there are only two possible options for staffing primary modern language teaching: either the pupils are taught by a specialist of some kind or they are taught by the generalist primary class teacher who is responsible for delivering all or most of the overall curriculum entitlement. In practice, the phrase 'specialist of some kind' has incorporated a wide variety of teaching personnel, including:

1   secondary-trained specialist MFL teachers who may seek employment as specialist MFL teachers in one or more primary schools, possibly in England under the terms of Local Education Authority (LEA) schemes;
2   specialist MFL teachers from neighbouring secondary schools who by arrangement teach classes in some of their feeder primaries;
3   secondary trained specialist MFL teachers who find employment in primary schools (maybe through phase retraining) and may operate as 'semi-specialists' taking some colleagues' classes for MFL on an exchange basis;
4   native speakers who are not trained teachers who are employed by schools to teach their mother tongue;
5   diverse MFL peripatetics such as MFL graduates who may not have undergone teacher training of any sort;
6   specialist *primary* teachers of MFL who followed a course of primary initial teacher education in which the subject was either a main or a subsidiary area of study.

At present in England specialist *primary* MFL teachers are in short supply. After the fateful conclusion of the final National Foundation for Educational Research (NFER) evaluation report on the 1967–74 pilot scheme that 'it is hard to resist the conclusion that the weight of the evidence has combined with the balance of opinion to tip the scales against a possible expansion of the teaching of French in primary schools' (Burstall *et al.*, 1974: 246), most primary initial teacher training (ITT) MFL specialists' courses disappeared along with the optimistic expectation that the whole primary French project would be extended nationally, and those who did at the time undertake such training and who stayed in the profession are now in the latter part of their careers. Many will have 'moved on'. Investigating how many are still actively engaged in primary MFL teaching today would be an interesting research study. Few providers of primary ITT undergraduate programmes offer MFL as a possible specialisation precisely because it is not a national curriculum subject at KS1 (Key Stage 1, i.e. pupils aged 5–7) and KS2 (Key Stage 2, i.e. pupils aged 7–11). At postgraduate level some modern language graduates do enter primary PGCE programmes, but until recently there was a stipulation that graduate candidates had to have specialist knowledge of a subject included in the sacred pantheon of the National Curriculum.

For the most part, therefore, the situation in England is that where it is being taught, MFL is delivered either by specialist teachers without primary training or primary teachers without specialist MFL knowledge. This is clearly an undesirable situation which cannot be justified in the long run, although it may be regarded as the inevitable outcome of the lack of a national strategy. Two nationwide organisations with a keen interest in this topic have recently issued policy statements intended to redress the situation. The Primary Languages Network (1997) argues that 'there are now strong arguments for building on the success of the Scottish project and extending it to *all primary schools* in England, Wales and Northern Ireland'. By contrast, the Association for Language Learning (ALL) in a revision of its earlier 1992 policy statement now advocates that:

> the introduction of a modern foreign language into the primary national curriculum for all pupils should be announced *as a long-term target* in order to allow adequate time and resources to establish the following:
>
> - initial teacher training in the primary sector;
> - revision of the National Curriculum in Key Stages 3 and 4;
> - publishers to develop new course books for Key Stage 2 and revise those for Key Stages 3 and 4;
> - continuing professional development not only in order to train primary teachers but also to develop secondary teachers to work effectively with Key Stage 3 pupils and liaise with primary colleagues.
>
> (ALL, 1997)

The position adopted is more moderate and restrained than the enthusiastic wholesale endorsement of primary MFL apparent in the 1992 document.

This seems to be because the ALL, the major national organisation of teachers and educationalist concerned with MFL, is anxious to promote a 'coherent strategy for language learning across the United Kingdom', a sort of national plan for MFL, of which primary MFL is only a part. To some extent this is driven by the concern that there is already a desperate shortage of MFL teachers for KS3 (Key Stage 3, i.e. pupils aged 11–14) and KS4 (Key Stage 4, i.e. pupils aged 14–16) and the system as a whole is having difficulties meeting the statutory entitlements. Back in 1990 during a House of Lords debate on MFL teaching, Baroness Lockwood, who later contributed to the 1992 conference where the joint policy statement of the Association for Language Learning and the National Association of Headteachers was promulgated, observed 'The two main problems affecting modern foreign language learning in the United Kingdom are the current crisis in teacher supply and the widespread lack of motivation and interest in foreign languages' (House of Lords Report, 1990: 562).

It is true that up to the present time providers of secondary ITT have had major problems recruiting suitably qualified candidates; places on Postgraduate Certificate in Education (PGCE) MFL courses are left unfilled. Some would argue therefore that to introduce statutory requirements for MFL to be taught at KS2 or even KS1 and 2 would make an already dire situation all but impossible. This argument has a surface plausibility, but it could be that it simplifies something which at the human level is more complex. Candidates for initial teacher training have varied, and often subtle, motives for their applications. Recruitment for primary teacher training in general continues to be very buoyant, especially at postgraduate level where the most prestigious institutions may have ten applications for every place. It is at least arguable that if there were a national strategy to introduce MFL in primary schools some candidates would apply for primary MFL specialist training who would not apply for secondary MFL training for reasons that include perceptions of what it is like to try and teach foreign languages to difficult adolescents who neither see any point in, nor harbour any desire to learn them. Such perceptions have been widely peddled throughout the British media in recent years. To the extent that this is so, it is not the case that new primary MFL ITT provision will necessarily 'hoover up' scarce potential secondary teachers. The fact of the matter is that the rejected primary applicants for each PGCE place are doing something else and not taking up empty secondary places in any un-recruited subject (MFL is not alone amongst secondary subjects failing in England to attract candidates for teaching). From September 1997 the Teacher Training Agency (TTA), the government agency responsible for teacher supply, has invited ITT providers to run specialist KS2/3 programmes and to use allocated secondary numbers to recruit students. It is too early for national figures to be available but it is certain that some MFL graduates have come forward who would not have applied for the straight secondary PGCE programme.

Thus while the caution implicit in the ALL position is understandable ('a long-term strategic plan should be in place *before* the subject is formally introduced into the primary curriculum'), and their wish for an overall coherence entirely correct, it may well nevertheless be possible to begin straightaway the process of training primary MFL specialists without tipping over too much further the already tottering applecart of shortages in MFL teacher supply.

The context of initial teacher training in England

Any proposal now to train primary MFL teachers needs to be set in the context of the requirements for all courses of ITT set out in the Department for Education and Employment (DfEE) circular 10/97 entitled *Teaching: High Status, High Standards*. This circular sets in place important reforms in teacher training generally among which the following are of particular relevance to the issue of preparing primary teachers of MFL.

First, it establishes a common framework of requirements for both primary and secondary teacher training courses, ending the tradition of differential treatment and replacing the separate sets of requirements for the two phases previously in force under Circular 9/92 (secondary) and Circular 14/93 (primary). This is a significant development not dissimilar from the *tronc commun* policy institutionalised in France when the Instituts Universitaires de Formation des Maîtres (IUFMs) were established to provide training for teachers destined for both the écoles élémentaires and the collèges and lycées. It signifies the unity of the teaching profession and gives recognition to the value of generic teaching skills and abilities.

Second, it establishes QTS (Qualified Teacher Status) as the first in a series of national professional qualifications which will provide a unified structure through which teachers' career progression can be systematically organised and promoted in post-qualification training and continuing professional development, from being a Newly Qualified Teacher (NQT) through to the award of NPQH (National Professional Qualification for Headship) and headship. Finally, it establishes clear and unambiguous 'standards' against which student teachers ('trainees') must be assessed before qualified teacher status can be awarded.

Circular 10/97 also incorporates an annex and the first two national curricula for initial teacher training (NCITT), an NCITT for primary English and an NCITT for primary mathematics. At the time of writing it is unclear how far this aspect of current educational policy will extend. The intention to produce NCITTs for information technology and for secondary English and secondary mathematics has been signalled, but it is unclear whether there will eventually be NCITTs for all subjects. What is generally significant about the concept of NCITTs, however, is that implicit in it is the notion that government can influence school practice by directly controlling the content of teacher training courses. In the present context what appears to be happening is that primary teacher training students are now being taught aspects of subject matter required by the NCITT for primary English, for example, which at the moment are not required to be taught to pupils by the existing National Curriculum orders for English at KS1 and KS2. There is currently a five-year moratorium on change in the school National Curriculum following the Dearing Reform of 1994, and it may well be that when this is over the changes which will be made will be those prefigured in the NCITT. What this suggests is that if ever/whenever, government policy shifts to promoting primary MFL, levers of control in the field of initial teacher training might well be used as a key part of the strategy.

Initial teacher training for primary modern foreign languages: a possible strategy

As far as subject specialisms within primary initial teacher training are concerned the emerging situation in England is one in which broadly five categories can be identified, as shown in Table 11.1.

The formal requirements of ITT providers in relation to subject specialisms are that for major specialisms candidates should by the end of their course have 'secure knowledge of the subject to at least a standard approximating to GCE "A" level in those aspects of the subject taught at KS1 and KS2' (DfEE, 1997: 8). This applies to students in categories 1, 2 and 3 above. Students whose relationship to the subject falls into category 4 above must have 'secure knowledge to a standard equivalent to at least level 7 of the pupils' national curriculum' (DfEE, 1997: 8). For category 5 no level specification is given in 10/97, nor is there any in the framework for inspection (OFSTED, 1997) against which the quality of ITT provision is judged by the government's educational inspection agency.

Table 11.1 Categories of subject specialist student teacher/trainees

Category	Subject specialism
1	trainee enters postgraduate training with degree level knowledge
2	trainee enters postgraduate training with sub-degree level knowledge
3	during undergraduate training trainee takes subject as major specialism
4	during undergraduate or postgraduate training trainee takes subject as non-specialist study
5	during undergraduate or postgraduate training trainees cover the subject as part of general primary curriculum studies

All forms of ITT are essentially concerned with two elements:

1   Subject Knowledge – ensuring that the future teacher knows and understands enough about what they are to teach to be able to teach it effectively.
2   Subject Application – ensuring that the future teacher knows and understands enough about how to teach what they are to teach to be able to do so effectively.

There are therefore different responses called for from ITT course providers in relation to each of the five levels described above. Students in each instance will need different programmes to enhance their subject knowledge and their understanding of its application in the classroom context. At this point, however, it is perhaps worth considering exactly what is meant by subject knowledge. Some would argue that in the case of MFL subject specialists ought to have a native mastery. In practice, however, this is more a statement of presumed ideal than a feasible policy prescription even when applied only to MFL specialists in the secondary phase. The qualifications of actual secondary MFL teachers in England and elsewhere vary enormously, ranging from native speakers and good single honours graduates to those whose mastery of the taught language is developed and accredited, if at all, only at modest levels. And, in fact, it is arguable whether the nature of the specialist subject knowledge in the case of MFL is much more than what is signified by native speaker competence. Effective MFL subject specialists know about the functioning of language as well as 'knowing the language' taught. Figure 11.1 suggests how the elements of subject knowledge and subject application underpin effective teaching of foreign languages.

These four elements are entirely interdependent. All need to be in place to some degree before anything approaching real MFL teaching can begin. A native speaker, *per se* only has SK1, and is therefore not the ideal. This is not of course to say that an MFL teacher's performance level in relation to linguistic and sociocultural skills should not be as high as possible. Nevertheless it is better to have a teacher with less than native command but with a more balanced profile across the four elements needed. It is for this reason that well-meaning local native speakers invited into schools to teach their language can, if left to their own devices rather than used as a resource by a competent teacher retaining what the French call 'responsabilité pédagogique', sometimes finish by creating little more than disaffected children with existing prejudices confirmed and with a determination at all costs to avoid the subject in the future. Of course fluency and accuracy in the language are important, but without effective teaching strategies their value cannot be applied. It is in this sense that it is possible to speak of the 'primacy of pedagogy'.

It is important therefore to be realistic about what it is possible to achieve

Figure 11.1 Subject knowledge and subject application in effective MFL teaching

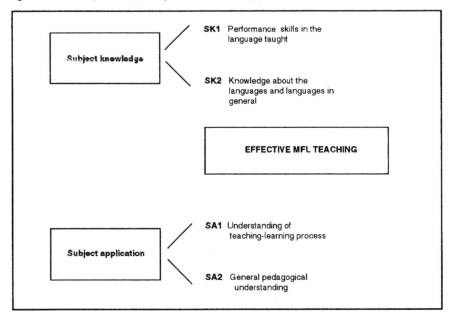

in primary modern language teaching. As far the UK is concerned, it is futile to imagine that in the near future it will be possible to recruit and train sufficient numbers of linguistically highly qualified MFL teachers who would teach in primary schools exclusively as specialist teachers, even if that were deemed desirable. There is some evidence from studies of projects where the specialists of some kind referred to at the outset of this chapter form the main basis of staffing that pupil response is markedly less positive than where the teaching is provided by the pupils' class teacher. It is probably making a virtue out of necessity therefore to advocate that training arrangements should be put in place to facilitate the development in the medium term of a primary teaching force which has amongst its ranks its own primary MFL specialists and in which the generalist primary class teacher is able to contribute to the teaching process. Ultimately, if there is to be a national commitment to primary MFL teaching as a basic universal entitlement at or during KS2 and/or KS1, the only solution to the staffing question is to empower primary teachers themselves to provide it. In places such as Kent, Croydon and within the Scottish Projects, where there are local schemes in operation, this is largely being managed through the provision of INSET/CPD, but increasingly providers of ITT are becoming involved, and if full national coverage is to be attained, MFL will need to become part of the overall primary ITT framework alongside other subjects outside the core of English mathematics and science. This implies designing courses which produce:

1   primary MFL specialists (categories 1, 2, 3 in Figure 11. 1);
2   generalists with an understanding of primary MFL (categories 4, 5 in Table 11.1).

The fundamental training needs of each of the categories are set out in Table 11.2.

Primary MFL training for specialists

There are of course certain things which all primary teachers need to know and to be able to do whether generalist or specialist in whatever subject. The specification concerning exactly what these are has become an increasing focus of concern by governments in most developed countries in recent years, largely under the stimulus of the perceived challenges and threats arising from globalisation. In essence, the concern is that during primary education that the 'basic skills' are acquired which are the key to later

Table 11.2 Training needs of specialist and non-specialist primary teachers of MFL

Specialist category	Non-specialist category	SK1	SK2	SA1	SA2
1 PG main degree or native speaker		Should be secure	Build on established understanding	Specific training needed	PGCE GPS and other programme elements
2 PG subsidiary degree		May need developing	Specific training needed	Specific training needed	
3 UG		Develop to A level +	Main focus of training and development	Main focus of training and development	UG GPS and other programme elements
	4 UG or PG	Develop to NC level 7	Subsidiary focus of training and development	Subsidiary focus of training and development	UG or PGCE GPS and other programme elements
	5 UG or PG	Basic structures and vocabulary	Application of general principles	Application of general principles	

Note: UG/PG refers to undergraduate or postgraduate students. GPS refers to general professional studies courses.

achievement and, in an increasingly harsh world economic climate, standards of basic numeracy and literacy must be raised to ensure the country produces a knowledgeable and skilled workforce able to face up to the market challenges coming from 'competitor countries'. The DfEE circular 10/97 referred to earlier is clearly intended to tighten central control over the training of primary school teachers and prescribes definitive content which ITT courses must cover. It represents a shift away from its immediate predecessor, Circular 14/93 (DfE 1993), which to some extent reinforced the traditional English preoccupation with breadth in the primary curriculum. It has a narrower emphasis focusing on the core subjects of English, Mathematics and Science and the requirement for all those awarded QTS to have one or more specialist subjects. As far as primary MFL is concerned, there is a 'technical' difficulty in that, although it is not made explicit, the requirements appear to assume that the specialist subject will be a National Curriculum subject or religious education (see 10/97, Section 2 d., i. and ii., page 8). In the present circumstances it would appear therefore that in England a primary student teacher/trainee can only take MFL as a second specialism. Providers of primary ITT will thus need to think creatively about how this might be achieved in student programmes already overcrowded with content. Of course in the event that after the current moratorium on change in the National Curriculum ends in 2000, primary MFL becomes part of it, the problem will be solved. It is, however, as yet far from clear whether this will happen. The chief executive of the Schools Curriculum and Assessment Authority (SCAA), Nick Tate, has recently declared that 'SCAA has no views on the future role of modern foreign languages in the primary school. We approach the issues with an entirely open mind' (SCAA 1997: 7). This is perhaps a policy equivalent of the half-empty or half-full glass: one is not sure whether to be optimistic or pessimistic. Certainly as far as the advocates of MLPS are concerned, this determinedly reserved tone strikes a rather dismal note and stands in marked contrast to the pronouncements of national curriculum policy-makers in other member states of the European Union on the issue. Nevertheless it is important to consider what should be offered to intending primary MFL specialists, both now as 'multi-specialists' and in the future possibly as 'single specialists', in relation to both subject knowledge and subject application.

The position for all other subjects is that student teachers/trainees have to have 'secure knowledge' of those aspects of the subject taught at KS1 and KS2. In the absence of statutory primary programmes of study for KS1/2 MFL, how is this to be interpreted? One apparent answer is maybe that under these conditions it does not need to be interpreted, and in effect ITT course designers might therefore follow their own inclinations without reference to any official constraints. Two notes of caution are, however, in order. First, all courses of primary ITT are subject to regular inspection and this has become an increasingly risk-laden experience for providers. Since 1995 a number of institutional providers of primary ITT have actually been closed down after failing inspection, their accreditation or licence to train teachers suspended and their government funding withdrawn. Second, course designers need to bear in mind that there is an MFL National Curriculum for secondary education to which primary pupils will be subject from the age of 11, and anything done in the primary school therefore clearly needs, to say the least, to be articulated with this. The interim report of the National Curriculum MFL working group (1991) specifically planned that levels 1–3 of the national curriculum might eventually be delivered in primary schools (see para 2.17, p.21). In point of fact both the substantive and formal content of these levels represents a version of a broad consensus apparent across a number of schemes (Pilote, *3-2-1...Los!*, *Salut La France!*, The Scottish Projects, PRISM) about what it is appropriate for learners to cover in the early stages. These common elements remain apparent in the current statutory orders for MFL, where clearly the two parts of the programmes of study and the level descriptions of the attainment targets include features which, although aimed at Key Stage 3 pupils, are actually being covered by many pupils during Key Stage 2 where primary MFL are taught. In particular the 'three areas of experience' designated for Key Stage 3, 'everyday activities', 'personal and social life', and 'the world around us' cover many of the functions, structures and vocabulary which make up the published schemes listed above. Similarly, the kind of performance in MFL described in the 'Exemplification of Standards' material for the level 2 pupil (SCAA, 1996: 11–19) might be achieved by many primary pupils currently being taught French.

If this is taken as indicative content of primary modern language, what exactly are the implications for ITT course designers regarding subject knowledge needed to teach it? In the case of MFL it really does not make much sense to say post-'A' level knowledge and skill on these elements is necessary. As far as SK1 is concerned, there is a certain 'wholeness' about any foreign language, and an appropriate programme of language study for student teachers needs to have regard more to established practices in the general assessment of foreign language learners levels than to merely having a deep knowledge of matters likely to be taught in infant and junior schools.

Postgraduate primary students taking a specialism in MFL should have their competence in the language audited. With students whose degree studies predominantly focused on a foreign language (category 1 in Table 11.1), further enhancement of SK1 is likely to be unnecessary, although it is not unknown for undergraduates to be strong on literature and therefore reading and writing, but weaker on speaking and listening which are the key skills needed in primary MFL. For graduates whose degree studies included a foreign language but whose principal focus was something else, the same auditing process is necessary but additional provision may more often be needed. It is, however, sometimes the case that category 2 (in Table 11.1) students are actually good on oral/aural skills since the foreign languages element in their degree was aimed more explicitly at facilitating communicative competence.

A perennial difficulty with SK1 (Subject Knowledge 1) in any subject on a PGCE primary course is lack of time. So much needs to be compressed into so short a course (currently 38 weeks of which 18 weeks are spent in schools). It is often possible to identify targets for improvement with students, following audit, which it then becomes their professional responsibility to meet. This kind of arrangement can be formalised in the shape of agreed learning contracts. Institutional providers of ITT, universities and colleges, have a range of learning support services, and it may be possible to arrange for students to join existing foreign languages courses or to take advantage of self-access study facilities to improve their overall competence.

For undergraduate students (category 3 in Table 11.1) the SK1 element clearly needs to be an integral part of the whole primary ITT programme. Before 1993 the prevailing official requirements laid down that students spend 18 months during a four-year course on advanced specialist subject study. While Circular 14/93 lifted this requirement, Circular 10/97 appears as something of a return to the status quo ante. However, there is no time specification, and there is a stronger steer towards only including professionally relevant content. Whereas, therefore, subject studies courses within any primary PGCE course will be mainly concerned with SK2 and SA1, those on undergraduate programmes will clearly need to address SK1 directly as well. Many will feel that a higher level than 'A level equivalent' should be aimed for both in recognition of the distinctive nature of the subject, and in order that the primary MFL specialist does have the confidence to act as a co-ordinator of the subject within a school. Where at all possible, time abroad in the country concerned is also desirable. With the extensive development of primary MFL in other European countries whose languages are mainly taught in England it is becoming easier to find partner ITT institutions willing to establish reciprocal exchange arrangements. While not needing to be native speakers, MFL specialists do need to be able to 'perform' their subject. It may be argued that music, art and physical education are in the same position, but it is important to remember that teachers in these subjects are able fruitfully to coach better performers than themselves. This is inconceivable in foreign language teaching: in particular cases successful teachers may be only one step ahead, but they do need to be ahead.

A lot of SK2 (Subject Knowledge 2) learning arises directly out of the experience of SK1 learning and it is thus to be considered to be an advantage for primary MFL specialists to be trained through the undergraduate route where awareness of how language works (SK2), and indeed how learners learn foreign languages SA1 (Subject Application 1), can be consciously raised at the same time as the student is actually learning the language. The tutor directing the teaching sessions can constantly have all these elements in mind in planning course content so that they can each be mutually reinforcing in an integrated and holistic programme. A major issue for primary ITT course managers and planners is what should be included in subject application (SA1), and *ipso facto* be specific to students studying that subject, and what should be included in general professional studies course which are common to all students SA2 (Subject Application 2). While issues often covered in general professional studies courses such as behaviour management, teaching strategies, assessment, recording and reporting, clearly have a 'generic' character, they also have specific applications in relation to each area of the curriculum. A related issue which is much more complex in primary ITT than in secondary ITT, given that primary students have to take courses in so many different curriculum subjects, is how the two (SA1 and SA2) should interrelate to provide a coherent experience for students. It is worth noting in this context, however, that the National Curriculum MFL working group considered that effective general primary teaching and effective MFL teaching had much in common. Having emphasised the importance of visual display, practical demonstration and active learning, they comment that 'this is one of the many areas in which teachers of foreign languages can learn from good primary practice' (NCC, 1991: 17). Thus, in the case of MFL, what is done in general professional studies dovetails to a considerable extent with subject application. It is arguable that shifts in policy and thought about primary methodology over the past five years have actually increased the congruence between the two. The growing emphasis on whole class teaching and the importance of memorisation through repetition, for example, fit neatly with the need for the MFL teacher to play a directive role in promoting learner progress.

Primary MFL training for non-specialists

Primary ITT providers can choose to include an MFL component in either the range of 'non-specialist' subject course they offer (category 4 in Table 11.1), or as part of a general course in primary curriculum studies (category 5 in Table 11.1). In either of these cases the aim might be to enable the eventual newly qualified teacher (NQT) to undertake some MFL teaching with support from more qualified and experienced colleagues. As suggested earlier, without the contribution of non-specialists, albeit under some kind of supervision and co-ordination, it is difficult to see how primary MFL can be *universally* provided, and it is therefore vital that this aspect of initial teacher education is carefully planned. A major challenge is of course the subject knowledge element. It could be said that the teacher with a category 5 (Table 11.1) relationship to the subject is the mirror image of the untrained native speaker. Such a teacher may have a sophisticated and informed understanding of effective primary teaching methods, but only a very rudimentary knowledge of the language to be taught. The training aim here needs to prioritise three main objectives:

1   equipping the student teacher with secure knowledge of basic structures and vocabulary which can underpin:
(a)   effective real use of the FL in routine events in the classroom;
(b)   some specific teaching of elements of the FL within a planned scheme which is part of a school MFL policy (possibly within an LEA MFL policy, and eventually within the framework of a national policy);
2   developing in the student teacher a positive and enthusiastic attitude towards primary MFL;
3   enabling the student teacher to apply principles of effective primary teaching to the specific instance of MFL teaching.

There is considerable evidence that where primary MFL projects have been successfully developed pupils' attitudes towards foreign language learning improve alongside their knowledge and skill. Indeed, this was the one really positive conclusion arising out of the otherwise strikingly desultory NFER evaluation of the ill-fated Primary French Project:

> Where the pupils taught French in the primary school do appear to gain is not in 'mastery' but in attitude. When they have been successful in their efforts to learn French, they do appear to retain a more favourable attitude toward speaking the language than do those who were not introduced to French until the age of 11.
>
> (Burstall, C., et al. 1974: 244)

This is not mere 'icing on the cake'. In the case of MFL it is scarcely an exaggeration to say that motivation is everything. Now that MFL teaching is overwhelmingly concerned with developing communicative competence, and mainly in speaking and listening rather than reading and writing, it is absolutely crucial that the learner actually desires to communicate. A positive attitude is vital for real success. This is one area where the old adage about taking horses to water but being unable to make them drink has a direct educational application. Not for nothing did the Primary Languages Network Working Party (1997) identify 'an enthusiasm for and interest in foreign language learning' as the first aim of teaching an MFL to primary pupils. It is possible to oblige pupils to be present at a foreign language lesson but it is not possible to force them to desire to communicate. In earlier times they might have been coerced into memorising, say, verb conjugations, against the threat of tests and punishments for poor marks, but to fall back on such tactics, when the whole point is to promote the engagement of the learner with the language and the culture in which it is embedded, is to undermine any meaningful purpose the lesson might have.

It is not my intention to rehearse the arguments in favour of including foreign languages in the primary curriculum, but one issue in that debate is of crucial importance to the present discussion. As HMI have argued:

> learning a foreign language should be primarily a matter of learning it for communication...Those activities which enable genuine communication to take place or which simulate it closely are the most effective. Such opportunities as are provided by the necessary business of the classroom should be fully exploited, for example, counting and spelling, noting absence, apologising, introducing people, asking permission and requesting an explanation.
>
> (HMI, 1985)

Once this is acknowledged, then the advantages of the primary school situation for language learning become clear. Hawkins (1987) has characterised the secondary situation, where the work of MFL teachers in isolated teaching periods is all too frequently deluged by all the other curriculum experiences delivered through the medium of the mother tongue, as 'gardening in a gale'. The image of delicate MFL seedlings swept away by a whirlwind of English need not be the picture in primary schools. Here the MFL can be integrated into the pupils' whole school and classroom experience, it can be valued and used as a real means of communication throughout the day, the week, the year, through both key stages. In this sense it is ironic that the statutory obligation to teach MFL falls on secondary schools but not on primary schools which are actually much better placed to deliver a programme of FL communicative competence (Sharpe, 1991). All non-specialist primary teachers could potentially be trained to conduct ordinary class routines in a foreign language – taking the dinner register, collecting dinner money, lining up, writing the date, distributing or collecting books and files, celebrating birthdays, setting the weather board, and the like can all be easily accomplished through the medium of a targeted FL by teachers whose training has made them committed to the importance of doing so. Given a willingness to do so, these are not difficult matters to master, and the constant repetition eases the learning process. Many classroom objects could be referred to using FL words in place of their English, or whatever mother tongue, equivalents. There is absolutely no reason in principle why FL vocabulary should not be incorporated by such non-specialist primary teachers within English sentences. The absorption of foreign vocabulary is in any case a naturally occurring process. What is the difference between talking about visiting the *café* or the *coiffeur* in everyday English and a primary teacher deliberately and for very good reasons asking pupils to undertake a written exercise in their *cahier d'histoire* or their *classeur*? In both cases an item of foreign vocabulary becomes an accepted and unremarkable element of a communicative process: this is a key objective for all language teaching. Primary teachers can 'embed' the FL in primary classroom life and the primary curriculum. In this way they can become remarkably successful gardeners whose pupils grow strong roots in MFL learning and may be better prepared to withstand the blast from the secondary curriculum.

Conclusion: the way forward

I have argued elsewhere that the essence of primary modern languages is to be found in the four 'C's of communication, culture, context and confidence (Sharpe, 1992). Ideally we need all our primary pupils to be able to *communicate* at some level in *culturally* appropriate ways in specific real *contexts* with *confidence*, and to do so with positive enjoyment and enthusiasm. Primary teachers are well placed to enable this to happen. Using the model of the undergraduate or postgraduate trained specialist MFL teacher as a whole school co-ordinator, supported by non-specialist generalists capable both of providing narrowly focused inputs which have been systematically planned and well resourced and of setting these within a supportive MFL school/class environment, such a vision is within our grasp. What is required is the political will to deal with the anomalies which now exist: what possible justification can there be for a situation in which the early learning of a foreign language is an entitlement of a pupil living in Maidstone but not in Manchester, in Glasgow but not in Gateshead? It was precisely concern about such inequities which led to the institutionalisation of fundamental pupil entitlements in the National Curriculum ten years ago. The infrastructural training framework is in place; what is needed now is a clear policy for the training of primary MFL specialists and the inclusion of MFL in primary generalist courses. In this way a timetable could be drawn up which would take us from the absurd anarchy of the present situation to the acceptance of primary modern languages for all early in the next millennium.

References

Association for Language Learning (1977) *Draft Policy on Primary Modern Languages*, Rugby: ALL.

Burstall, C., Jamieson, M., Cohen, S. and Hargreaves, M., (1974) *Primary French in the Balance*, Slough. NFER.

Department for Education and Employment (1993), *The Training of Primary School Teachers* (Circular 14/93), London: HMSO.

—— (1997) *Teaching: High Status, High Standards*, (Circular 10/97), London: HMSO.

East Sussex LEA (1989) *Salut La France!*, E. Sussex / Stanley Thornes.

Edelenbos, P. and Johnstone, R. (1996) *Researching Languages at Primary School*, London: CILT.

Hawkins, E. (1987) *Modern Languages in the Curriculum*, Cambridge: Cambridge University Press.

—— (ed.) (1996) *Thirty Years of Language Teaching*, London: CILT.

HMI (1985) *Modern Foreign Languages 5–16*, London: HMSO.

House of Lords (1990) *Debate on European Schools and Language Learning*, Hansard.

NCC (1991) *Modern Foreign Languages Working Group Initial Advice*, York: NCC.

Office for Standards in Education (1997) *Framework for the Assessment of Quality and Standards in Initial Teacher Training*, London: OFSTED.

Primary Languages Network (1977) *Draft Policy on the Introduction of Foreign Languages into the Primary School Curriculum*, London: CILT.

Rumley, G., Rowe, I. and Killbery, I. (1992) *Pilote: Kent Primary French Project*, Dover: KCC/KETV.

SCAA (1995) *Modern Foreign Languages in the National Curriculum*, London: HMSO.

——(1997a) *Exemplification of Standards in Modern Foreign Languages*, London: HMSO.

——(1997b) *Modern Foreign Languages in the Primary Curriculum*, London: HMSO.

Sharpe, K. (1991) 'Primary French: More Phoenix than Dodo Now', *Education 3–13*, 19: 1.

——(1992) 'Communication, Culture, Context, Confidence: The Four "Cs" of Primary Modern Language Teaching', *Language Learning Journal*, 6.

12

Developing primary MFL
A teacher-led, community-focused approach

David Frost

Readers who might have turned to this chapter in the hope of finding a ready-made training package to support the implementation of modern foreign languages (MFL) in the primary school may well experience disappointment. Unless, of course, they are persuaded by my argument for an alternative way of thinking about the problem of teacher expertise and curriculum development.

The pilot scheme launched in England in the 1960s demonstrated that primary MFL was not a cost-effective proposition (Burstall *et al.*, 1974). The input/output approach to evaluation used at that time suggested that the somewhat modest gains in linguistic competence could only be sustained by vast expenditure on training which, in the light of an economic downturn, seemed unjustified. The final decision was that it was simply not worth it. Hawkins' account of these events draws upon a report written by Peter Hoy, the staff HMI for Modern Languages at the time, who said that, even if Burstall had recommended an expansion of the scheme, the consequences would have been financially crippling (Hawkins, 1996). So we could say that the attempt to introduce modern languages into the primary curriculum failed in England because of the expense of addressing the problem of the shortage of teacher expertise.

Hawkins and others called for 'radical solutions' like that adopted in Sweden in which the second language became a compulsory part of the entry qualification at the initial training stage. I want to suggest that this remains an unrealistic proposition for us when we continue to have a chronic shortage of expertise at the secondary stage where the statutory obligation to teach modern languages is already established. If having expertise in modern languages were to become a requirement to enter the profession, we would almost certainly be plunged into a crisis of teacher supply. In any case, even if it were possible to ensure a supply of newly qualified teachers with appropriate language skills, it would still be many years before we could expect to see that expertise translated into an established programme in every school in the UK and, as Johnstone argues, however well qualified primary teachers might be at the outset, they would not have the benefit of the constant reinforcement and practice that secondary languages specialists have and would need to be provided with the means to update their professional knowledge and maintain their expertise throughout their teaching careers (Johnstone, 1997).

So, in the course of this chapter, I would like to argue for radical solutions of a quite different nature; solutions which focus on the continuing professional development (CPD) of serving teachers in the context of a community-based developmental approach.

The idea of a national training strategy

It seems to me unlikely that the UK government is going to commit itself in the foreseeable future to a national training programme for primary MFL when there is already a major commitment to literacy, ICT and numeracy. The costs of such programmes are considerable and funding is limited. However, besides these financial arguments, I want to suggest that there are more compelling reasons for rejecting the idea of a national implementation and training strategy. I believe that such a strategy would fail to embed modern languages in the primary curriculum in such a way as to make it self-sustaining. My argument is rooted in a particular view of curriculum reform and teacher professionalism which draws heavily on John Elliott's analysis of the model of curriculum development underpinning the present National Curriculum. He argues that the 'logic of technical rationality pervades the Educational Reform Act' (Elliott, 1991: 144). According to this logic, education is seen rather like a manufacturing process having fixed targets for the product. Standards are pre-specified by the parent company (the state) and the producers (schools) are forced to compete on the basis of their relative ability to meet those specifications. This drive towards standardisation leads to training scenarios which are expensive and not necessarily effective. There is a fundamental assumption in this way of looking at the problem that the responsibility for the decision to develop a particular aspect of the curriculum is firmly located at the centre; national policy must then be implemented through a fully-funded training programme designed to produce uniform practice.

I want to argue that there are profound difficulties with an approach based on this model and that we need an alternative vision of curriculum development which faces up to the present realities as far as primary MFL in England is concerned. We need instead a vision of curriculum development which takes seriously the role of the 'agency' of individual teachers and the capacity of schools to manage change within their particular social and cultural contexts. In the 1970s, that seminal figure of the curriculum development movement, Lawrence Stenhouse, coined a memorable phrase: 'But there can be no educational development without teacher development; and the best means of development is not by clarifying ends but by criticising practice' (Stenhouse, 1975: 83). Much later, voices from the school improvement movement played with Stenhouse's words and argued that 'there can be no teacher development without school development'. I shall now explore in greater detail these two interdependent dimensions of curriculum development.

The teacher as an agent of change

The term 'agency' I take to mean the human capacity for independent judgement and practical action, which is arguably at the heart of professionalism. I find Michael Fullan's research on the process of educational change helpful here (Fullan, 1991). He has pointed out that there are three dimensions to the change process. The first two dimensions – *materials* and *pedagogical practices* – are easily identified as being part of the same thing; they clearly go hand in hand although I dare say that we can all think of cases where it has been falsely assumed that change can be managed by simply distributing new materials. But even where there may be sufficient understanding of the way in which certain innovations demand a rethink of teaching methods, we are still likely to come across attempts to manage change which fail to recognise the extent to which an innovation requires a significant shift in teachers' fundamental *values and beliefs* – Fullan's third dimension. This seems to be particularly true in the case of primary MFL in that the UK's full participation in the European Union is still brought into question at the political level and thus to consider teaching modern languages in the primary school when it is not a compulsory part of the National Curriculum requires a considerable degree of conviction on the part of the teachers involved.

It is also arguable that the kind of knowledge required for primary MFL is different to that required for other aspects of the primary curriculum in that it seems to demand so much in terms of the teacher's personal knowledge. The teacher's ability to speak the language is such a significant resource and so the 'subject content knowledge' (Shulman, 1986) is of a different kind to that required in most other subjects.

So, any model of development we might adopt in relation to primary MFL has to be responsive to questions of the teachers' beliefs about, for example, the value of language learning, the importance of intercultural activities, and the politics of European identity. It has also to take full account of the widespread assumption that an extraordinary degree of personal mastery in the target language is required in order to begin to teach it.

The nub of the problem is this: in order successfully to implement primary MFL we need to increase quite radically the number of primary teachers having sufficient expertise and the confidence to tackle the job of teaching a modern foreign language. This is a problem of a wholly different nature to that of requiring teachers to review and develop a policy for something which was already a taken-for-granted part of current provision to ensure compliance with the National Curriculum statutory orders. Primary MFL requires a massive commitment in terms of cultural values, political beliefs and personal knowledge, on the part of those teachers who may have only GCSE (General Certificate of Secondary Education) French and it may well prove extremely difficult to mobilise that sort of personal commitment particularly given the financial implications of mounting a national training and implementation package.

So there are issues to do with the agency of the teachers but they cannot be considered independently of issues to do with the role of the school as an organisation in managing the process of change, mobilising individual teachers and providing the ongoing support they will surely need.

The school's capacity for change

Following the Educational Reform Act of 1988 the teaching profession in England and Wales became accustomed to a rapid pace of change on so many different fronts that the collegial and collaborative cultures developed in the 1980s began to yield to the forces of managerialism and directive leadership (Webb and Vulliamy, 1996). Now, if my argument about the agency of teachers stands up, we would have to say that the conditions generated by these forces cannot be ideal for the development of primary MFL. Headteachers may well be able to direct members of their staff to attend meetings for the purposes of agreeing the levels of attainment to be reported to parents, for example, but they are unlikely to achieve the desired outcomes in MFL by simply instructing them to develop good French accents or positive attitudes to a foreign culture.

So, if primary MFL is to flourish, headteachers and governing bodies need to be adopting change strategies which can empower teachers as curriculum developers and professional learners rather than ones of which the teachers will feel themselves to be the victims. This means avoiding the shortcomings of those top-down staff development strategies designed to achieve implementation of a particular innovation in record-breaking time and choosing instead to concentrate on developing a climate for successful curriculum and professional development. In Fullan and Hargreaves' words this involves the development of 'total teachers' through strategies which take seriously 'the teacher's purpose, the teacher as a person and the real world context in which teachers work' (Fullan and Hargreaves, 1992: 27).

A useful model of educational change linked to whole school improvement is to be found in the IQEA (Improving the Quality of Education for All) Project, a research-based support strategy in which academics from universities such as Cambridge and Nottingham work with schools throughout the UK and a variety of other countries. A key assumption in the IQEA project is that maximum benefit is to be had when schools identify a small number of clear and well-focused priorities for development (the development of modern languages would be a good example) which are then pursued through a strategy which involves the simultaneous development of what the project team refer to as *the internal conditions* for school development (Ainscow *et al.*, 1994: 10).

The internal conditions which the IQEA team suggest need to be developed are as follows:

- enquiry and reflection,
- collaborative planning,
- involvement,
- staff development,
- co-ordination,
- leadership.

The last item on the list must surely be the starting-point but we need to approach the concept of leadership with some caution. It has been identified as a key characteristic of effective schools (Sammons *et al.*, 1995) but school effectiveness research in general has its critics and in particular, the much vaunted notion of 'firm and purposeful leadership' has been seen by some as arising from values which are anti-educational (Elliott, 1996). What I want to argue for is a view of leadership which is based on a commitment to the maximisation of teachers' agency; one which assumes first of all a proactive role for the Head but assumes also that the Head will encourage and support collaborative decision-making and collaborative planning. This means that leadership has to be shared – not abnegated in favour of some kind of sloppy, in-house democracy – but systematically devolved so that a range of individuals are asked to take on leadership roles according to their particular enthusiasms, knowledge and experience.

I want also to take issue with the inclusion of *staff development* in the list of internal conditions. Barbara MacGilchrist and her colleagues in the London Institute of Education's school improvement team remind us that, 'support for teachers' own learning and development is a key characteristic of the intelligent school' (MacGilchrist *et al.*, 1997: 54) but for me the term *staff development* suggests an approach to professional learning in which the sense of purpose and the initiative rests with someone other than the classroom teacher. Perhaps this is just a matter of the terminology accumulating negative connotations in the way indicated by the following quotation. 'Many staff development initiatives take the form of something that is done to teachers rather than with them, still less by them' (Fullan and Hargreaves, 1992: 27).

My preference would be for a way of thinking about professional learning as a process which is integral to the professional work of teachers. I would suggest that if we concentrate on the development of the kind of *leadership* and *co-ordination* which leads to *collaborative planning* based on thorough *reflection and enquiry*, we are most likely to produce the conditions which favour the sort of professional learning arising from teacher-led developmental activities. In order to maximise that professional learning, we need to provide support for teachers' participation in decision-making and for the expression of their sense of purpose as individuals; in short we need to ensure their *involvement*.

However, the principle of involvement should not just be applied to teachers and it would be wrong to suggest that teachers' voices should be paramount. Certainly, we need, for the sake of an enhanced professionalism, to recognise and sponsor the teacher's voice but, at the same time, we need to recognise the legitimate role of the wider society in shaping a vision of what our children's education should be. This tension between *voice* and *vision* is arguably a key characteristic of post-modern society (Hargreaves, 1994) and it is one which can be made to work for the development of primary MFL. For the IQEA team, *involvement* is meant to include, in addition to the teachers, the students/pupils, the parents, the governors and the community and I believe that if we focus on the local community and its role in curriculum innovation and development, not only will we be able to resolve the tension between vision and voice but we may also be able to identify a source of practical help for the development of primary MFL.

One of the most damaging effects of the reforms of the late 1980s and early 1990s has been the undermining of the place of the concept of community in educational endeavours. According to Husbands, these reforms introduced 'market-led concepts such as competition, purchaser-provider distinctions and the empowerment...of consumers...Schools were encouraged to think of themselves as competing businesses, providing services and purchasing support and supply systems as they required them' (Husbands, 1996: 9). Within such a competitive environment it has been increasingly difficult for schools to collaborate with each other and for schools to work with their local communities in ways which are authentically educational rather than focused on marketing the school. Nevertheless, the arguments for the idea of community have been consistently voiced and I want to draw on these to explore ways in which the concept of community can serve the development of primary MFL.

The importance of community

First, as I have already suggested, it is important that the school acts as a community in which teachers are working together to support change. The development of *communities* in generating the school's capacity for improvement and the creative energy which can transform the curriculum is well documented (Woods, 1993). In addition, the benefits of integrating modern languages into the primary curriculum and into the fabric of the social life of the school have been argued elsewhere in this volume and this must surely depend on a high level of collaboration among the teaching staff. There is currently a great deal of rhetoric about the transformation of organisational cultures for the sake of change but there is a difference between a collaborative organisation and a community in which persons and their differences are respected and valued (Fielding, 1996).

Second, it is important that schools extend their sense of community to include other schools in their locality. Professor Maurice Galton is just one of many voices calling for the development of collaborative arrangements whereby schools organise themselves into clusters or consortia. 'There are sound arguments for clusters developing their own joint planning structures and supporting these development plans by establishing common staffing policies whereby a range of curriculum specialisms are covered by the cluster itself' (Galton quoted in Webb and Vulliamy, 1996: 448).

Not only do such arrangements enable schools to share scarce resources such as teachers with expert knowledge and expensive curriculum materials but they also provide a context for professional learning. Staff development budgets in primary schools are pitifully small but a cluster of schools which includes at least one secondary school would be able to support a development project in which expertise is used creatively to support those whose expert knowledge may be slight.

The third sense in which I want to invoke the idea of community relates to the long if not particularly well established tradition of community schooling (Poster, 1982; Allen *et al.*, 1987). It is perhaps regrettable that innovation under the banner of community education has been motivated to a great extent by the need for desperate measures in socially disadvantaged areas (Midwinter, 1975) but the principles underpinning this tradition are sound and are particularly applicable to primary MFL. Community education assumes that the school exists to serve its local community directly, to reflect its values to some extent and to draw upon it as a resource. I suggest that primary MFL is most likely to be successful when the decision to include it in the curriculum is rooted in the expressed desires, needs and values of the local community. There is already plenty of evidence referred to elsewhere in the volume that many primary schools in the UK are responding to the local community in this way. It follows that, if there is a certain level of enthusiasm within the local community, then there is also likely to be some expertise which could be brought into the school either on a voluntary or professional basis. Members of the community who might, for example, be native French speakers or trained linguists could be deployed to work with classroom teachers to embed the target language in the curriculum and to teach children directly. However, it may be more effective in the long term to help the teachers to develop their own linguistic competence. There is some evidence of the enormous potential of community involvement in educational projects. Peter Woods, for example, has documented the way in which members of the community can be drawn into primary schools projects which not only have dramatic learning outcomes for pupils but also for the teachers involved (Woods, 1993). Reaching out into the community in this way has been encouraged by the Educational Business Partnerships movement although such activities have tended to flourish more in the secondary school context where local arrangements have ensured the provision of work experience placements and some additional funding to support desired initiatives. Clearly, this sort of development makes more immediate sense when there is a direct flow of school leavers into local industry but there is no reason why primary headteachers should not seek help in a similar way. There are doubtless other points of contact such as twinning associations which primary headteachers can approach with a view to securing financial or practical support for the development of primary MFL.

So far I have talked about what the community can do for the school but there is no doubt also that the school is well placed to provide a service for the community. There is evidence of continuing enthusiasm amongst adults for 'lifelong learning' and, according to a recent Audit Commission report (Crequer, 1988), local authorities are not keeping up with demand. There is an opening here for schools to provide modern languages courses for adults who may be prepared to learn alongside pupils or alongside teachers. This may be simply a way for a cluster of schools to recoup the costs of employing a languages specialist but the effects could be more far-reaching. The involvement of adults other than teachers in the life of the school can be seen to have a range of benefits; the experiences which adult members of the community can bring to the life of the school open up possibilities for making the curriculum more relevant and help to encourage parents to become less suspicious of schools and more involved in their children's education (Nixon et al., 1996).

So what are the implications for national policy of an approach to the development of primary MFL which is focused on the local community?

A national framework of support for local government

Given the present circumstances, perhaps we should be calling on the government not to include primary MFL in the National Curriculum but rather to provide support for those communities wanting to develop it for themselves. This would mean change strategies which empower schools and their communities and recognise their differences. Schools, like individual teachers, are all different, each school having its particular social context, which means a particular catchment with particular expectations and assumptions on the part of parents and governors. Each school has its particular history in terms of the professional culture, the quality of collaborative relationships within the school, between schools in the local area and with the local authority (Nias *et al.*, 1989). Most crucially, it also means that each school has particular resources in the community which can be drawn upon in the ways suggested above.

There is a precedent for this rather more open-ended approach to managing development; in the 1980s the government's Training Agency (formerly the Manpower Services Commission) launched the Technical and Vocational Educational Initiative (TVEI). The agency established broad criteria and then offered funding through a bidding system referred to as *categorical funding* (Dale *et al.*, 1990). A great deal of local creativity was stimulated as schools, consortia and local education authorities (LEAs) devised development schemes shaped by their local conditions and aspirations but which also matched the national criteria. One of the most significant outcomes of TVEI was the development of a new approach to the funding of staff development. This approach now underpins the current Teacher Training Agency's policy on the distribution of funds to support in-service training courses for teachers. The strength of the approach is that it offers choice so that teachers, schools and local authorities do not become demoralised and over-stretched by imposed change. It is significant that, at the time of the launch of the government's cherished literacy hour, the teacher unions called for a delay, insisting that the Secretary of State should provide extra training if he wants to see it established in the primary schools. Because the government has taken this action and imposed its will on the nation's schools, it has diminished the scope of teachers' professional judgement and provided those who are reluctant to examine their own practice with a perfect alibi which no amount of costly training will remedy.

I want now to set out proposals for an approach to the development of primary MFL which rests on the collaborative actions of teachers and others at a local community level.

Initiating a local development of primary MFL

First of all, it is important for a local grouping to form itself around a secondary school partly because it will have a significant repository of linguistic expertise and partly because it will already have in place liaison arrangements with the feeder primary schools. The question of primary–secondary transfer is central and stands in need of urgent attention. This cluster formation around a secondary school has been the bedrock of the Scottish primary MFL development (see accounts elsewhere in this volume) because of the need to try to achieve coherence in the language learning experience of pupils throughout the years of compulsory schooling. However, this is not to say that the secondary school should assume the leading role, rather that it should see itself as an equal partner with as much to learn from primary colleagues as it has to contribute. The secondary school is in a good position to communicate with the primary schools, to invite them to participate in a development project and to host an initial meeting. For this reason it may well be the case that the first steps in the initiation of a project would be taken by a senior manager in the secondary school who might call a meeting of representatives of all the primary feeder schools. Following such a meeting it is suggested that some kind of working group is formed in order to pursue a number of steps towards the establishment of a development project; these would include locating sources of external support, identifying expertise and the co-ordination of strategic planning.

Locating external support

One of the crucial choices to be made would be concerned with the nature of external support. Development in schools is more likely to succeed if it is supported by external agents who should have a broader view and can provide advice which is relatively uncluttered by the inevitable vested interests and traditions of the local situation (Somekh, 1988) although it must be said at the outset that the cluster itself must retain the initiative and exercise ruthless discrimination about the services that external agencies might be offering. The LEA is an obvious source of such support although this provision has diminished over the past few years because of the Conservative government's policy of 'marketisation' in educational services (Bridges and Husbands, 1996). University departments of education can also provide support for curriculum research and development and have the added advantage of being able to offer accreditation towards further academic awards for the teachers involved.

So, what kind of help might external agencies be able to provide? First, they might be able to bring to bear fresh *curricular and pedagogical knowledge* and are likely to have the skills to help teachers explore these (Hargreaves and Hopkins, 1991). This knowledge is likely to be both based on research and developed through contact with large numbers of schools and through wider professional networking on a national and even international scale. Linked to the provision of specialist and up-to-date knowledge is the notion of *leadership*: the framing and articulating of a vision. This is the sort of provision which LEAs are most likely to offer in that they have always been in the business of developing policies and providing leadership, or at least co-ordination, to schools in their constituency. Clusters need to be particularly wary of LEA officers bearing visions of course and in the case of primary MFL can afford to be choosy, only taking on such visions if they make a good fit with the circumstances in the cluster and if the LEA is offering a partnership arrangement which is likely to be empowering rather than dictatorial. The local HEI (higher education institution) might also be a source of a vision about primary MFL but this would depend on whether the subject is part of their research agenda.

Given what I have argued about empowerment, it is important to recognise the value of forms of external support which are likely to enhance the *process* of development. For example, an external agent can act as a 'critical friend' able to challenge colleagues' thinking within a supportive and constructive framework (Hargreaves and Evans, 1997). They might offer this by attending meetings of a steering or planning group or they may offer more elaborate arrangements involving support in the classroom or ongoing support for enquiry and reflection within the cluster schools. HEIs in particular are more likely to be able to offer this kind of support either as part of a *collaborative research* project or as part of an *accreditation* package. I suggest that an ideal scenario is one where a cluster invites both the LEA and the HEI to work with them so that the project can tap into CPD funding and research funding to support a research and development initiative in which the teachers engage in *action research*. The evidence arising from such a process would constitute the data base for a university-led research project and can also be compiled by teachers and submitted for the purposes of accreditation. Accreditation towards further academic awards is seen by many teachers as an irksome irrelevance which is simply bolted on to the practical business of curriculum or professional development in a way which is inauthentic and unhelpful. However, there have been significant developments such as *'reflective action planning'*; a process in which teachers are provided with a framework of guidance and support leading to more systematic enquiry-based development work, evidence of which is presented in the form of a portfolio. I have previously published a detailed package of guidelines, facsimiles and workshop materials which can be used as a framework by a collaborative group such as the one proposed here (Frost, 1997).

The second strategic step which the proposed working group would want to consider would be the identification and recruitment of sources of expertise in languages.

Identifying and using languages expertise

There is evidence that where schools are working in an isolated and non-developmental way they often choose simply to 'buy in' a trained languages teacher or even a native speaker without any teacher training or experience either to run an extra-curricular activity or to teach a series of discrete language lessons. This is likely to have limited impact on the school concerned and is inefficient as far as the community of schools is concerned. I suggest that there are more efficient ways to deploy such expertise; a cluster could find trained linguists or native speakers living within the community and deploy them in support and training roles so that the widest possible range of teachers can draw upon their expertise. One school employed native speakers to build a bank of materials including tape recordings which were copied and made available to all the teachers across the cluster. Such linguists are invaluable to help teachers with very limited language skills to develop their repertoire through language workshops which could be combined with adult study sessions for other adults in the community.

A word of warning, however: there is some anecdotal evidence which suggests that bringing in language specialists can have a markedly disempowering effect on the primary generalist teachers. It is perhaps inevitable that, in any field of endeavour, from changing a tap washer to operating new computer software, if there are experts to hand we are liable to become passive and wait for them to take the lead. Such passivity leads to a diminution rather than a growth in capability. It is absolutely vital, therefore, for all members of the partnership to be self-conscious about this and to ensure that the specialists do not have the leading role thrust upon them because of a lack of confidence on the part of the non-specialists.

Strategic planning

Once the personnel has been identified, the cluster group is in a position to proceed but it is essential that the development is co-ordinated; this means mandating an individual or small group to plan the development work. It may be that one of the external agencies can be asked to fulfil this function or it may be possible to deploy shared resources to provide a teacher within the cluster with extra time to devote to such a role. A co-ordinator or co-ordinating group should produce a development plan in which there is clarity about:

- the scope of the project;
- the roles and responsibilities of all participants;
- the resources available and how they are to be used;
- the costs of the operation and the sources of funding;
- the arrangements for support;
- the time scale after which the project will be reviewed;
- the outcomes with some idea of success criteria;
- the procedures for evaluation and review of the project.

The development plan needs to be the instrument by which intentions are made visible and agreement of all interested parties secured.

Evidence-based development

I suggest that any such development plan should foreground the role of systematic enquiry and reflection and ensure that it is focused on the classroom. The essential point is that there can be no single, fixed solution for every set of circumstances and so the cluster and the individual teachers within it have to determine what works for them. This may mean a period of experimentation where evidence of what is currently being tried out in classrooms across the cluster is opened up to scrutiny by the whole group. This might be achieved by teachers visiting each other's classrooms to observe according to some agreed schedule or it might be that the cluster can draw upon the services of a researcher or LEA adviser who can carry out a series of observations. The cluster group can then enter into a debate about the benefits of the variety of aims, strategies and outcomes in evidence and move towards a more consistent approach. This is likely to entail some joint decisions about the deployment of available resources; for example, a cluster may decide that the specialist languages teacher employed in one of the cluster schools could be better deployed across the consortium in a support role or that a joint scheme of work could be developed. If there is a low level of languages teaching at the beginning of the project or no languages teaching at all, the decisions will have to be concerned with rather more basic questions such as what could be taught and by whom.

The process of collaborative enquiry can be enriched and made more powerful by the use of the 'reflective action planning' model in which the teachers develop their own portfolios of evidence and engage in critical debate about their own classroom practice. For the teachers concerned, the systematic action planning and documentation of the process of enquiry, reflection and strategic action support a high level of professional learning and the subsequent accreditation towards further professional qualifications is an added bonus (Frost et al., forthcoming).

Such a local, enquiry-based approach to development may be said to be dangerously inward-looking, likely to be conservative and based on the taken-for-granted and perhaps limited assumptions of the particular participants. For this reason it is important that clusters seek support from external agencies such as LEA advisory units or from university departments of education. However, even then, insularity may still be a problem. Research has shown that *networking* with practitioners in other schools is a powerful source of teachers' professional learning (Leiberman and Grolnick, 1996) and an essential part of the process of opening up curriculum proposals to wider scrutiny. It is important therefore for local primary MFL clusters to ensure that they have sufficient contact with a range of other practitioners and interested parties. Fortunately recent developments in information and communication technology (ICT) have transformed our ability to engage in such networking. The Internet provides an efficient means by which local primary MFL clusters can link up with each other and with other networks across the world. These links enable all of us to examine the widest possible range of alternative practices and to open up our own practice to scrutiny and challenge.

In concluding this chapter I want to summarise my argument and locate it within an emergent discourse about 'rebuilding teachers' professionalism' (McLaughlin, 1997). McLaughlin's contribution to this discourse is based on the American experience but seems none the less valid here in the UK.

Though the outlines of a new policy paradigm for professional development are appearing, the hand work of developing concrete exemplars of policies and intersecting practices that model 'top-down support for bottom-up reform' has just begun. In this reform era, old models of 'staff development', 'in-servicing' or 'teacher training' are well and truly understood as inadequate and wrongheaded.

(McLaughlin, 1997: 81)

What I hope I have demonstrated here is that there could be a way to develop the teaching of modern languages in the primary school which, while it may not lead to blanket implementation within a short time span, is nevertheless realistic and likely to be more productive in the long run. It requires the central authorities to provide leadership and support aimed at enablement rather than compulsion and which empowers teachers and other members of local communities to build programmes reflecting their actual circumstances and aspirations. It makes significant demands on teachers and others in terms of their commitment to their own professional learning but it at least enables them to exercise a choice and to develop the curriculum according to their professional judgement. It therefore stands a far greater chance of being successful than an approach which denies teacher professionalism and does nothing to enhance it.

But this approach cannot be made to work in isolation; it has to be seen as part of a general rethink about the teachers' role in curriculum development. If we have learnt anything about in-service teacher education, it must surely be that we need to avoid such expensive follies as training programmes designed to shoehorn a new government initiative into the primary curriculum. We need instead to focus on strategies which are part of a 'new deal for teachers' (Hargreaves, 1997) in which the pursuit of a mature and robust professionalism becomes the main priority.

References

Ainscow, M., Hopkins, D., Southworth, G. and West, M. (1994) *Creating the Conditions for School Improvement*, London: David Fulton Publishers.

Allen, G., Bastiani, J., Martin, I. and Richards, K. (eds) (1987) *Community Education: An Agenda for Educational Reform*, Milton Keynes: Open University Press.

Bridges, D. and Husbands, C. (1996) *Consorting and Collaborating in the Education Market Place*, London: Falmer Press.

Burstall, C., Jamieson, M., Cohen, S. and Hargreaves, M. (1974) *Primary French in the Balance*, Slough: NFER Publishing.

Crequer, N. (1988) 'Ridges and Troughs in the Spread of Adult Learning', *TES*, 13 March.

Dale, R., Bowe, R., Harris, D., Loveys, M., Moore, R., Shilling, C., Sikes, P., Trevitt, J. and Valsecchi, V. (1990) *The TVEI Story: Policy, Practice and Preparation for the Work Force*, Milton Keynes: Open University Press.

Elliott, J. (1991) *Action Research for Educational Change*, Buckingham: Open University Press.

—— (1996) 'School Effectiveness Research and its Critics: Alternative Visions of Schooling', *Cambridge Journal of Education*, 26, 2, 199–224.

——(1998) *The Curriculum Experiment: Meeting the Challenge of Social Change*, Buckingham: Open University Press.

Fielding, M. (1996) 'Beyond Collaboration: On the Importance of Community', in Bridges, D. and Husbands, C. (eds) *Consorting and Collaborating in the Education Market Place*, London: Falmer Press.

Frost, D. (1997) *Reflective Action Planning for Teachers: A Guide to Teacher-led School and Professional Development*, London: David Fulton Publishers.

Frost, D., Durrant, J., Head, M. and Holden, G. (forthcoming) *Teacher-led School Improvement*, London: Falmer Press.

Fullan, M. (1991) *The New Meaning of Educational Change*, London: Cassell.

Fullan, M. and Hargreaves, A. (1992) *What's Worth Fighting For In Your School?*, Buckingham: Open University Press.

Hargreaves, A. (1994) *Changing Teachers, Changing Times: Teachers' Work and Culture in the Post-modern Age*, London: Cassell.

——(1997) 'From Reform to Renewal: A New Deal for Teachers', in A. Hargreaves and R. Evans (eds) *Beyond Educational Reform: Bringing Teachers Back In*, Buckingham: Open University Press, 105–25.

Hargreaves, D. and Hopkins, D. (1991) *The Empowered School: The Management and Practice of Development Planning*, London: Cassell.

Hawkins, E. (1996) 'The Early Teaching of Modern Languages: A Pilot Scheme', in E. Hawkins (ed.) *Thirty Years of Language Teaching*, London: CILT.

Husbands, C. (1996) 'Schools, Markets and Collaboration: New Models for Educational Polity', in D. Bridges and C. Husbands (eds) *Consorting and Collaborating in the Education Market Place*, London: Falmer Press, 9–20.

Johnstone R. (1997) *Case Study Notes: Researching Primary MFL in Scotland*, paper presented at Euro-Conference CELTE, University of Warwick, April 1997.

Leiberman, A. and Grolnick, M. (1996) 'Networks and Reform in American Education', *Teachers College Record*, 98, 1, 7–45.

MacGilchrist, B., Myers, K. and Reed, J. (1997) *The Intelligent School*, London: Paul Chapman Publishing.

McLaughlin, M. (1997) 'Rebuilding Professionalism in the United States', in A. Hargreaves and R. Evans (eds) *Beyond Educational Reform: Bringing Teachers Back In*, Buckingham: Open University Press, 77–93.

Midwinter, E. (1975) 'Curriculum and the EPA Community School', in M. Golby *et al.* (eds) *Curriculum Design*, London: Croom Helm.

Nias, J., Southworth, G. and Yeomans, R. (1989) *Staff Relations in the Primary School: A Study of Organisational Cultures*, London: Cassell.

Nixon, J., Martin, J., McKeown, P. and Ranson, S. (1996) *Encouraging Learning: Towards a Theory of the Learning School*, Buckingham: Open University Press.

Poster, C. (1982) *Community Education: Its Development and Management*, London: Heinemann.

Sammons, P., Hillman, J. and Mortimore, P. (1995) *Key Characteristics of Effective Schools: A Review of School Effectiveness Research: A Report by the Institute of Education for the Office for Standards in Education*, London: OFSTED.

Shulman, L. (1986) 'Those Who Understand: Knowledge Growth in Teaching', *Educational Researcher*, February, 4–14.

Somekh, B. (1988) 'Support or Interference: Observations on Working with School-based INSET', *Cambridge Journal of Education*, 18, 2, 191–207.

Stenhouse, L. (1975) *An Introduction to Curriculum Research and Development*, London: Heinemann Educational Books.

Webb, R. and Vulliamy, G. (1996) 'Impact of ERA on Primary Management', *British Educational Research Journal*, 22, 4, 441–58.

Woods, P. (1993) *Critical Events in Teaching and Learning*, London: Falmer Press.

13

A research agenda for modern languages in the primary school

Richard Johnstone

Introduction

The Fourth General Objective of the European Commission (EC) White Paper (1995) advocates that school systems should aim to help all learners develop proficiency in three Community languages, which for many though not all pupils would be national languages of member states of the European Union. Where possible a start should be made with the second language during pre-school education, so that this may be developed throughout the primary period and a third introduced at secondary. The White Paper indeed implies that much more than language competence is required: personal development, intercultural learning and the cultivation of a European identity to complement children's existing local and national identities will also be at stake. This overarching policy objective sets the scene for a rich and varied research agenda in relation to languages in primary education.

In keeping with the above policy, DG22 of the EC invited a group of six researchers to review the recent research on languages in primary and pre-primary education across the various member states of the EU. The group (Blondin *et al.*, 1998) were able to identify over sixty publications that represented genuine research. Many others contained some research but were more developmental, speculative or political. Since the review is a separate publication, it would not be appropriate to present its detail here. However, as one of its authors, I shall refer briefly to a small number of the research projects mentioned in it, not in order to describe these but rather to discuss what they might mean for our future research agenda.

The review sets out to chart the relationship between 'contextual factors' and 'outcomes'. The context for languages at primary school can vary enormously both across and within countries and hence care has to be taken in interpreting outcomes. In addition, 'outcomes' must also be interpreted in relation to 'intentions', and the review indicates that a range of different intentions were at play. In some cases there was a clear intention to develop an initial competence in one foreign language, so that secondary education could build further on this; but in other cases the intention was to expose children to a variety of languages so as to help them develop an underlying metalinguistic and intercultural awareness that would support their subsequent learning of one or more languages.

From now on, although the acronym MLPS is a Scottish invention, I will use it when referring to the teaching of a modern foreign language at primary school in any member state where the agenda is one of language learning rather than language awareness and where there is a relatively modest allocation of time per week, falling far short of partial immersion for example. So far as 'outcomes' are concerned, the review does not provide evidence of MLPS making a substantial difference to children's language attainments at secondary. Such positive evidence as there is (e.g. Low *et. al.*, 1995; Kahl and Knebler, 1996) is tentative and matched by more cautionary evidence elsewhere (e.g. Genelot, 1996). It should be noted, though, that thus far very little research has been published on this key aspect.

A major component of any future research agenda for MLPS must therefore be to follow children's progress through their primary education and into at least the initial years of secondary, in order to ascertain whether (and if so, in what ways and to what extent) their experiences at secondary do actually build on what the research has indicated they experienced at primary. The review presents a more positive picture of 'outcomes' when these are evaluated within or at the end of primary education, with some studies suggesting considerable progress in learning the foreign language and others pointing to development of metalinguistic and intercultural awareness. However, the group of six were not able to find any research which showed a clear connection between the development of metalinguistic and intercultural awareness at primary and consequent success in learning a particular foreign language at secondary. This does not imply that an effect of this sort does not occur, but again it simply means that this potentially important link has not yet been established by research.

A second item on the research agenda for the future then must be to explore the relationship between exposure to a variety of languages at primary (with the intention of engendering metalinguistic and intercultural awareness) and the subsequent learning of one or more foreign languages. Does the one create a useful precondition for the other, e.g. in the case of children with difficulties in their (or their school's) first language?

Reports

I shall now turn to a small number of fairly recent publications (most of them featuring in the review), in order to highlight certain issues that will be important for our future MLPS research agenda.

One of the boldest innovations in recent years has taken place in France in the second phase of national development. In the first phase, piloted during 1989–92, teaching was done from CM2 onwards (with pupils aged

10) by a variety of teachers, including visiting native speakers. In view of the difficulties in establishing this model convincingly across the country it was decided to develop video material that would be available to primary school teachers in CE1 (pupils aged 7), that would initiate a four-year introduction to a foreign language at primary. The video material was made available in various languages and with a range of native-speaker equivalent models, including children of the same age. It would provide a major source of foreign-language input, thereby allowing class teachers, many of whom would have only limited proficiency in the language, to play a more facilitative role in the fifteen minutes per day devoted to this purpose. The 1997 report of the National Expert Group of the Ministry of Education indicated that initially 13,400 cassettes for CE1 had been distributed for English, 3,600 for German, 1,800 for Spanish and 1,600 for Italian. The videos were of good quality, liked by the children and favoured by their parents. However, problems were identified: the objectives pertaining to the use of video had not been thought through with sufficient clarity; the phonological quality of much of the classroom interaction involving teachers and pupils left much to be desired; and English was widely adopted as the foreign language, even in some cases by teachers who in fact were stronger in Spanish or German.

Within the Ministry initiative a special study was conducted by Luc and colleagues (1996), drawing on classroom observations, discussions and lesson transcriptions. Their report shows that the teachers made only limited use of the textual support material that accompanied the videos, e.g. lists of language functions, and had only a vague notion of what their pupils should have been expected to acquire by the end of their first year. They also noted a disparity between the apparent level of foreign-language competence of the class teachers and the levels which they as researchers noted in class. When used more or less on their own by teachers who showed limited competence in the language, the videos had hardly any positive effect on children's learning. The children were able to gain a general sense of the contexts represented on screen, but they needed to learn how to focus more on words, i.e. on the verbal as well as the non-verbal aspects of meaning.

The above account, which is not intended to cover all aspects of this important initiative, allows me to highlight three issues pertinent to an MLPS research agenda. First, how might video best be utilised for the benefit of children aged 7–11 learning a foreign language? What strategies of information-processing do they possess and what ones do they need to acquire in order to comprehend verbal as well as non-verbal meaning? What competences do teachers need in order to facilitate this process? Second, how might busy class teachers with limited proficiency in a foreign language acquire the knowledge and skills necessary for evaluating their own contribution to lessons, so that there are no worrying disparities between their apparent and their realised performance? Third, what might be done in order to develop a research-based picture of what children may reasonably be expected to do after each year of their primary school experience?

Although I have chosen the French initiative in order to illustrate these research agenda items, experience elsewhere shows they are in no way limited to one country. Let me explore the third of these items in more detail. Will our picture of what children 'can do' be based on specially devised tests? (If so, exactly what abilities will these be testing, and what procedures, criteria and rating scales would be appropriate?). Or, would it be preferable to rely on teachers' professional judgements in relation to speci-fied national levels? (If so, how are these levels to be validated, and how reliable can teachers' judgements be?). Or, would it be more appropriate to find ways of providing a linguistic analysis of children's performance, ideally on a range of tasks and over a period of time, in order to understand more clearly how progression takes place? (If so, what tools would be appropriate for the analysis of children's productions? Might it be possible to use concor-dancing software, for example?) Or, would it be possible to make use of all three of these approaches, using the first (tests plus criteria and rating scales) and the third (linguistic analysis) in order to find ways of refining and ulti-mately validating the second (nationally prescribed levels)?

It is appropriate to mention one other recently published research report on MLPS in France, by Genelot (1996), this time based on the pre-video phase, centred on the Dijon area. The evaluation sought to measure the extent to which MLPS had contributed to effective improvement at secondary. The use of multivariate analysis permitted an estimation to be made of the relative weighting of different groups of variables, with three main groups being found to be children's socio-demographic background, their general ability as measured by performance in French (their own or their school's first language) and the organisation of material and teaching. Another influential factor was the amount and distribution of time. The longer the period of initiation, the better the level attained by the pupils, though there did appear to be a saturation threshold above which increased time was less effective, particularly with slower learners; and frequent short lessons were more successful than less frequent longer ones. After one year at secondary the MLPS pupils were slightly ahead of the comparison group but this advantage had disappeared by the end of the second year. Moreover, MLPS was significantly linked to less success in French, possibly because of the reduced amount of time for French because of the need to make space for the foreign language.

So far as our research agenda is concerned, let me signal three key issues that arise from the Genelot research. First, the effects (positive or negative) of MLPS on performance in the child's (or at least the school's) first language. In principle, there ought to be a two-way flow of transferable skill, so that each supports the other. Genelot's research indicates this does not necessarily happen, and therefore it becomes important to identify the sorts of organisation and approach that will allow gains rather than losses to be made at the L1–L2 interface. Second, the notion of a saturation threshold is interesting and has also been mentioned by teachers outside France as a possible factor. This is an area well worth exploring. What does this apparent threshold consist of? Is it similar to the notion of threshold or 'plateau' that is a well-attested characteristic of second-language acquisition? What are the factors that appear to cause this threshold, and can they be manipulated in such a way that children progress beyond it? Third, however, this research has one self-acknowledged limitation. It was not possible to assess pupils' competence in speaking their foreign language. This was a pity, since spoken language was central to the MLPS initiative in France. To my mind, MLPS evaluation research should be grounded on the particular aims of the MLPS initiative, and if competence in spoken language is an aim, then it is important to find some way of building up a valid and reliable picture of what children can do in this respect.

In fact, the assessment of spoken language in MLPS has begun to receive serious attention from researchers. In Kahl and Knebler's (1996) meticulous study of children learning English in Hamburg, the assessment of spoken language was central. Children in classes 3 and 4 were assessed in groups of six, whereas children in Classes 5 and 6 were assessed individually. The procedures, criteria and rating scales they developed will be a useful model for researchers elsewhere. It was praiseworthy that pupil performance was audio-recorded to allow for a more detailed analysis and a check on inter-rater reliability. The report presents real insight into what children, the weak and the strong, could do in classes 3–6. The approach adopted in Scotland (Low et al., 1995) attached similar importance to the assessment of speaking, in their case from Primary 6 (aged 10) to Secondary 2 (aged 13), though the means of achieving this differed from the Hamburg model in certain respects. A linguistic description of pupil production was favoured, based on extensive transcription of what was said during the assessment interviews, leading to an analysis of the transcripts, e.g. number and range of nouns, verbs, adjectives, pronouns, structures used by pupils in the four years from P6 to S2. The same test format was applied to these four year-groups, to see if there was linguistic progression. Would children in S1 and S2 (who had experienced MLPS when at primary) be able to put a richer mixture of language into this common task than children in P6 and P7 (who were still experiencing MLPS)? The Scottish approach is very time-consuming and can only be adopted by research teams with appropriate resources. However, the Kahl and Knebler approach that was subsequently adopted in Hamburg is of considerable interest to the Scottish team in a new national project, this time geared to assessment in modern languages for children aged 11 and 14. For this, simpler yet still valid and reliable procedures will be needed and we are intending to adapt the Kahl and Knebler set of procedures, criteria and rating scales.

It is worthy of note that neither of the above two approaches drew on national or other levels of progression of the sort set out in the UK in the National Curriculum for England and Wales and in Scotland for the national 5–14 programme. These levels are based on a 'climb the ladder' approach and were generated by groups of competent professionals. As such, they are of great interest, though at present for languages they are geared to secondary and neither is designed to take account of MLPS. However, even if they did exist for languages at primary, the problem in principle in using them as a basis for research would be that levels of this sort have not been validated against a properly research-based analysis of what children are actually able to do. This aspect is well exemplified by a study of children's foreign language progression in the initial years of secondary education (in the South of England) by Mitchell and Dickson (1997) which presents a research-based model of progression that in some key respects does not sit well with the hypothesized rungs of the National Curriculum ladder.

The above discussion makes it clear that a substantial component of our future research agenda must pertain to the description, analysis and assessment of children's developing competence in a foreign language during their primary and early secondary education. Among the many problems to be tackled would be: what purposes should assessment serve, at what points should assessments be implemented, and by whom? In what ways may the validity and reliability of the assessments be maximised? How might children's spoken production be assessed in ways that are sensitive and systematic but not too time-consuming? How are we to build up a picture of how children progress from one year to another? How are we to identify suitable procedures, criteria and rating-scales? On what basis might a linguistic description of pupil performance be achieved, and can computers help in this? If children are to be assessed across a number of schools and parts of the country (and perhaps even internationally), how are we to establish the ground that they have all covered in common? To what extent is it fair to assess children on knowledge and skills that they may not have been taught but that they might possibly have acquired incidentally in the MLPS process?

These are not the only questions to ask about assessment but they are sufficient to show how complex the domain is. To my mind as an MLPS research community we will all benefit if there are both macro-studies by large research teams covering a number of schools and more micro-studies by individual researchers that explore in depth one clearly targeted aspect, even if this is in one location only. But why is it important to assess children learning a foreign language at primary? Objections have often been raised that this would be premature, that it would reduce children's enjoyment, that it would put undue pressure on teachers at the very time when their confidence needs building up, that many primary teachers lack the relevant specialist skills and that it would be better to wait until pupils reach secondary. On the other hand, all over Europe national ministries have made a huge commitment to MLPS, and it seems to me that they are entitled to know what sort of return this investment is generating in respect of children's learning. It is equally important that teachers, parents and pupils should learn in a sensitive yet systematic way what it is that children are actually able to do as they progress from one year to another. This will provide vital diagnostic feedback that will inform subsequent teaching. What we therefore need to put on the research agenda is the development of sensitive, user-friendly assessment instruments that can be used comfortably by busy teachers and that will do a valid and reliable job.

Thus far my discussion has centred mainly on MLPS as a means of developing an initial competence in a foreign language. I shall now briefly discuss two other models: metalinguistic awareness and partial immersion.

Metalinguistic awareness and partial immersion

The EC review (Blondin *et al.*, 1998) points to a number of research studies which confirm that children can gain valuable insights into language and culture if they are deliberately introduced to more than one other language at primary and their teacher uses the school's first language in order to encourage them to reflect on and discuss what language is, how it is organised, how languages resemble and differ from each other, what it might be to be a speaker of another language and so on. One study (Charmeux, 1992) in fact brought eight different languages into the pupils' experience with a particularly beneficial effect on children from minority ethnic–linguistic backgrounds, which included the raising of their self-esteem. A major two-volume study (Luc, 1992; Bailly and Luc, 1992) provides fascinating insight into children of 9–10 years of age in a monolingual French environment engaging in a three-language approach (English, German, French) aimed at enhancing their metalinguistic awareness. In this, the children learnt to make a distinction between actual reality and how particular languages classify this. The intention was to prepare them for moving in an unstressed way to a system of representation other than their mother tongue, and so they were engaged in a set of conceptual activities that exploited the skills of observation and reflection that 10-year-old children possess, while also receiving actual practice in the two foreign languages. The second volume provides a detailed account of the underlying cognitive skills that were being developed and illustrates this with extensive transcriptions of lessons and commentary on these. A striking characteristic of the transcripts, however, is the very high level of French as L1 that is used, though there may well have been many lessons, not transcribed, that were based on L2 use. However, a legitimate and thus far unanswered research question does arise concerning the optimum balance between the development of metalinguistic awareness through L1 and the implementation of classroom activities in L2.

For our future research agenda it will be essential to explore what metalinguistic awareness is for different ages and levels of cognitive and other maturity, how it may be taught and (most importantly) what its relation is to the development of actual proficiency in one or more languages. Would it help, for example, if some initial degree of metalinguistic awareness were developed before children begin learning a particular foreign language? Or, should the two run alongside each other? Or, should it be periodically slotted into an overall language learning approach? If the two run alongside each other, what will be the short-term as well as the long-term effects? Will it help children or will it confuse them? The Luc and Bailly volumes take us into fascinating territory but stimulate us into asking questions about the link between language learning and metalinguistic awareness that thus far have not been answered. My visits to Croatia, where in the pilot experiment centred on Zagreb children begin learning French, German or English at age 6, suggest strongly to me that if young children are introduced to grammatical concepts through their own language at around the age of seven, they can transfer these to the learning of their foreign language the following year in ways that benefit their creativity, fluency and accuracy. We would benefit from further studies on this aspect.

It is beyond the scope of the present task to include 'early total immersion', since this is vastly different from MLPS. However, 'early partial immersion', as in bilingual education, does merit discussion, since it is nearer to MLPS, and some MLPS projects could under certain circumstances move in that direction. One of Europe's best-known bilingual programmes is in Vienna. The research report (Peltzer-Karpf and Zangl, 1997) provides classroom data on the key functions exercised by teacher-talk, with transcriptions of actual lessons and a rich set of examples of pupils' utterances at various stages of their development of English as a second language, plus commentary on these. A major advantage of the research was its longitudinal aspect which meant that the same children could be followed through for all four years. The key elements of pupils' linguistic progression are helpfully set out in tabular form. For each of the four years there is detailed information on their spoken output in both natural communication and specially devised psycholinguistic tests. 'Natural communication' contained data organised under the headings of 'teacher-input and interaction', 'pupil–pupil interaction' and 'spontaneous speech', while the psycholinguistic tests contained data organised under 'morphology', 'syntax' and 'semantic/lexicon'.

To offer but one example of the above system in order to demonstrate one aspect of how linguist progression actually occurred: Psycholinguistic Tests data on children's command of 'morphology'. In Year 1 among the key features were 'dominance of stored elements produced with high degree of correctness', 'strong linkage between L1 and L2, with hybrid utterances' and 'production that was hardly self-initiated'. By Year 2 among the descriptors for the same category were: 'manifest system turbulence through creative speech activities linked with production of errors', 'over-generalisation of frequently occurring, simple rules', 'decrease of L1-responses'. By Year 3: 'increase of error production', 'strengthening of creativity', 'decrease of unanalysed chunks', 'extensive stabilisation of simple morpheme flexions'. By Year 4: 'stable morphological framework for the formation of grammatically conditioned modulations of form and new words', 'production of errors is limited to the later development of complex sub-systems of rules'.

Data of this sort teach us a great deal about children's actual progression in a second language. We begin to see, for example, that in highly favourable conditions such as these, accurate control of a grammar system is something that develops only over time. Before this phase is reached, pupils go through quite a lengthy period of what the researchers call 'system turbulence' in which they learn to move beyond the production of stock phrases in order to manipulate language with increasing range and creativity but without at the same time being able to impose complete formal control.

Our research agenda for the future, then, will ideally contain many more studies of this sort, so that as a research community we can build up a picture of how progression operates at different ages and in different contexts. This would give us information which is better than that we have at present concerning whether or not, and if so to what extent, progression follows a universal sequence.

One study of partial immersion conducted in the USA suggests something to us about the difficulty or otherwise of learning particular languages. It is well known, for example, that western adults take longer to develop the same level of proficiency in Japanese than they do in French. Does the same apply to children at primary receiving partial immersion? Thomas, Collier and Abbott's (1993) study involved 1,007 pupils in Fairfax County Primary Schools (FCPS), one of the largest-ever immersion samples in the USA. There was strong parental support from English-speaking parents who wished their children to acquire proficiency in another language. A model of 'early partial immersion' rather than 'early total immersion' was chosen, in order to satisfy possible concerns about the development of children's English. Most of the schools began in Grade 1 but some began in Grade 2, so that the evaluation after two years covered Grades 1–3. Four schools did Spanish, three did Japanese and one French. There was no formal teaching of the target language. It was simply assumed that children's oral proficiency in it would develop through their being taught important subject matter through the language. The target language was used exclusively for teaching mathematics, science and health while English was used for English language arts and social studies.

In the research, account was taken of the performance of three groups of children: the partial immersion (PI) group, a comparison (Comp) group and FCPS children across the county. The Comp group was chosen on the basis of similar performance to the PI group on a Cognitive Abilities Test. The findings after two years showed that the PI and Comp groups significantly outperformed the FCPS group on all measures, even though the FCPS mean was well above the national norm. Moreover, the PI group did as well or slightly better than, the Comp group in mathematics and significantly outperformed them in English language arts. The PI groups in addition were considered to be making excellent progress towards oral proficiency in their particular target languages.

Of particular interest must be the performance of the PI children in Japanese who seemed to be making as much progress as their counterparts in Spanish and French. Young children on total or partial immersion programmes appear to be much less 'fazed' than adults by languages that are very different from their first language. Our future research agenda would benefit greatly from further exploration of this issue.

For our future research agenda the research of Peltzer-Karpf and Zangl provides one of the most sophisticated descriptions of children's L2 development that I have read. The frames of reference and concepts that they use are grounded in educational or psycholinguistic research and will be of value to many researchers elsewhere. Further reports of this sort will gradually help us in Europe to achieve what Canadians have already achieved as a result of some thirty years of researching different forms of immersion: a research-based understanding of the different sorts of outcome that arise from different models such as 'early total', 'early partial', 'delayed total' and 'delayed partial' immersion. In Canada it is possible to make a reasonable prediction as to what the outcomes of each of these models will be, and so the emphasis in Canadian research has recently swung somewhat to researching the classroom processes that occur within these models, so that the best possible outcomes are generated.

I therefore see a major need in Europe for research to be further exploring the relationships between different input models (e.g. 'MLPS', 'early partial immersion' and points in between these), process factors (what takes place overtly and covertly when the language is taught, learnt and used) and outcomes (in terms of language proficiency, metalinguistic awareness and attitudes).

Thus far, my discussion has assumed that the research will be done by researchers working in collaboration with teachers, pupils and others. Very little research has been published that has been undertaken by teachers themselves. Our research agenda for the future surely ought to envisage teachers themselves having an increased role in research, particularly when this relates to their own practice and probably within an action research framework. One positive example of teacher as action-researcher is provided by Smith (1996) who took his small-scale study through to the stages of writing it up and having it published. Many classes in Scottish primary schools are 'composite', i.e. they contain children of different age-groups, often a reflection of the rural situation. In this case the class had seventeen pupils in four age-groups from seven to eleven. With guidance from a supporting national development officer, Smith drew on pupil diaries, his own teacher's diary, audio- and video-recordings, and a pupil questionnaire in order to collect data pertaining to the learning strategies that his pupils used in this composite class. His analysis of video-recorded lessons involving his pupils and a native speaker showed that the 6–8 year-olds relied to a great extent on guessing strategies in order to make sense of the native speaker's input. His brief report shows real insight and is a model of small-scale action research that is closely related to a specific context. It is designed to illuminate an issue that was considered to be important in that context, and is for the benefit of those most immediately involved, i.e. the pupils and teacher.

A major component of our future research agenda then must be to find ways of encouraging busy teachers to investigate aspects of their practice and to communicate their findings to professional colleagues, thereby fostering a culture of professional reflection, exchange and communication that at present is hardly there.

New directions

Thus far I have been arguing that the research of the future can and should arise out of the research of the present. However, to leave it at that would be to offer only a limited vision of a future research agenda for MLPS. What we must also do is anticipate the new directions that the MLPS innovation should take and work out what the research implications of these might be. I offer one possible innovation that in my view would make a major differ-ence. This would consist of primary schools in the UK developing real, everyday working links with primary schools in other European countries. These links would involve large amounts of Information and Communications Technology exchange (via e-mail and Internet) as well as reciprocal visits. They would affect the entire life and ethos of the primary schools partici-pating in the link, including the school staff. Primary schools would then become brokers of intercultural learning and exchange, and the various languages of the partnership would be central to the success of the opera-tion. This view of MLPS as the medium of intercultural learning and exchange is very different from what we have at present and would raise a large number of new and potentially interesting research questions. Among these would be: in what languages will the interactions take place? What will be the actual language needs of the participating teachers? One way of making the initiative work would be for each community to express itself for the most part in its own language. If so, then UK teachers would need to develop good levels of comprehension skill in the language(s) of their part-ners but would have less need to develop high levels of speaking or writing.

However, this is only a starting thought. What would be of interest to the researcher would be to follow this through in order to establish the levels of partial competence that were actually needed.

My final thought concerning a research agenda arises from the fact that much of the best research on MLPS, bilingual education and metalinguistic awareness to which I have referred in this chapter has not been written in English. Perhaps some of the important findings will eventually be published in some form or other in English, but in a way I hope that this will not be the case. English-speaking researchers of MLPS, as part of their personal research agendas, will benefit from possessing or acquiring a high level of reading ability in at least French and German as well as English, in order to keep up with the best work in the field and offer a shining example to the multilingual community of young people that the EC White Paper rightly commends.

References

Bailly, D. and Luc, C. (1992) *Approche d'une langue étrangère à l'école. Volume 2: Étude psycholinguistique et aspects didactiques*, Paris: INRP.

Blondin, C. *et al.* (1998) *Modern Languages in Primary and Pre-primary Education: A Review of Recent Research Within the European Union*, London: CILT.

Charmeux, E. (1992) 'Maîtrise du francais et familiarisation avec d'autres langues', *Repères*, 6, 155–72.

European Commission (1995) *Teaching and Learning. Towards the Learning Society. White Paper on Education and Training*, Luxembourg: Office for Official Publications of the European Commission.

Genelot, S. (1996) *L'enseignement des langues vivantes à l'école primaire: éléments d'évaluation des effets au collège*, Dijon: IRÉDU (Institut de Recherche sur l'Économie de l'Éducation).

Groupe National d'Experts (1996) *L'initiation à une langue vivante au cours élémentaire, première année. Rapport d'étape, mai 1996*, Paris: Ministère de l'Éducation nationale, de l'enseignement supèrieur et de la recherche.

Kahl, P. W. and Knebler, U. (1996) *English in der Grundschule – und dann? Evaluation des Hamburger Schulversuchs English ab Klasse 3*, Berlin: Kornelsen.

Low, L., Brown, S., Johnstone R. M. and Pirrie, A. (1995) *Foreign Languages in Primary Schools: Evaluation of the Scottish Pilot Projects: 1993–98. Final Report*, University of Stirling: Scottish CILT.

Luc, C. (1992) *Approche d'une langue étrangère à l'école. Volume 1: Perspectives sur l'apprentissage*, Paris: INRP.

——(1996) *Première année d'initiation à une langue étrangère au cours élémentaire: constats, analyses, propositions*, Paris: INRP.

Mitchell, R. and Dickson, P. (1997) *Progression in Foreign Language Learning: Report of a Project Funded by the Econcomic and Social Research Council, 1993–96*, Southampton: University of Southampton, Centre for Language in Education, Occasional Paper No. 45.

Peltzer-Karpf, A. and Zangl, R. (1997) *Vier Jahre Vienna Bilingual Schooling: Eine Langzeitstudie, Zoom: Extraheft 1: Fremdsprachenlernen in der Grundschule*, Vienna: Bundesministerium für Unterricht und kulturelle Angelegenheiten.

Smith, S. (1996) 'Learning about Pupils' Strategies in a Composite Class', in A. Hurrell and P. Satchwell (eds) *Reflections on Modern Languages in Primary Education: Six UK Case Studies*, Reflections on Practice series. London: CILT.

Thomas, W. P., Collier, V. P. and Abbott, M. (1993) 'Academic Achievement through Japanese, Spanish or French: The First Two Years of Partial Immersion', *The Modern Language Journal*, 77, 2, 170–9.

Appendix I

This appendix has been prepared by Shelagh Rixon and is discussed in Chapter 8.

Section I: Useful addresses and points of reference

Associations and information centres

Association for Language Learning (ALL)
150, Railway Terrace
Rugby
Warwickshire
Tel: 01788 546443
e.mail langlearn@aol.com

Central Bureau for Educational Visits and Exchanges (CBEVE)
10, Spring Gardens
London SW1A 2BN
Tel: 0171 389 4004

3, Bruntsfield Crescent
Edinburgh E10 4HD
Tel: 0131 447 8024
Fax: 0131 452 8569

16, Malone Road
Belfast BT9 5BN
Tel: 01232 664 418
Fax: 01232 661 275
Web site http://www.britcoun.org.cbeve

Centre for Information on Language Teaching (CILT)
20, Bedfordbury
Covent Garden
London WC2N 4BT
Tel: 0171 379 5110
Fax: 0171 379 5082
Web site: http://www.ncet.org.uk/projects/linguanet/cilt/

Education Business Partnerships
National Secretary
June Ritchie
Durham Business and Educational Executive
Broom Cottages
Ferry Hill
Co. Durham DL 17 8AN
Tel: 01740 652 681
Fax: 01740 657 005

National Centre for Educational Technology (NCET)
Millburn Hill Road Science Park
Coventry
West Midlands
CV4 7JJ
Tel: 01203 416 994
Fax: 01203 411418
e.mail: enquiry_desk@ncet.org.uk
Web site: http://www.ncet.org.uk

Cultural institutes

French Embassy Cultural Department and Bureau de Coopération Linguistique et Éducative (BCLE)
23, Cromwell Rd
London SW7 2EL
Tel: 0171 838 2055
Fax: 0171 838 2088
Web site: http://www.francealacarte.org.uk

Goethe Institut London
50, Princes Gate
Exhibition Road
London SW7 2JR
Tel: 0171 411 3400

Fax: 0171 581 0974
e.mail: goethe.lon@dial.pipex.com
Web site: http://www.goethe.DE/

Italian Cultural Institute/Istituto Italiano
39, Belgrave Square
London SW1X 8NX
Tel: 0171 235 1461
Fax: 0171 235 4618
e.mail: italcultur@martex.co.uk
Web site: http://www.italcultur.org.uk

Spanish Embassy Consejería de Educación/Education Office
20, Peel Street
London W8 7PD
Tel: 0171 727 2462
Fax: 0171 229 4965
e.mail: conseduca.lon@dial.pipex.com
Web site: http://www.spanishembassy.org.uk/education.office

Publishers and distributors

Channel 4 Schools
PO Box 100
Warwick CV34 6TZ
Tel: 01926 433 333
Fax: 01926 450 178

Chivers Press Ltd
Windsor Bridge Road
Bath BA2 3AX
Tel: 01225 335 336

European Language Institute (ELI)
Recanati, Italy
[distributed in the UK by European Schoolbooks Ltd]

European Schoolbooks Ltd
Unit E, Ashville Trading Estate
The Runnings
Cheltenham
Gloucestershire GL51
Tel: 01242 245252

Eurotalk
Tel: 0171 371 7711

Little Brown and Co Ltd
Brettenham House
Lancaster Place
London WC2 7EN
Tel: 0171 911 8000

Lively Learning Ltd
Woodington House
East Wellow
Romsey, Hants SO51 6DQ
Tel: 01794 322415/324054
http://www.lively-learning.co.uk

Mary Glasgow Publications Magazines
1, Oxford Street
London WC1A 1NU
Tel: 0171 421 9050

Scope International
230, Peppard Road
Emmer Green
Reading
Berks. RG4 8UA
Tel: 01189 483 444

Usborne Books
Usborne House
83–5 Saffron Hill
London EC1N 8RT
Tel: 0171 430 2800

Bookshops

Grant and Cutler
55–57, Great Marlborough Street
London WIV 2AY
Tel: 01071 734 2012

Heffers
20, Trinity Street,
Cambridge CB2 1TY
Tel: 01223 358 351
e.mail: orders@heffers.co.uk
Web site: http://www.heffers.co.uk

KELTIC Bookshop and Information Centre
25, Chepstow Corner,
Chepstow Place
London W2 4XE
Tel: 0171 229 856
Orders: Tel: 01932 820 485
Fax: 01932 854320
e.mail: shop@keltic-london.co.uk
Web site: http://www.keltic.co.uk

Web sites for further information

Tel*Lingua Virtual Language Centre
[for information on primary languages]
http://www.ncet.org.uk/linguanet/tel lingua/wp3/primary.html
[for update on CD-ROM in schools project]
http://www.ncet.org.uk/projects/CD-ROM/schools/summary/html
[for evaluations of Primary CD-ROM materials]
http://www.ncet.org.uk/projects/CD-ROM/schools/evaluations

Web sites with language experience material

Dictionnaire Encyclopédique
[read and contribute to children's definitions of words in French]
http://www.imaginet.fr/momes/dictionnaire/index1.html

Halloween!
[Illustrated pages about Halloween from Canada in simple French]
http://www.quebectd.com/halloween/000fr.html

Schools On-Line Project – modern languages home page
http://sol.ultralabl.anglia.ac.uk/pages/schools-online/languages/mflhome.
html

This leads to several options, many of them in simple enough language to appeal to primary children. For example, an on-screen interview in text form with the driver of a Eurostar train:

Un chef de bord d'Eurostar parle
http://sol.ultralabl.anglia.ac.uk/pages/schools-online/languages/euro.html

Section 2: Select annotated list of resources

This list features all the resources referred to or discussed in the body of the chapter, and also some similar resources not specifically mentioned. Selection has been made mostly for relevance to the themes I have highlighted in Chapter 8.

Exclusion from the list implies no criticism of particular materials. The interested reader is recommended to follow up the sources of information that I mentioned in the chapter when investigating other materials and resources.

I have listed resources under headings that give the most obvious description of their major components. Under the main headings, I have organised the materials by language. French and German predominate, and this reflects the state of MFL in the UK at the moment. There are, however, many sets of resources that directly cater for other languages or can be adapted for use with other languages.

I have departed from strict bibliographical practice by listing materials according to title, rather than author, since this seems to be the most user-friendly approach. I have tried to include accurate prices at the time of writing [1998] but these should be seen only as indications of the price range, since prices will change over time. The information given should be enough for ordering from your suppliers but where relevant, especially for material published outside the UK, I have given indications of the main distributors, where known. Please also see the List of Useful Addresses, which will give further clues to tracking down resources.

Text-based teaching resource packages

French

Gaston!
ELI [distributed by European Schoolbooks]
Three level course for 8 to 11 year olds, with Pupil's Book, Teacher's Book and two audio cassettes for each level, and special kit of Flip Posters for level 1.

Pupil's Book	£ 5.50
Teacher's Book	£ 7.95

Audio cassettes   £11.95 + VAT
Gaston! Flip Posters   £ 22.50 + VAT.

Salut La France!
East Sussex County Council / Stanley Thornes (1989)
Resource pack including teacher's manual and book, audio cassettes and workbooks.
Price: £54.36.

German

Mach Mit!
ELI [distributed by European Schoolbooks]
Three level course with activity books and Teacher's Guides for 8 to 11 year olds.
No cassettes.
Pupil's Book   £5.50
Teacher's Guide   £5.20
Audio cassettes   £5.95 + VAT.

Tamburin
Max Hueber Verlag [distributed by European Schoolbooks]
Three level course with Pupil's Book, Teacher's Guide and song and listening cassettes for each level.
Pupil's Book   £7.30
Pupil's Workbook   £5.75
Teacher's Guide   £6.05
Cassettes   £17.75 + VAT
CDs   £18.50 + VAT.

Italian

Evviva
ELI [distributed by European Schoolbooks]
Three level course with activity books and Teacher's Guides for 8 to 11 year olds.
Pupil's Book   £5.50
Teacher's Guide   £5.20
Audio cassette   £5.95 + VAT.

Spanish

¡Bienvenidos!
ELI [distributed by European Schoolbooks]

Three level course with activity books and Teacher's Guides for 8 to 11 year olds.

Pupil's Book   £5.50
Teacher's Guide   £5.20
Audio cassettes   £5.95 + VAT.

Games and visual kits

Two or more languages

Cartoons for Classroom Communication Miniflashcard Language Games
Miniflashcard Language Games
Copy masters of cartoon pictures with suggestions for use and vocabulary lists in English, French and German. Price: £25.00.

ELI Kits
ELI [distributed by European Schoolbooks]
Five sets of flash cards, bingo cards and counters for topic-based activities. Each set covers one theme: animals, the house, food, verbs, clothes. Teacher's guide included with each set. Available for French, German, Italian, Spanish.
Price: £17.50 each + VAT.

Miniflashcard Language Games
Miniflashcard Language Games
Kits of cards and dice-games, with Teacher's Notes giving hundreds of suggestions for use. Most of the cards can be used for games and activities in any language but cards are also available with the following languages as labels on the backs: English, French, German, Italian, Latin, Spanish, Russian, Welsh. Different combinations of cards can be purchased, making these a highly flexible resource.
Price: £25.00.

French

Allez France!
European Schoolbooks publishing
Photocopy masters for topic-based activities
Price: £39.95.

Flip Posters France
ELI [distributed by European Schoolbooks]

Size: 70 x 100 cm
Price: £52.00 + VAT
Size: 50 x 70 cm
Price: £34.95 + VAT
Pupil's Book   £7.95
Teacher's Book   £11.95
Audio cassette   £8.95 + VAT.

Spanish

Splendid Ideas for Spanish Teachers
Collins Educational
Copymasters for a wide range of activities.
Price: £9.99.

Song and story collections on audio or video tape

French

Chante avec moi
ELI [distributed by European Schoolbooks]
16 traditional songs on audio cassette + words and music booklet
Price: £6. 50 + VAT.

Le Français en Chantant
Didier [distributed by European Schoolbooks]
10 specially written songs designed to appeal to the 5–8 age range, but attractive to older children. With Teacher's Book and Activity Book.
Cassette   £15.95 + VAT
Activity Book   £4.75
Teacher's Book   £ 7.65.

Muffin Song Cassettes
Muffin Record Co., Toronto [distributed by European Schoolbooks Ltd]
Comment ça va? and Quand tu seras grand?
Combinations of specially written and traditional songs
Cassette   £14.95 + VAT
Songbook   £7.50
Teacher's Kits   £35 + VAT and £45 + VAT, respectively.

Un kilo de chansons
Mary Glasgow Publications
Audio tape collection of songs
Price: £20 + VAT.

Viva le Karaoke!
ELI [distributed by European Schoolbooks]
Three video tapes with cartoon animations of well-known songs. 'Rose, Bleu' and 'Le Karaoke de Noël'.
Price: £14.95 each + VAT.

German

Das Weinachtskaraoke
ELI [distributed by European Schoolbooks]
German Christmas songs on video tape.
Price: £12.95 + VAT.

Singspiel
Mary Glasgow Publications
12 songs in German on a cassette with Teacher's Notes and lyrics printed on the cassette liner.
Price: £20 + VAT.

Video resources

Multilingual or available for several languages

Eurokids
Channel 4 TV Broadcasts for Primary Schools in 10, 15-minute episodes. General European and Cultural Awareness, but with individual programmes [with subtitles] dedicated to: French, German, Italian and Spanish.
Teacher's notes   £4.95.
[No longer available, but copies on video worth seeking out.]

Muzzy video language courses
Early Advantage, published in association with BBC.
World-famous 'Muzzy in Gondoland' animated cartoon EFL course, first produced by the BBC. Believed to be out of print but copies may still be for sale and available in good resource centres.
Price: £75.67.

French

Bonjour Les Amis. Levels One and Two Wonderland Entertainment Ltd.
Wonderland Entertainment Ltd.
Level One is aimed at toddlers, Level Two is aimed at 6–9 year olds.

Marketed mainly for home use, but the simple animated cartoon-supported presentation of basic French phrases and some songs, with the invitation to 'Join in' and 'Repeat' is attractive to most ages. Stars 'Moustache' the cat.
Price: £11.00 each.

French for Children, and More French for Children
Creative Media Marketing
Two videos, starring Marcus the Mole, the Channel Tunnel mascot, with on-screen activities in French, following his adventures in computer game style. The first is intended for children of 4 to 11 years, and the second for older Primary schoolchildren. Endorsed by L'Alliance Française.
Price: £15 each.

Learning and Teaching: French for Primary Schools
Scope International
Videos and Teacher Support notes and class activities pack. Specially designed to support Scottish teachers of French at the Primary level. Good on-screen activities encouraging repeating and responding to language, and use of authentic speakers and settings. INSET video also available.
Price: £28 + VAT and p&p.

Le Petit Monde de Pierre
Channel 4
TV broadcasts for primary schools in 10, 15 minute episodes. Fantasy story in simple French [with subtitles] for primary children.
Contact Channel 4 for details of broadcast times. Current details also available on the Channel 4 website [see Useful Addresses]. Not on sale on video, but recording is legal by schools with an ERA licence.
Teacher's notes   £4.95.

Pilote
Invicta Media
Three Teaching videos and Teacher's Notes and class activities pack. Originally produced to support the Kent schools Primary MFL initiative. Good on-screen activities encouraging repeating and responding to language, and use of authentic speakers and settings. INSET video also available.
Price: £35.95 + VAT + p&p.

Tots' TV
Independent Television
Puppet-based series general children's entertainment programmes broadcast for very young children. One of the puppets, Tilly, speaks only French. Probably not to be used in school, but pupils could be recommended to try

to watch it to catch Tilly's words. Contact Independent Television for current times of broadcasts.

Video-France
ELI [distributed by European Schoolbooks]
Video about Paris and France, designed for younger learners.
Price: £12.95 + VAT.

German

Anna Schmidt und Oskar: Ein Fernsehen und Videosprachkurs für Kinder
Langenscheidt [distributed by European Schoolbooks]
Aimed at learners of 7–8 years old upwards.

Audio cassettes	£6.30 + VAT
Students' books	£7.95
Students' workbook	£6.45
Videos	£31.95
Teacher's guide	£7.25.

Der Wolf und die Sieben Geißlein
Goethe Institut
Story-based video with language activities
Price: £8.00.

3-2-1...Los!
Invicta Media
Three Teaching videos and Teacher's Notes and class activities pack. Originally produced to support the Kent schools Primary MFL initiative. Good on-screen activities encouraging repeating and responding to language, and use of authentic speakers and settings. INSET video also available.
Price: £45 + VAT + p&p.

Learning and Teaching: German for Primary Schools
Scope
Videos and Teacher Support notes and class activities pack. Specially designed to support Scottish teachers of German at the primary level. Good on-screen activities encouraging repeating and responding to language, and use of authentic speakers and settings. INSET video also available.
Price: £28 + VAT and p&p.

Video resources for teachers

European Awareness in Primary Schools
Central Bureau for Educational Visits and Exchanges
Video and notes showing good practice in UK primary schools, for promoting
European Awareness across the curriculum.
Price: £19.85.

Lehrer Erzahlen
Didier [distributed by European Schoolbooks]
The first of two videos + activity books on the same model as the 'Instit'
materials above, featuring German primary school teachers. Publication of
the second, classroom language, element (Lehrer in Unterricht) is planned
and a course for Spanish is in production.
Workbooks   £5.95
Videos   £51 + VAT.

Une Vie d'Instit' and Travail d'Instit'
Didier [distributed by European Schoolbooks]
Two videos with accompanying workbooks, presenting authentic French, to
provide language development resources for primary teachers who wish to
build their own confidence in the target language. The first video features
interviews with a number of French primary school teachers on topics such
as Personal Information, Hobbies, the School Day, and the second shows the
same teachers at work in their classes and focuses on authentic classroom
language in French.
Activity booklet   £8.95
Videos   £47.95 + VAT
User's guide   £11.25.

Magazines

[The distributors will send specimen copies on request]

French

Allons-Y!
Mary Glasgow Publications
School annual subscription price per pupil [workbook included]   £6.50
Individual annual subscription price [workbook included]   £13.50
Audio cassettes   £6.00.

Voilà!
ELI (distributed by European Schoolbooks Ltd)
Price for six issues £12.00
Audio cassettes   £7.50 + VAT.

German

Das Rad
Mary Glasgow Publications
School annual subscription price per pupil [workbook included]   £6.50
Individual annual subscription price [workbook included]   £13.50
Cassettes   £6.00.

Fertig – los!
ELI [distributed by European Schoolbooks Ltd]
Price for six issues   £12.00
Two or more subscriptions   £8.00
Cassettes [two]   £9.50 + VAT.

Italian

Azzurro!
ELI [distributed by European Schoolbooks Ltd]
Price for six issues   £12.00.

Spanish

¿Qué Tal?
Mary Glasgow Publications
School annual subscription price per pupil [workbook included]   £6.50
Individual annual subscription price [workbook included]   £13.50
Cassette   £6.00.

¡Vamos!
ELI [distributed by European Schoolbooks Ltd]
Price for six issues   £12.00.

Readers and story books

French

I can read French...Language Learning Story Books
b. small publishing [sic]
Series of bilingual English/French story books including:

'Goodnight everyone/Bonne nuit à tous'
Price: £5.95 each.

Learn a Language Storybooks
Chivers Press Ltd
Series of bilingual French/English story books with cassettes.
Price: £8.99.

Où est Spot mon Petit Chien?
Nathan [distributed by European Schoolbooks Ltd]
Other 'Spot' raise-the-flap story books available in the same series.
Price: £12.95.

Usborne Bilingual Readers
Usborne Books
Les Métiers/Things People Do, Château Mystère/Mystery Castle, L'Île Fantôme/Phantom Island
Price: £3.99 paperback, £5.99 or £6.99 hardback.

German

Leseskiste [A]
Mary Glasgow Publications
Boxed kit of 60 short readers with Teacher's Notes
Price: £103.50.

Language awareness books

Toto's Travels
Little Brown
Three books recounting Toto's Adventures in Paris, Rome and Spain
Stories in English with target language words and phrases integrated into the text, and some basic cultural information incorporated.
Price: £7.99

Word and phrase books and picture dictionaries

ELI Picture Dictionaries
ELI [distributed by European Schoolbooks]
Bilderwörterbuch Deutsch, Diccionario illustrado Español, Dictionnaire illustré Français, Vocabulario illustrato Italiano.
Price: £5.95 each.

Usborne First Thousand Words series
Usborne Books
Picture dictionaries organised according to topics, available for French, German, Italian, Spanish, Russian and Hebrew, with bilingual English/ target language word lists at the back.
Price: Between £4.99 and £7.99.

Usborne Language Guides
Usborne Books
Topic-based attractively illustrated language learning books, simple grammar explanations. Accompanying puzzle books are also available. Sold for children to enjoy at home, so motivating enough to be popular in the school library. Available for French, German, Spanish, Italian, Irish, Welsh and Latin.
Books   £4.99.
Book and audio cassette £9.99.

Computer and CD-Rom multimedia materials

Multilingual, or available in more than one language

Adventures of Muzzy Series
Apple/PC CD-ROM
Vektor
Series of four disks: Muzzy at the Seaside, Muzzy at the Disco, Muzzy and the Clockmaker, Muzzy at the Gondoland Games. Each one presents an animated story with text and soundtrack support to be used in any combination chosen by the user. Users can switch between seven languages or varieties: British and American English, French, German, Italian, European and Latin American Spanish.
Price: £22.00 each disk.

The Asterix series
Apple/PC CD-ROM
Eurotalk Ltd
An Asterix cartoon strip presented in a flexible way with possibility of text alone, sound alone, text and sound, and voice-recording facility. Available for English, French, German, Spanish, Italian and Latin.
Price: £29.99.

At Home with KC
Apple/PC CD-ROM
English Quest
A 'rescue game' in which the user solves spelling and other language puzzles to save the 'hero'. Soundtrack and own voice-recording facility. Produced at

the moment for practising English as a native or foreign language, but with translation facilities on screen for several languages. There are plans possibly to produce the game in the future with focus on French and German learning.
Price: £25.00.

Multilingual Talking Picture Dictionary
Apple Mac/PC CD-ROM
TLC
Pictures and word-matching activities, with soundtrack and own voice-recording facilities. Covers English, French, German and Spanish on one disk.
Price: £22.00.

Rosetta Stone
Apple/PC CD-ROM
Apple Computer U.K. Ltd
Picture-matching of words and phrases with spoken and written stimuli. Covers English, French, German and Spanish, suitable for KS1 and 2. No voice-recording facility.
Price: £39.95.

French

ADI French 11/12
Amiga/ PC floppy disk
Europress
Intended for KS3 level but basic enough for primary use. Mostly very simple word and phrase-matching activities.
Price: £ 22.11.

Friendly French
PC CD-ROM
Lively Learning Ltd.
Different vocabulary matching games with text and soundtrack support and voice-recording facility. Comes with a kit of Banana Bluff cards to play using the computer or alone.
Price: £24.99

Learn French
PC CD-ROM
Library/Schools Directory
Introduction to French culture. French and English appear together on screen and on soundtrack. Voice-recording facility.
Price: £29.99.

Spanish

Friendly Spanish
PC CD-ROM
Lively Learning Ltd.
Different vocabulary matching games with text and soundtrack support and voice-recording facility. Comes with a kit of Banana Bluff cards to play using the computer or alone.
Price: £24.99

Appendix II

The structure of schooling of England, Wales and Northern Ireland

KS1 Key Stage 1   Years (Reception) 1 and 2. Aged 4/5: 5/6 : 6/7
KS2 Key Stage 2   Years 3, 4, 5, 6. Aged 7/8 : 8/9 : 9/10 : 10/11
KS3 Key Stage 3   Years 7, 8, 9. Aged 11/12: 12/13 : 13/14
KS4 Key Stage 4   Years 10, 11. Aged 14/15 : 15/16

The French system

CP Cours préparatoire   aged 6/7
CE1 Classe élémentaire 1   aged 7/8
CE2 Classe élémentaire 2   aged 8/9
CM1 Cours moyen 1   aged 9/10
CM2 Cours moyen 2   aged 10/11

The Scottish system

P1 Primary 1   aged 5
P2 Primary 2   aged 6
P3 Primary 3   aged 7
P4 Primary 4   aged 8
P5 Primary 5   aged 9
P6 Primary 6   aged 10
P7 Primary 7   aged 11
S1 Secondary 1 aged 11/12
S2 Secondary 2 aged 12/13
S3 Secondary 3 aged 13/14
S4 Secondary 4 aged 14/15
S5 Secondary 5 aged 15/16

Index

Lightning Source UK Ltd.
Milton Keynes UK
02 October 2009

144439UK00003B/52/A

9 780415 183833